J. E. NEALE

The Age of
Catherine de Medici

and Essays in Elizabethan History

JONATHAN CAPE
THIRTY BEDFORD SQUARE LONDON

The Age of Catherine de Medici
FIRST PUBLISHED 1943
England's Elizabeth AND
Essays in Elizabethan History
© 1958 BY SIR JOHN NEALE
THIS EDITION FIRST PUBLISHED 1963
REPRINTED 1965, 1970

ISBN 0 224 60566 6

*Reprinted by Lithography in Great Britain
by Jarrold & Sons Ltd, Norwich*

CONTENTS

PREFACE

This paperback volume includes *The Age of Catherine de Medici*, first published in 1943, and a selection from *Essays in Elizabethan History*, first published in 1958. A newcomer among the Essays is 'England's Elizabeth', a centenary lecture included by permission of the Folger Shakespeare Library, Washington.

THE AGE OF
CATHERINE DE MEDICI

I

THE RELIGIOUS BACKGROUND

OUR story begins in March 1559 with the Peace of Cateau-Cambrésis. It was primarily a peace between Spain and France, though England too was a party, for Mary Tudor had entered the war in the train of her husband Philip II, and had lost Calais. This peace marks the close of an epoch in European as well as French history.

The most obvious change in the European scene was its new rulers. Only three to four years before, Philip II had taken over Spain and the Spanish Netherlands from his father, the Emperor Charles V; in England Elizabeth had become Queen the previous November; and in France celebrations connected with the Peace were to result in the death of Henry II and thus lead to the gradual emergence of the Queen-Mother, Catherine de Medici, as the director of French policy. By a striking coincidence all three of these rulers were long-lived. Catherine de Medici died at the turn of the year 1588–9: she was sixty-nine. Philip II died in 1598: he was seventy-one. Elizabeth died in 1603: she was sixty-nine. The second half of the sixteenth century was dominated by these three personalities, and, according to one's national standpoint, is the Age of Philip II, of Elizabeth, or of Catherine de Medici.

The Peace of Cateau-Cambrésis closed the period of the Italian Wars, which had gone on intermittently for over sixty years and ended, from the French point of view, in complete humiliation. France finally gave up the challenge to Spanish hegemony in Italy, and Italy was left to itself and Spain. The Italian states could no longer disturb the peace by playing off one great power against another; they passed out of the main current of international affairs.

The Italian Wars were ended. So also was the second great theme of that period of history — the German Reformation. After years of disorder and civil war, in which the Emperor had tried and failed to accomplish the miracle of uniting rival theologies in a compromise, exhaustion and realism had propounded their own solution — the solution which is described by the Latin tag, *cuius regio eius religio*: the prince determines the faith of his kingdom. The sixteenth century was totalitarian in its political creed: its motto was 'One King, One Faith'. Germany preserved this creed in its Reformation settlement, but paid a heavy price. It shattered itself. The Prince, not the Emperor, was the beneficiary of the German Reformation; and a country which in law was a federal state became in consequence a confederation of states. German unity had to wait until the nineteenth century — or perhaps one should say, until the twentieth. The Reformation settlement was embodied in the Peace of Augsburg in 1555; and thereafter Germany, like Italy, receded from the main current of European affairs and did not re-emerge until the eve of the Thirty Years War, half a century or so later. In that half-century it is western Europe that occupies the stage of history.

Modern research, with its emphasis on economic factors, has a very up-to-date reason for the making of the Peace of Cateau-Cambrésis: money, or rather, the lack of it. Of that I must say a word in a later chapter. But in the mind of the King of France, Henry II, who wanted peace so desperately that he was prepared to surrender almost anything, money was not the only reason. He had an overwhelming desire to tackle a domestic problem, the urgency of which had been growing in recent years. That problem was heresy; and it is the theme of this chapter.

We have all heard, maybe to the point of staleness, about the causes of the Reformation; about the state of the Catholic Church in the early sixteenth century, about worldly and non-resident bishops, ignorant and unspiritual clergy, and the monasteries. The story is the same in France, only perhaps more so, for there, in addition to the general slackness of the age, there was a peculiar reason for the deplorable condition of the Church. It was the Concordat of 1516; an agreement made between the French monarchy and the Papacy, which can only be described as a deal in the spoils of the Gallican Church. It gave the King the nomination to bishoprics, abbeys, and conventual priories in France; and its effect can be put quite briefly. Not a single French bishop obtained his post because of religious zeal or spiritual worthiness. Fifty per cent of benefices were given for Court services, the rest to please influential local magnates; and benefices were actually given to two Italian princes to further French diplomacy in Italy. These appointments were regarded, not as ecclesiastical preferment, but as grants of revenue, a conception that was blatant enough when the grants consisted of all future vacant benefices until their combined revenue should reach a certain sum.

Pluralism was of course scandalous; though it made little odds how many benefices bishops held when they were non-resident. Take as an example the most princely of French churchmen, the Cardinal of Lorraine, who rivalled England's Wolsey in his pluralism. He was Archbishop of Rheims, held the revenues of the bishoprics of Metz and Verdun, and was abbot-in-commendam of eleven abbeys, including the famous abbey of St Denis which was usually reserved for a member of the royal family. And in addition he controlled an immense amount of ecclesiastical patronage. His income has been estimated at 300,000 *livres* per annum. Most of his appointments were inherited from his uncle — a still greater pluralist — like family estates. He was made Archbishop of Rheims at the age of fourteen, and was a cardinal at twenty-three. He happened to be, in his own way, a rather good churchman; but that fact has the irrelevance of an accident.

Among the lower clergy almost all benefices were part of the patrimony of local families, descending from uncle to nephew, like the Cardinal of Lorraine's holdings. In such circumstances priesthood could not be regarded as a calling, in the evangelical sense: it was merely a qualification to hold a benefice, lightly regarded and lightly conferred. In addition · to those with benefices awaiting them, an increasing number of smaller folk took orders as a means of escaping misery and want. They were the hangers-on of the Church, roaming from place to place. Some, by making the highest bid, might farm the benefices of non-resident clergy, and after paying dearly for their posts set about recouping themselves. Pluralism and non-residence were rampant. There were many priests in France, but a wholesale neglect of the spiritual needs of the people. According to a contemporary, there was not one of fifty parishes in Brittany that had its rector resident; while another contemporary, writing from Périgord, declared that near Bordeaux there were forests fifty leagues in extent where the inhabitants lived like beasts of burden, without an idea of heavenly things. There were persons — he went on to say — fifty years of age, who had never heard a Mass nor understood a word of religion. The ignorance, as well as the low spiritual quality of the clergy, was in no small way responsible for this state of affairs. It was said that there was scarcely one priest in ten who was able to read; an estimate which, if inaccurate, was not far wrong. There is little reason to be surprised at the spread of the Reformation in France.

In its early phases the French Reform movement was moderate and respectable. It was the spiritual facet of Humanism, a blending of Erasmian and Lutheran impulses, and had the King's sister for patron. Though admirable in many ways, it lacked the qualities to shape a great rebel cause. Indeed, neither Lutheranism nor Humanism possessed the practical genius required for sustained and successful rebellion. This may seem a strange remark when one thinks of the explosive force of the Lutheran Reformation in Germany: it had been dynamic enough to rouse a whole nation and had accomplished a revolution. But the practical success of the movement had been due to the support of the secular princes. It was they and not Luther who had supplied the Lutheran Church with its organization. Luther was a mystic, not an administrator. To him the Church was not an organized, earthly society, but an invisible body, the mystic communion of saints; and it needed the mundane mind of the Prince to fetch the Church down from the heavens, where Luther had left it suspended, and clothe it in the necessary garments to move about the earth. There were no essential Lutheran doctrines about the form of church organization, and everywhere the Prince supplied that form. Consequently we find the Lutheran Church episcopal in one state and non-episcopal in another.

By the middle of the sixteenth century Lutheranism had lost its revolutionary fervour, become respectable in its dependence upon secular rulers, and shown its essential conservatism, a conservatism reinforced by the worldly timidity of secular policy. The second half of the century was to make this still more evident, for there were times when it seemed as if European Catholicism was uniting in a formidable crusade to smash Protestantism, and attempts were made by Queen Elizabeth and others to form a rival Protestant League. The Lutheran princes met these approaches with fair words but nothing more. Perhaps the wily Elizabeth deserved little else; yet it was all too clear that the crusading spirit had gone out of Lutheranism. If French Protestantism had remained Lutheran it would indeed have been a weak plant.

It would have been weak because in the nature of things the Reformation in France could not count on the support of the King. However much on occasions the French monarchy might seem to wobble, there can be little doubt that it was fated to remain Catholic. What had it to gain from going Reformist? In the all-important business of appointing to bishoprics and wealthy abbeys, the King of France, under the Concordat of 1516, was as much the Head of the Church as Henry VIII of

15

England. A government that was desperately and permanently bankrupt, as France was for the next half-century, that relied on its ecclesiastical patronage to pay officials and courtiers, and that in dire need was able to tax the Church without mercy, could not afford to discard a system which served it so well.

True, the French King might have broken with Rome and, like Henry VIII, become the titular as well as the practical Head of the Church. There was an old and strong tradition of Gallicanism in the French Church, a tradition of national independence which might seem to have suggested a move of this sort; and in the first year or two of our period there actually was an occasional hint to the Papacy that if it did not mind its p's and q's France might follow the example of England. But even if such a change had been practical policy, it would not have satisfied the Reformers. On doctrinal questions a breach with Rome would no doubt have brought some concessions to Protestants, but the last thing the Reformers wanted was the perpetuation of that scandalous laxity and irreligion associated with royal control of the Church. No. The French monarchy was fated to remain Catholic. Its vested interests in the *ancien régime* were too great, and so also were those of powerful elements in the country. Moreover, though Protestant communities developed in Paris and were troublesome, this city was always staunchly, nay fanatically Catholic. It was not an accident that England ultimately took the religious complexion of its capital: London was worth a sermon. Nor was it an accident that France ultimately took the religious complexion of its capital: Paris was worth a Mass.

Thus the French Reform movement, being opposed to the interests of the monarchy, was bound to assume the shape of rebellion. Now, there are certain essentials for prolonged and successful rebellion; and the chief is organization. Here lies the significance of Calvinism. If I am inclined to stress organization over against doctrine or anything else, the reason is my profound conviction of its vital importance. Much of English history, Scottish history, and Dutch history in the second half of the sixteenth century might be written round the organization of Calvinism; and I am often tempted to speak of this period as the Age of Calvin, although in fact Calvin died in 1564.

In Calvin, France produced its own prophet of the Reformation. He fled from his home country in 1534, and did two outstanding things: first, he wrote the bible of the new Protestant movement, his *Institution of Christian Religion*, published in Latin in 1536 and afterwards in French and other languages; secondly, he founded at Geneva the Protestants' New Jerusalem, the City of God on earth.

The theological or doctrinal aspect of Calvinism need not detain us. On this subject it is sufficient to note that at a moment when the inherent individualism of the German Reformation was producing confusion in Protestant theology, Calvin, with his legal training and the clarity and rigour of the French genius, rethought Protestant theology into an ordered and logical system. The Gallic qualities of his mind naturally fitted his teaching to become the Protestant gospel of the French people. There was one doctrine of Calvinism — that of pre-destination, to which Calvin was driven by the relentless logic of his thought — which deserves mention because of its value to a fighting faith. In time of hazard and persecution it was no small fortification to the spirit to know that one was among the elect, predestined by God to salvation.

But it is not the theology, it is the organization of this Church that is the most striking feature in the history of the French Calvinist, or, as it was called, Huguenot movement. Unlike Luther, Calvin did not regard the organization of the Church as a negligible consideration and let the State have its own way. It was an integral part of his teaching. After all, the secret of the power wielded throughout the centuries by the Catholic Church lay in its organization and discipline as well as its dogma. And, as one eminent French historian has put it, Calvin's unique achievement, the sign of his originality, was to construct a new Catholicism outside the old and opposed to it.

This organization, which is better known to most of us by the name Presbyterian, must be examined in some detail. The officers of Calvin's Church were divided into three categories: ministers, elders, and deacons. The elders joined with the ministers in the government and discipline of the Church, while the deacons had charge of the sick and poor. In appearance the scheme had a democratic basis, since each minister — and the same was true of elders and deacons — had ultimately to be elected by the particular congregation that he was to serve. But in fact Calvin's Church was oligarchic and conservative. The real choice of candidates for the ministry was in the hands of the body of ministers, who put them through a preliminary and searching examination of their doctrinal views and knowledge of scripture, their preaching ability, and their moral fitness. In Geneva Calvin gave the title of the Venerable Company to his ministers, and he meant them to live up to the title. Discipline was the very essence of his Church, among both officers and rank and file.

Each individual church, in the scheme of ecclesiastical government for countries like France, was governed by its minister and elders, the laity in the persons of the elders joining with the ministry here as throughout the whole organization. Minister and elders together formed a disciplinary committee known as the Consistory, which, by domiciliary visits or otherwise, maintained a constant supervision over the mode of life of every member of the church; an activity which Queen Elizabeth, to whom the Genevan system was anathema, described as an intolerable inquisition to pry into people's lives. This committee might even, and in France did, exercise a minor police power.

Above the Consistory, or ruling body of the single church, was another committee known in France as the Colloquy. It consisted of the ministers and elders of a number of neighbouring churches, grouped into a district, over which they exercised a general supervision, dealing with business brought to them by the individual churches. Above the Colloquy was the Synod, also a governing body of ministers and elders. In a large country like France there would be Provincial Synods, and, capping the whole ecclesiastical organization, a National Synod.

Think what this organization meant; think, especially, how well it was adapted to the cause of rebellion. Isolation, which breeds fear, doubt, and surrender in all but the most courageous, was impossible. No sooner was a community formed than it was organized; no sooner were there several communities than they were linked together by the Colloquy; and on top of this came the Provincial Synod and finally the National Synod to weld all the churches into a single unit.

Throughout every grade of this organization ran the remarkable Calvinist discipline, which maintained unity of belief and a high code of personal conduct. At the meetings of each governing committee there were always two items of procedure in addition to business matters: an exposition of some passage of the Bible, and what was called a censure. In Colloquy and Synod a different minister undertook the biblical exposition at each meeting, and when he had finished, his colleagues proceeded to criticize. Two important objects were achieved by these scriptural exercises: first, uniformity of doctrine — and the Bible was there on the table, as at all Calvinist meetings, the ultimate authority of the Church in case of disagreement; and secondly, a decent level of preaching ability, no small matter in that sermonless age.

At the conclusion of meetings, whether of Consistory, Colloquy, or Synod, there took place an 'amicable and brotherly censure', in which those present reviewed each other's conduct and life, offering friendly criticism. It may strike us as a humourless procedure, and we may wonder how much 'amicable censure' brotherly feeling could really stand. But we must not forget the appalling spiritual and moral laxity of the age, against which it was a reaction; nor should we forget that the totalitarian states of our own day, which in some respects Calvin's Geneva resembled, intrude into the private lives of citizens with their party discipline. The discipline had more than its ordinary value in France, for, as we shall see, in the early days of the Huguenot movement congregations had often to meet at night. As Calvinism had thrown over the Catholic doctrine of salvation by works, its adherents easily laid themselves open to a charge of libertinism, and these secret night-meetings were liable to provoke much the same slander as was levelled against the early Christians.

Here are some examples of censures from French Consistories: M. Manget, the preacher, was told that he did not preach popularly enough and repeated himself too much; another minister was told not to preach so quickly. As for laymen: M. Rozel was urged to go to the sermon more frequently, manage the maids in his house better, and be less ready to air his opinions; another was censured for avarice; another for lending money at usury; another for ill-treating his wife; another for playing piquet; others for dancing and drinking. Though severe, the discipline was beneficial in its results. In France the Consistory often acted like Justices of the Peace and stopped much useless litigation in a litigious age. Morals were reformed, a purposeful and industrious way of life encouraged, and material prosperity followed in the wake of godliness. In the words of Tyndale's Translation: 'The Lorde was with Joseph, and he was a luckie felowe.'

So much for the organization and discipline of the Calvinist Church. We must next see how Calvin meant his Church to fit into the State. Once more he was precise and logical. State and Church were separate powers, but they were fused, first by the assumption that every citizen would be a member of the Church, and secondly by the unique position accorded to the Bible. Calvin regarded the Bible as the word of God, in the full and literal sense. Consequently, in a godly society it should be the fundamental law both of the State and the Church. Now, the Bible is full of moral injunctions, and the Old Testament in particular, with its Mosaic laws, embodies a whole penal code. These injunctions and this code, being the word of God, should therefore be part of the law of the State: for example, death is the punishment for adultery in the Old Testament, and it should be the same in the Calvinist State. From our point of view the conception reveals a monstrous confusion of morality and law; the sort of confusion which, in a minor degree perhaps, the contemporary totalitarian State has made. But it is not my object to condemn or praise; and I hasten to make a final point about Calvin's State. It is this: since the Bible was to be the fundamental law of the State, and since the professional expositors of the Bible were the ministers, it followed that the ministers would in fact dominate State as well as Church. In other words, Calvin's State would be a theocracy; a natural conclusion, for he drew his inspiration from the Old Testament and the Israelitish theocracy.

This in brief was Calvin's theory of Church and State — his vision of Utopia. In the course of the centuries many authors have written Utopias; few indeed have had the opportunity and the ideal conditions for putting them to the actual experiment. This perfect and rarest of Fortune's gifts was Calvin's. Geneva became his theocracy. It would involve me in unpardonable irrelevance if I stopped to explain how that city came to be the ideal laboratory for his ideas. I can only say that a theocracy, more or less as Calvin planned, was established there.

That simple fact is of profound importance. We ourselves have seen and still see, in the recent past and the present, the infectious character of ideas translated into political institutions. Communist and Fascist states have shaken the world by the enthusiasm they have aroused in other countries; and also, it must be added, by the detestation. The same contagious emotional quality belonged to Calvin's Geneva. To puritans in every land it represented the New Jerusalem, the godly society in actual working order; a demonstration that their dreams were realizable. The missionary value of this model state can hardly be exaggerated. Making allowance for the differing scale of the world, its influence was perhaps more formidable than that of Communist Russia in our own day.

Moreover, Geneva was a small state, standing outside the system of great nation-states and therefore well suited to be the centre of an international movement. In this it was like Rome, its religious rival; but with a difference that was to Geneva's advantage, for by long tradition Rome was also a centre of national diplomacies and its prestige as a spiritual metropolis suffered from the notorious and very unspiritual clash of national interests there.

The metropolitan character of Geneva was revealed in many ways. Its school and university became international institutions, attaining the fame and more than the influence of Wittenberg under Luther and Melancthon. It became the training college of ministers, especially for France. And the correspondence that Calvin carried on, immense in volume and international in scope, was perhaps the most remarkable personal correspondence of the age.

As wave after wave of religious exiles fled now from this country and now from that, Geneva took on the role of a city of refuge. Many English Protestants fled there in Mary Tudor's reign; and as the French religious troubles developed, the city was overwhelmed by Huguenot refugees and was subject to an almost unbearable strain. Here are some figures that give an idea of the increasing influx of refugees. They are from the registers of new inhabitants, and show, in 1549, eighty-one; in 1550, one hundred and forty-five; in 1551, two hundred and sixty-four; in 1557, five hundred and eighty-seven; and Geneva, let us remember, was only a small city-state. A letter in December 1572 gives some idea of the refugee problem after the Massacre of St Bartholomew, which had taken place in the previous August. There were, the letter says, more than seven hundred people in the city ordinarily needing assistance; and this figure did not include a great number employed on public works, who for the moment, but for the moment only, could support themselves; nor did it include those passing through the city and requiring help *en route*; while there were also fifty refugee ministers, all poor. The parallel with our own times will be obvious. Paris, into which Russian, Italian, German, and Austrian political refugees were pouring between 1918 and 1939, has perhaps in this respect been most like Calvinist Geneva.

It was from Geneva that the French Huguenot movement was organized. From here and neighbouring Protestant cities, Protestant literature was carried secretly through France by *colporteurs* and distributed surreptitiously by booksellers. It is significant that between 1549 and 1557 no less than fifty-six printers and booksellers sought refuge in Geneva. From here also missionaries went forth. As Huguenot congregations were formed it was to Geneva that they applied for ministers, and it was there that they sent their young men to be trained for the ministry. On questions of government and policy they were continually writing to Calvin. Once more I think that a contemporary parallel may be helpful. Calvin's Geneva was in many ways like Moscow during those years after the war of 1914–18 when the Soviet State dreamed of a world Communist revolution: it was as much a thorn in the side of the French government as Moscow in the side of capitalist Germany before 1933.

Though this account of Calvin and Geneva has not, I hope, exceeded the length that their place in French history warrants, it is time that we examined the growth of the Calvinist movement in France itself.

First, let us look at the classes of people who responded to Reformist propaganda. We can best begin with the one class that it scarcely touched — the peasantry. With certain exceptions they were hostile. They were completely illiterate and thus could not be affected by the clandestine literature that played so large a part in Huguenot propaganda; and as was inevitable with people rooted to the soil, they were profoundly conservative. They were attached to the worship of saints and the cult of the dead; and it was only when Reformist ideas began to grip the nobility and gentry that any of them were won over to the cause, and then by tenant-loyalty rather than religious conversion.

As might be expected, it was among the educated, at the universities, that the new doctrine spread first. Many university teachers and also tutors in noble households were converted, and in due course influenced the minds of their pupils. Medical men, lawyers, and notaries, and other professional men figured prominently in Huguenot ranks. The lawyer class in France was very large and, in comparison with the less bureaucratic government of England, was used in great numbers in the administration of the country. They formed almost an estate in themselves, and their traditions were anti-clerical. It was generally from the rank and file of the profession that Huguenot converts were obtained. They played an important part in the movement, for they were able secretly to shelter heretics from the operation of the laws against them.

These professional men were mostly the sons of merchants, whose trade connections with other countries brought them into touch with new-fangled ideas, and who, by their independent spirit and quality of mind, as a class were everywhere inclined to anti-clericalism and heresy. In France they had additional cause for discontent in the grave financial drain caused by the Italian Wars. Their professional sons had no small part in converting them to Calvinism; and the organization of the Huguenot Church, by providing through the offices of elders and deacons for bourgeois laity in church government, appealed to their *amour-propre*. The spirit of Calvinism was, as I have said, essentially oligarchic and bourgeois.

Among the clergy, the bishops kept more or less clear of the infection. Only four went over to Geneva; five more were restless. Otherwise, in contrast with the English Reformation, the episcopacy was the great obstacle to heresy. It was the lower clergy and especially the Friars who became Huguenots. For three centuries the Friars had been the militia of the Church. They thronged the universities, and by their preaching, their mysticism, and their contacts with the people, were the true leaders of the crowd. They were a great asset and a great nuisance: speculators in doctrine and rebels against discipline, their tradition was one of independence and turbulence. They proved readily accessible to Genevan ideas, and were invaluable in the early stages of the Reform movement as peripatetic preachers of heresy, profiting by the non-residence of bishops and the immunities of their orders to overrun the country. They provided the new Church in France with its first ministers. But their indiscipline and their democratic spirit, both of which Calvin loathed, detracted from their service. One of Calvin's correspondents described them as 'these horrible beasts'; and Calvin himself was far from enamoured of such turbulent pioneers.

The nobility — a class which included what we in England would term the country gentry — was the last class to be won over in large numbers. Very few were Calvinists in 1547, but twelve years later the situation had changed remarkably. Education and the influence of their women-folk were important factors in their conversion. With the women it was religious feeling — a revulsion against the moral and religious laxity of Francis I's reign; but with their men-folk the motive was often revolt against a social and political regime of which they were the victims. Moreover, they had lost a good deal by the Concordat of 1516, before which they had been able to secure high ecclesiastical positions for their sons. They tended to be anti-clerical and anticipated spoils for themselves in the form of Church lands if the Reform movement triumphed.

The recruiting of the lesser nobility — the country gentry — was of great practical service. They might be described as the

Storm-Troopers of the Huguenot movement. As a class they were entitled and accustomed to carry swords, and they therefore constituted a natural protection for meetings of heretic congregations. There was need for this. At first Huguenot congregations met in secret and often at night, in cellars or in the countryside outside the towns. Their meetings were illegal and liable to be broken up by the authorities. A more frequent danger was attack by hostile bands of Catholics, for, as the movement spread, it inflamed passions, as the growth of the Nazi movement did in Germany; and just as there were incessant clashes and fights between Communists and Nazis in the days before Hitler succeeded to power, so there were clashes and fights between Catholics and Huguenots. The gentry were needed to protect the Huguenot ministers and their flocks from assault, and congregations often met with a body of armed protectors forming a circle of defence round them. The churches came to place themselves, each under some nobleman as their protector.

As the number of converts increased, the situation deteriorated, breeding further aggression on both sides, for there were few ministers available in the earlier stages of the movement and congregations were therefore apt to grow so large that they were forced to meet in public. Secrecy was no longer possible. An extract from the minutes of the Consistory of Mans, dated August 6th, 1561, illustrates this transition to public meetings: 'It has been decided that M. Merlin shall commence to preach publicly under the town hall of this town on Sunday next at 7.0 a.m. Superintendents will make haste to warn faithful noblemen (*gentilshommes*) so that all the faithful of this town shall be at the meeting.' After this beginning, the minister at Mans preached in public four times a week.

Naturally, when secret meetings gave place to public, ministers were no longer able to exercise adequate control over the recruiting of their audiences, and rowdy elements appeared, only too ready to start image-breaking. Moreover, there was an impulse, which the ministers could not well restrain, to seize buildings, especially churches, for Huguenot services. This was often done in a hot-headed and riotous way. In Languedoc and Guienne bands of fanatics drove priests and worshippers out of churches and attacked convents. Similar happenings took place in other parts of the country, though occasionally, where Catholics were lukewarm, amicable arrangements were made with them and churches were shared between the new and the old faiths.

The change from secret to open worship — a significant stage in the Huguenot story — took place during the years 1560 and 1561. Disorder spread through France. Where Catholics were in a majority they turned on the Huguenots and engaged in bloody strife; where the Huguenots were strong, extremists often got out of hand and terrorized the Catholics.

Speaking in general terms — for it would be wearisome, and not very illuminating, to discuss the question in detail, province by province — the Huguenot movement tended to be strong in centres of international trade; for example, at Lyons, the great entrepôt near to the Genevan and German centres of Protestant-ism, and in the east in Brittany where trade connections with England and the Netherlands encouraged its growth. Normandy too was badly infected with heresy, though here the chief inducement was social and political discontent among the gentry of a province where the evils of French government were exceptionally rife. The movement also flourished in the south, from the Rhône and Provence through Languedoc to the King of Navarre's territory in the south-west. Paris had heretics, but remained predominantly and fervently Catholic: the Huguenot stronghold over against Catholic Paris was Orleans, where some idea of the numbers may be gathered from the fact that in May 1561 five to six thousand persons attended Communion and more than ten thousand followed Protestant funerals. In May 1561 there were said to be two thousand one hundred and fifty separate Huguenot churches in France.

The important years for the organization of the Church were 1555 to 1559. Since 1555 the separate churches had been organizing themselves, largely under the influence and direction of Calvin, who wanted to put a stop to disorder and establish a responsible ministry and proper discipline. Then in May 1559 the first National Synod was held in Paris. The meeting was in a lodging-house, so that the coming and going would not attract attention; and the number present may have reached fifty. They were obscure men, for as yet the nobility had not imposed itself upon the leadership of the Church; and all of them risked death by their presence. They drew up a confession of faith and articles of discipline, including a constitution or organization for the whole Church.

Orderly development upon a settled model could now go forward. That model I have already described. At the base was the Consistory, the governing body of the single church, comprising the minister and lay elders. Its meetings were frequent, sometimes every fortnight. Next there was the Colloquy, the assembly for the combined churches of a district, meeting from twice to four times a year. Then came the Provincial Synod, the province coinciding with the political divisions of France: the number of such Synods was fifteen or sixteen, and they met once or twice a year. Finally there was the National Synod, consisting of two ministers and two elders from each province. It was supposed to meet once a year, and, in accordance with Calvin's insistence on equality among both ministers and churches — a deliberate reaction against the primacy of Rome and the hierarchy of the Catholic Church — to meet at a different town on each occasion. Actually, there were sixteen National Synods between 1559 and 1601, which, considering the chronic state of civil war, was a striking sign of the vitality of this, the supreme governing body of the Huguenot Church.

Such an organization — the organization of a rebel movement within the State — would be remarkable at any time in any State. It is nothing short of astounding to find it within the sixteenth-century State.

That is not all. I have already noted how the nobility, when they joined the movement, naturally took over the protection of congregations. During the turbulent years 1560 and 1561 most of the individual churches placed themselves under a noble protector. Consistories and Synods encouraged this, and the nobility took their place, by right of birth, on the governing bodies of the churches they protected.

The dangerous possibilities of this development were soon evident. The French nobility still retained the old feudal traditions which grouped the lesser nobles under the leadership of greater noblemen, and these in turn under still greater, until the few greatest noblemen in the land were reached — a feudal pyramid. Obviously, this grouping of the nobility fitted perfectly into the pyramid organization of the Huguenot Church, with its district, provincial, and national bodies. And so the Church was able and indeed tempted to create a military organization coinciding with its ecclesiastical organization. The individual church had its captain, the Colloquy its colonel, and the Province its general (*chef-général*). This was the military organization devised in November 1561 for the provinces of Bordeaux and Toulouse.

At this point I can, for the moment, leave my story, for I am verging on the political problem of the age — the subject of my next chapter. I would merely ask you to consider the amazing character and terrifying possibilities of this organized heretical party; consider also the passions that its growth had aroused in France. And I know no better way to secure an imaginative grasp of the situation than to reflect on the turbulent history of the ideological movements in our own days — the history of the Fascist movement in Italy, and better still of the Nazi movement in Germany. Governments have collapsed before them.

II

THE SOCIAL AND POLITICAL
BACKGROUND

EARLIER in this narrative I said that modern research has
a very up-to-date reason for the making of the Peace of
Cateau-Cambrésis: money. We may take this as the
starting point for examining the condition in which the long
period of the Italian Wars, and their last phase in particular,
had left France. For some time — in fact, since the reign of that
extravagant and picturesque king, Francis I — war had become
ruinously expensive. Henry VIII of England had discovered
this in the latter years of his reign, and, although he had the
wealth of the monasteries on which to fall back, his by-no-means
spectacular military adventures undermined English government finance. It was the misfortune of Europe, and especially of
Spain and France, that the disastrous business of war, with its
new and costly methods, could go on because international
business and credit were just developing on a modern scale and
could be made the means by which kings might impoverish their
own and other countries. As yet the evil of credit inflation had
not been realized, and bankers and others were therefore the
easy victims of a royal rake's progress.

Now it so happens — and this is significant for our study of
the Age of Catherine de Medici — that the first great credit
inflation of modern times, with its nemesis of state bankruptcy,
took place in the years 1557 and 1558, setting in motion a series
of financial crises that were to last through the rest of the century
and on into the next. This inflation was the result of the last
phases of the war between France and Spain. Both countries
had needed very large sums of money — far beyond their
immediate or, with safety, their prospective revenues — to

carry on the war. And both countries had developed the instrument of credit. They had established what we term funded debts — permanent state loans, the interest on which formed annuities for those investing in them. The French call these *rentes*, and quite small people had their savings invested in them in the sixteenth century as today. The *rentier* class in France had been in existence and had been growing since the 1520s.

However, the main monetary resources for war came, not from permanent but from short-term loans, raised by the French king mainly at the great banking centre of Lyons, and by the Spanish king at Antwerp. At first these loans had been regarded by individual bankers with suspicion, but the habit of making them grew, and as the interest that kings were ready to pay increased to twelve per cent and then sixteen per cent, the prospect of a fine bargain broke down restraint. In 1555 Henry II of France carried through a transaction, the name of which we may translate as the Great Deal. He renewed his immense loans at Lyons, some of which had been at twelve per cent interest, contracted new loans, and put both old and new on a sixteen per cent interest basis. The transaction created a kind of South Sea Bubble. Everyone rushed to share in the Deal, layman and professional, widow and merchant, prince and gentleman, French, Swiss, German, even the Turk.

At the same time Philip II of Spain was working the money market at Antwerp for all that he was worth, or rather, for a great deal more. Both kings had outrun their resources, though their war needs were by no means satisfied. Nemesis followed. In 1557 Philip went bankrupt. Henry II managed to fool his creditors for a few months by asserting that the King of France would not break his word; and oddly enough there were people ready to believe him. Then he too defaulted. The credit inflation burst; and to put it rather crudely both kings had to make peace because wars then as now were fought on paper — paper-credit — and supplies had disappeared.

Financial stability is of course one of the main sources of the strength of a State; and here was the French State about to enter a critical period in its history with its credit ruined and colossal debts. The debt at the death of Henry II was over forty million *livres*; the royal income then, much of which never reached the Treasury, was approximately twelve million. The *livre* equalled about two shillings of contemporary English money, and perhaps some idea of the meaning of these sums may be obtained by remembering that Queen Elizabeth's annual revenue at the beginning of her reign averaged little more than a quarter of a million pounds.

A desperate budgetary position was not the only lamentable consequence of the war period. Naturally enough, the French monarchy had exploited taxation as well as other devices for raising revenue, to their extreme limits; and these limits, it is worth noting, were much greater than in England, where direct taxation could only be levied through parliament. The French king could tax on his own authority. So heavy, in fact, did the main direct tax — the *taille* — become that peasants left their lands and fled from it. There were certain sections of the country, of which Normandy was an example, where for various reasons the exactions and abuses of the government could go further than elsewhere; and these provinces readily lent themselves to Huguenot propaganda. Generally speaking, social discontent found an outlet for itself in religious and political unrest.

The machinery of government itself suffered from the financial straits of the monarchy. French local government was already very different from that in England, which remained in the unpaid hands of the landed gentry; and while the rapid increase of governmental activity associated with the rise of the modern state was accompanied by a remarkable expansion of the administrative duties of the English gentry as Justices of the Peace, in France the nobility or landed gentry were stripped of their feudal share in the government of the country, and more and more the business of local government, like that of central government, was placed in the hands of lawyer-officials of the State. This growing bureaucracy ought to have been a source of strength to the French monarchy, to which the professional administrator owed office, salary, and career. But in its overwhelming need for money, the Crown had taken a page out of the Papacy's book and had recourse to the sale of offices: officials were compelled to purchase their posts. Control was inevitably sacrificed, for a bureaucracy cannot be disciplined without the right of dismissal, and this had virtually gone. Thus when the severe trial of civil war fell on the French monarchy, one of the chief means of governing was deficient.

The mere sale of offices was not all; for Henry II, again like the Papacy, had taken to the creation of new offices and the multiplication of old, not because the administration required an increase of officials, but because the Crown needed ready money for new wars and could obtain it in this way. The policy was hopelessly short-sighted. Salaries were small, yet were often not paid. In 1559 the whole royal pay-roll, from high officials to common soldiers, was badly in arrears, in many instances for years. Officials had to recoup themselves from the wretched people who came under their charge or needed to use their services. And thus to the crippling burden of taxation was added the vexatious weight of official exactions.

Another element of weakness was the state of the lesser nobility or country gentlemen. As a class they were vulnerable at two points where the English gentry were protected. In the first place, the system of entail of estates, with descent to the eldest son only — a system which, whatever its injustice, has the advantage of preserving the wealth and standing of a family through generations — was not rigorously applied. Estates were constantly being broken up and the wealth of the main line of a noble house diminished. Secondly, in the sixteenth century a final ban was placed on the entry of French noblemen and their children into trade. In contrast with the custom of England, all the sons of the nobility were noble. They were thus precluded from that salutary participation in commerce which refreshed the wealth of the English gentry. For the younger sons of the gentry, cursed with the empty dignity of nobility, war was the only career; and as that career was closed by the termination of the Italian Wars in 1559 they were left without employment. And to make matters worse, they had latterly been fighting without pay since the royal Treasury was empty.

The lesser nobility in 1559 were in a very bad way. Their social functions had largely gone with the transfer of local government from them to lawyer-bureaucrats. They were immune in theory from the main tax, the *taille*; but in practice this was not entirely true, and in any case they had to bear an appreciable part of the financial burden. They had been compelled to contribute to forced loans; they had been victims of the great speculation in royal loans at luring but unpaid interest; in 1555 they had been cruelly hit by a heavy royal levy of money. And they found themselves in a ruinous age. Their rank compelled them to spend money on the education of their children and burdened them with the growing luxury in dress and display, while the great price-revolution in the second half of the sixteenth century, which caused a slump in the value of money at least as drastic as that in our own lifetime since 1914, played havoc with their finances, since rentals tended to remain fixed. Last blow of all, peace brought an end to their career of war.

They raised mortgages, they went bankrupt. And as in England in the sixteenth century, though to a far greater extent, they saw merchants and the lawyer-sons of merchants ousting them from their estates, becoming country gentry, and receiving patents of nobility. Some noblemen in desperation took to brigandage, forming those bands of marauders who were recruited for the Conspiracy of Amboise and were later to help in making the Religious Wars scenes of murder and rapine.

The picture which I have drawn is that of a country needing above all things a period of peace, firm government, and retrenchment. This was not to be. In June 1559, during a tilt at celebrations connected with the Peace of Cateau-Cambrésis, the King, Henry II, whose folly and prodigality had brought France to the verge of ruin, was mortally wounded. He left a family of four boys, the eldest of whom and the successor to the throne, Francis II, was only fifteen.

In the New Monarchies of the sixteenth century, government was essentially personal. Its whole mechanism, from the core of councillors whom the King chose to advise him, reflected the personality of the monarch. Loyalty was a personal feeling towards the King, not towards the abstraction of the State; and the secret of successful government was that power should rest on this loyalty and both be merged in the Crown. Obviously, a boy could be no more than the titular repository of power. The reality must be somewhere else. Consequently, power was bound to become an object of competition among the various claimants to it at Court.

England under Edward VI demonstrated this sixteenth-century truth; and the rivalry of the great lords, Somerset and Northumberland, for the control of power is one of the notorious passages of our history. Who, then, were the Somersets and Northumberlands of France? Who were the leading personalities at Court and what Court parties were there at this time?

The answer must begin with the Queen-Mother, Catherine de Medici. She was just forty years old at the death of her husband, Henry II. She was a daughter of the Medici, the ruling House of Florence, and niece of the Medici Pope Clement VII. Her marriage at the age of fourteen and a half to Henry, then only the second son of Francis I and unlikely to succeed to the throne, had been a move in Francis I's Italian diplomacy. It was a *mésalliance*: indeed, how else could the marriage of a French king's son to the daughter of an Italian merchant family — for that was the origin of the Medici — be regarded? But it was to be justified by Papal policy. Unfortunately Pope Clement died in less than a year, and the justification did not mature. Then, the death of the Dauphin made Henry the heir to the throne, thus aggravating the blunder of the marriage; and, final catastrophe, for seven years Catherine remained childless. For a time there was talk of repudiating her, and, no doubt, if she had continued childless we should have had a 'divorce' that might have helped to make the marital adventures of Henry VIII of England a little more understandable to modern writers. The situation called for all Catherine's skill and sweetness to postpone a decision. Children alone could save her. And at last they came. In rapid succession she bore ten. The danger was past.

Life with her husband, while not so total an eclipse as has often been said, needed much tact, for Henry II was dominated by his mistress, the notorious Diane de Poitiers, who though twenty years older than himself managed to maintain her hold on him till the last. It says much for Catherine that she tolerated this situation, without loss of dignity and without forfeiting her husband's respect. It says still more for her that when her chance came of revenge, which everyone expected and which the mercenary nature of Diane would have justified, she was content merely to dismiss the woman from Court and make her surrender the jewels that she had acquired.

A fairly stern school of experience: life had certainly been that for Catherine. She never overcame the sense of her inferior origin, and her exaggerated respect for royalty was time and again to influence her policy. She pursued crowns for her children as wealthy American matrons — according to repute — once pursued titled husbands for their daughters. She was not an intellectual, nor was she genuinely cultured, but as a true daughter of the Italian Renaissance she liked to patronize the arts and have the trappings of culture about her. She had a live sense of the splendour of royalty, derived from the extravagant Court of her father-in-law, Francis I, and, being a very rich woman in her private fortune, she indulged her taste for showiness and was insatiate in her love of building. Her reckless extravagance in the midst of the terrible financial distress of her country is not a pleasing aspect of her character.

She was undoubtedly a woman of great qualities, if not a great woman. Her vitality was boundless: she was always ready, with tireless energy, to tackle every difficulty that arose. But she lacked any grasp of principles, and was apt to see political problems in terms of a Palace intrigue which could be solved by getting folk together and making them shake hands. She was, in fact, a politician, a very able politician, not a statesman; and her charm coupled with her vitality made her most successful at the game.

Modern psychologists would shake their heads over her possessive maternalism. She loved her children and dominated them with her affection and personality in a way that was ruinous to them. The blackest event in her whole story — the Massacre of St Bartholomew — had its root in this instinct. To a certain extent it was her desire to mother her children that led her to desire the regency of France, though once she had tasted political power her energy led her to guard and monopolize it with passion.

Among the high nobility at Court there were three parties. The first was that of the Bourbons, who were princes of the blood, heirs to the throne should the reigning House of Valois die out. Their head was Anthony of Navarre, who had married the Queen of that small state, situated in the south-west corner of France. He was a wretched specimen of a leader, fickle, shifty, backboneless, easily twisted round Catherine de Medici's little finger; and characteristically his one ambition in life was to get back the portion of his kingdom of Navarre that Spain had conquered. It was always possible to divert his. attention from French politics by talk of inducing Philip II to restore his lost territories, a prospect the utter hopelessness of which he ought to have had the wit to see. When he was mortally wounded in the first Religious War his death removed a futile personality.

The real leader of the Bourbons was Anthony's younger

37

brother, Louis, Prince of Condé. Here was the true figure of a faction-leader: a brave fighter, a good companion, but a hot-headed, restless, ambitious person who in a struggle for power would inevitably assert the claims of his family, as princes of the blood, to the first place at Court.

The second party was that of the Guise family. They were a younger branch of the House of Lorraine, and therefore half foreign; but it had been the policy of Francis I and Henry II to neglect the princes of the blood and raise this foreign family, along with certain of the French nobility, to the dignity of dukes and peers, ranking in all but blood with the princes. The Guise family had profited enormously from the favour of Francis I: its lands were immense and so were its ecclesiastical holdings. Moreover, the Duke of Guise was allied by marriage to the French monarchy, while Mary of Guise was Queen-Mother of Scotland and Regent for her daughter, Mary Queen of Scots, whom the Guise by a brilliant coup had married to the Dauphin of France, now the new king, Francis II. They talked of being descended from Charlemagne; and had the two leading members of the House, the Duke of Guise and the Cardinal of Lorraine, not been such attractive personalities, their pride would have been insufferable. They pretended to a place in the Kingdom, lower of course than the King but above everyone else, even the princes of the blood. Frenchmen distrusted their ambition and their foreign strain.

Francis, Duke of Guise, was a brilliant soldier, with the laurels of Calais, which he had taken from the English in 1558, still fresh on his brow. Charles, Cardinal of Lorraine, his brother, was the wealthiest ecclesiastic in France, a highly-cultured churchman, an eloquent preacher, and the statesman of the family.

The third great family was the Montmorency. Its head was the Constable, Anne de Montmorency, the supreme military officer of France. He had been raised to high favour by Francis I, and then, after an eclipse, had returned to power under

Henry II. He owed his position and wealth to the monarchy, and Henry II's dependence on him as his chief minister had been constant. But the Guise family had always been present to play the role of rivals, and the last phase of the Italian Wars had not only been a triumph for Guise war policy over the Constable's counsel of peace, it had also seen the Constable defeated and taken prisoner at St Quentin — a striking disaster for French arms — while the saviour of the country had been the Duke of Guise, victor of Calais. The Montmorency accordingly had good reason to hate the Guise, and they hated them no less because their own tradition, in contrast with Guise ambition, was one of inflexible loyalty to the Crown.

The Constable had three nephews. Unlike their uncle, whose orthodoxy was as unswerving as his loyalty, they were all converted to the Huguenot faith. The eldest of the three was Gaspard de Coligny, the Admiral of France. He inherited all the fine qualities of the family. His conversion was a genuine act of faith, not a move in factional strife or personal ambition; and in the whole sordid story of the Religious Wars he is the one great leader who stands out as the man without reproach.

These three leading families practically divided France between them. Through a system of patronage and clientage, there was scarcely a nobleman, great or small, who was not attached, directly or indirectly, to one or other of them. The lands and influence of the Guise family, the largest of the three, covered the whole eastern provinces of the realm; those of the Bourbons covered the west; and the Montmorency held sway in the centre.

As Guise and Bourbon each claimed priority of the other at Court, it was impossible for the monarchy to satisfy both at the same time; and the situation, disconcerting enough in itself, had by 1559 become dangerous when this clash of political ambitions aligned itself with the religious divisions of the country.

Condé was converted to the Huguenot faith in 1558, though indeed religion sat lightly on him and he exercised a prince's licence in his private life that would have shocked Calvin. He naturally assumed the military leadership of the Huguenots when that aspect of their movement revealed and developed itself in the next two or three years, thus becoming their evil genius, for his inclinations and his rank as a prince of the blood lent impetus and respectability to all aggressive impulses. Anthony of Navarre, the head of the Bourbons, was also a Huguenot. But in religion as in everything else he was spineless: it was his wife, a woman of great force of character and an ardent Protestant, who had converted him.

With the Bourbons now at the head of Protestantism, the Guise naturally assumed the leadership of the Catholics. The Montmorency, however, remained divided. The Constable was not to be divorced from his faith, nor his nephews from theirs. Creed in this instance was stronger than family; a new phenomenon in French history, and one which increased the difficulties of the French government, for the obvious way of maintaining political equilibrium was dependence on the Montmorency in alliance with one of the other two parties, thus keeping the third party under control.

A final point. All these men, who were to play a prominent part in the opening phases of the Religious Wars, were, with the exception of the Constable, young, or at any rate not old, men. The Duke of Guise was forty in 1559, the Cardinal of Lorraine thirty-four, Anthony of Navarre forty-one, Condé twenty-nine, and Coligny forty-one. Their lieutenants were younger: all less than thirty. And young men are not servants of tranquillity.

Though technically of age, Francis II was only fifteen and a half when he succeeded to the throne in 1559, and it was obvious that there would have to be a regency, in fact if not in name. This was the opportunity of the Guise family. Through their niece, the new Queen, Mary of Scots, Francis was persuaded to place himself and the government of his country in their hands. They made friendly advances to Catherine de

Medici, and found her ready to acquiesce in the situation. France passed under Guise control.

Their task was an unenviable one. The end of the Italian Wars — as we have seen — had brought an insoluble financial problem, failure to meet debts, widespread social distress, the dismissal of soldiers who had not received their pay. The odium of it all descended on the Guise, and stuck more easily because there was the taint of the foreign adventurer about them and their personal ambition was thought to be limitless. Then, too, the religious problem had reached a crisis. This they tried to solve by continuing with increased energy Henry II's savage policy of persecution, thus adding to their unpopularity and piling on themselves the hatred of the Huguenot party.

The way was no smoother at Court. The restless Condé had seen, in the accession of a boy to the throne, the chance of making the political fortunes of himself and his family. The King, he contended, was legally still a minor, a Regent ought therefore to be appointed, and by the constitution of France one person and one only had the right to that post — the first prince of the blood, Anthony of Navarre. In his eyes the Guise brothers were mere usurpers of power, who, by the device of proclaiming the King of age, had evaded the necessity of appointing a Regent and so had excluded Condé's brother from the government of the country.

With much persuasion Condé induced his brother to come to Court to claim his rights; but when he arrived, Anthony's nerve failed him and he returned to his estates without playing the game that had been planned. As Condé could make no constitutional claim in his own name, he was left, after his brother's defection, with the alternative of acquiescing in Guise rule or turning to conspiracy. He chose conspiracy.

This was the origin of the Conspiracy of Amboise, the first outward sign of that civil strife towards which France was drifting. The Conspiracy was talked of as early as September 1559; and gradually preparations spread throughout the country. The nominal leader was a member of the lesser nobility named La Renaudie, but the real head was Condé, the 'silent chief', that mysterious great lord of whom the government heard and whose identity they could easily guess, though they were unable to secure adequate proof of his responsibility. The conspirators' plan was for a small group to make their way into the royal palace while the Court was at Amboise in March 1560, and seize the King and the Guise brothers, killing the latter if they resisted. This palace revolution was to be consolidated by the support of a large army which was to arrive at Amboise in small bands from all over France and hide in the woods till the signal was given. Captains were to be stationed in the principal towns of the country to stir up trouble and so prevent the passage of troops going to the aid of the government. Once the Guise had been seized, Condé was to arrive at Court, voice the country's grievances to King and Council, and secure the punishment of his rivals.

The Conspiracy was prepared by widespread propaganda, especially among the Huguenots who were urged to revolt against the increasing religious persecution. But though many Huguenots responded, Calvin and responsible ministers were flatly opposed to co-operation. As yet, the Huguenot Church was true to the political theory of Calvinism which taught passive obedience and forbade rebellion. Modern research has definitely exploded the old idea that this Conspiracy was a Protestant revolt. It was political, not religious, its purpose being to replace the Guise by the Bourbons in the government of the country; and most of the armed bands directed to assemble at Amboise consisted of those professional soldiers who were unemployed and in distress. Condé appears to have had plenty of money to hire them; indeed, the financial backing of the Conspiracy so far exceeded anything that the leaders could have raised from their own resources that one French historian has voiced the suspicion the Elizabeth of England was paymaster of the forces.

The plot miscarried; one armed band after another was captured. At first the government was merciful, but as more and more soldiers were seized and the true extent of the Conspiracy became apparent, mercy was replaced by rigour.

But the government was shaken by the evident signs of unrest and discontent, for on top of the Conspiracy came a spate of seditious pamphlets, peddled secretly through the country and even thrown into the royal apartments. These attacks on Guise rule gave Catherine de Medici her excuse to intervene and virtually assume the guiding authority in the State. She sought the advice of Coligny, stopped the operation of the edicts of persecution, released those imprisoned for their religion, and inaugurated a policy of conciliation by which the secular authorities, though ordered to suppress Huguenot assemblies, were forbidden to try any individuals for heresy. They were to leave such trials to the ecclesiastical authorities, which in fact meant that heresy as such would go practically unpunished. So far as the secular law was concerned, the policy amounted to liberty of conscience, but not liberty of worship. In actual practice conciliation went further, for the amnesty to religious offenders and the stopping of the old persecution tended to paralyse the whole secular attack on heresy; an effect which Catherine, in her pursuit of appeasement, was not inclined to prevent. The Huguenot movement took fresh courage; it grew in numbers and in turbulence.

Pacification was a hopeless quest. Though Condé, by putting on a bold face and denying all complicity in the Conspiracy of Amboise, had narrowly escaped punishment, like an inveterate gambler he set to work to build up a new conspiracy. It was on much the same lines as the old, and once more he made his appeal to Protestants, within and without France. This time, significantly enough, the Huguenot movement was more ready to entangle itself. Bands of armed men were raised, and their instructions, as finally evolved, were to join the King of Navarre and Condé as they marched on the Court from

Navarre's capital in the south-west. Again the plot miscarried. The Guise got wind of it, secured evidence with which to convict Condé, and then acted vigorously. At Lyons their troops fell on one of Condé's bands which was to have seized the city, after which they set out to crush the Huguenots in that area of France. It looked as if the Religious Wars had already begun.

With equal vigour the government ordered the King of Navarre to bring Condé to Court; and, caught between an army advancing from the north and another that Philip II was assembling in the south, and beguiled by reassuring messages which Catherine de Medici unscrupulously sent him, Anthony obeyed the order and delivered his brother to his fate. Condé was arrested and steps taken to try him for treason; extreme measures for which Francis II may have been personally responsible.

But Fortune had not yet deserted Condé. At this very juncture Francis II was taken ill. In a few days it became evident that he was unlikely to recover, and, with dramatic suddenness, the whole situation was reversed. The new King would be a boy, not yet ten. There could be no pretence this time that the King was of age, nor could the appointment of a Regent be evaded. It looked as if the position for which the Bourbons had twice plotted rebellion was theirs by the constitutional theory of the country. How, indeed, was the claim of Anthony of Navarre, as first prince of the blood, to be denied? And yet that is what Catherine de Medici was determined upon. She wanted the regency for herself, and with masterly skill used the last days of Francis II to secure it. By a mixture of cajolery and coercion, reminding the King of Navarre of the threatening situation in which their last plot had placed his family, she persuaded him to acquiesce in her plan. For his reward she promised the release of Condé and oblivion as to the past, and the title of Lieutenant-General of the Kingdom for himself, a title giving prestige but little or no power.

From the point of view of the country's welfare, it was

thoroughly sound policy. Power was slipping from the Guise. They were preparing to leave Court, and if Navarre had become Regent would certainly have done so, thus placing France once more at the mercy of the factions, with the roles of Bourbon and Guise reversed. The Guise were too wealthy and too mighty for Catherine to let them depart to their estates, there to brood in pensive discontent. Her aim was to make friends all round, and with this object in view she assured Anthony that neither she nor the Guise had persuaded the dying Francis to arrest his brother, while Anthony in turn protested his own innocence. The Guise and he embraced one another. All was going well and according to Catherine's plan. On December 5th, 1560, she secured Anthony's renunciation of the regency in writing, and that night the King died. Charles IX, a boy of nine and a half, was now King. Catherine placed herself at his side to receive the homage of the nobility, and placed her bed in his bedroom to symbolize that dominance over the King from which he was only to escape once in his unhappy reign.

One more obstacle in the way of Catherine's regency had still to be surmounted. At the time of the Conspiracy of Amboise it had been decided to summon the Estates General, the national representative assembly. This body had not met for nearly eighty years, and it is eloquent proof of the desperate political and financial condition of the country that the French monarchy, which had hoped to obliterate the memory of such assemblies, was now forced to call them up from the grave.

During the recent troubles, anti-Guise tracts had, among other arguments, declared that the right of appointing Regent and Council during a royal minority belonged to the national assembly; and in Geneva Calvin was at this time supervising an agitation directed to wresting the regency from Catherine de Medici and giving it to the Huguenot King of Navarre. When the Estates General met at Orleans a few days after the death of Francis II, deputations arrived from the Huguenot churches to stimulate the demands of the Estates. But to Calvin's disgust and to the amazement of Bourbon supporters, the King of Navarre refused to play their game, and instead supported Catherine's retention of the regency. The silly man had been completely bamboozled by the Queen-Mother. He was vowing eternal love and friendship for the Guise and complete content-ment with everything. The agitation collapsed and Catherine kept the regency.

Appeasement was now the ruling idea, and the year that followed was to see this policy put to its crucial tests. Peace depended on the solution of two problems: Court faction, and religion. Catherine's solution for the first was to keep both Bourbons and Guise at Court, behaving like bosom friends. When their real feelings betrayed themselves in squabbles, she hurried to make them friends again, as one might try to keep two naughty quarrelsome boys in order by love and sweets. It was a nice, motherly policy; but it was not statesmanship, and we shall later see its fatal error.

Catherine's solution for the religious problem, while bound to command respect in the more tolerant atmosphere of later centuries, was no more statesmanlike in its own *milieu* than her handling of the political problem. She contemplated a temporary policy leading to a permanent solution. Temporarily, she determined to continue that partial toleration of Huguenots which had been inaugurated on her initiative during the troubles at Amboise. With this in view she issued a new amnesty, releasing religious prisoners, even those imprisoned for causing disturbances; and at the same time she urged officials to exercise a toleration beyond the terms of her edict. The practical consequence, of course, was to encourage the growth of the Huguenot movement, increase the bitterness of religious feeling everywhere, and make the religious problem graver than ever. The Easter of 1561 was a time of great disorder through-out the land.

It would be a signal error to imagine that Catherine meant

either to recognize the Huguenot faith or permanently to tolerate two faiths. Both Calvinists and Catholics would have regarded the latter as sacrilege, and to politicians of that epoch it would have been an assault on national unity. Toleration, as that age saw it, was not homage to the rights of conscience, but the recognition that one of two faiths was not strong enough to suppress the other, or that it would only succeed in doing so at the cost of wrecking the State.

If, then, toleration was merely a temporary policy, what was Catherine's permanent solution for the religious problem? It was a National Council of the French Church with a programme of reform, doctrinal and disciplinary, that would unite Catholic and Protestant.

For some years sovereigns had been urging the Papacy to summon a Council of the whole Church. Such a Council had sat twice at Trent, the last time in 1551–2, when it had adjourned to another meeting. Now this Council had come to decisions that made a compromise between Catholicism and Protestantism, desired by an influential section of Christendom, impossible. Consequently, in demanding another Council those who still hoped for compromise were emphatic that the Council of Trent must be allowed to lapse and an entirely new one be summoned, not bound by its decisions. The Papacy gave no signs of action; and Catherine de Medici and the Cardinal of Lorraine, who in this matter was for compromise with Protestantism and a broad Church settlement, hit upon the plan of calling a National Council of the Gallican Church. They hoped to arrange a compromise with Protestantism, and thus be ready with a *fait accompli* when the Oecumenical Council of the whole Church was at length summoned. The condition of the French Church, they argued, could not wait on Papal dilatoriness.

From the Papal point of view the policy was not only wholly unacceptable but also extremely dangerous. It might lead to schism; and the notorious independence of the Gallican Church

47

made a breach between France and Rome seem far from impossible. The Papacy met the danger by issuing a Bull announcing the continuation of the old Council of Trent, at the same time using all the vigour and threats of which it was capable to prevent the meeting of a French Council.

What was to be done? Catherine could not hold a National Council when an Oecumenical Council was summoned. On the other hand, to acquiesce in the re-summoning of the Council of Trent was to renounce all hope of settling the religious problem in France. She resolved the dilemma by dropping the name of Council from her assembly, disguising her intentions under the term 'Colloquy'; and she proceeded with her plans in secret to avoid a direct Papal veto. Her Colloquy — the Colloquy of Poissy as it was called — was launched on an assembly of the French Church which met at the end of July 1561.

Catherine was playing with fire: there can be no doubt about it. And the Cardinal of Lorraine, who is credited by his latest biographer with responsibility for the scheme of a National Council, revealed, one may admit, a well-meaning tolerance but hardly great foresight or astute statesmanship. In order to arrange the representation of the Huguenot Church at the Colloquy, Catherine naturally turned to the Admiral Coligny, whose charm of manner and unselfish loyalty to the monarchy pleased her. She kept him at Court for advice, agreed to his suggestion that Calvin's right-hand man, Theodore Beza, should be brought from Geneva for the Colloquy, and herself suggested Peter Martyr of Zürich. She actually received these notorious heretics at Court; and inevitably the Huguenots in Court circles, with such leaders present and in high favour, flaunted their faith and worship as never before. Nor could or did all this happen without encouraging the Huguenot movement everywhere.

Catherine's policy could only be justified if it had an appreciable chance of success. In fact it had none. Neither the Catholic

Church nor the Calvinist was purely national. Each was controlled from a headquarters over which the French King had no control; and force or cajolery was incapable of imposing a settlement on Rome or Geneva. The truth is that Catherine was blind to the difficulties that she was up against. Her Colloquy would necessarily handle doctrinal problems; but, as a contemporary said, she herself had no idea what the word 'dogma' meant.

The assembly opened. Catherine succeeded in her trick of turning it into a Colloquy. And then the trouble started. Orthodox Catholics cried out in horror at a figure of speech used by Beza. She smoothed this out. Then, when further difficulties arose, she tried to overcome them by gathering the leading Catholic and Protestant divines together in private. She was under the illusion that differences over the Eucharist could be solved as she had been solving the quarrels of Bourbon and Guise in the last nine months — by bringing the quarrelsome people together and persuading them to be friendly. She meant well; she laboured hard; she failed. Fundamental differences of principle are not to be resolved by mediators who have no principles.

Catherine's policy was a catastrophe. On the one hand, by seeming to give recognition to their faith she had bred in Huguenot ranks a new spirit of daring that displayed itself in the wholesale seizing of churches. On the other hand, she had enraged the Catholics, who turned on the Huguenots and massacred them. But in spite of all this, Catherine persisted in her policy of seeking for a peaceful settlement. She kept Beza and Coligny at Court to pacify the Huguenots and check excesses by their influence. What wonder if this merely added to the demoralization, apparently confirming the impression that the Court supported the Huguenots? So thoroughly did she play her game that Beza himself thought that he was about to convert the King and the Queen-Mother to Calvinism!

The extent of the catastrophe has been only half told. In

49

tackling the problem of political faction, Catherine had concentrated all her attention on maintaining friendship between Bourbon and Guise and keeping both parties at Court. Time and again she patched up their quarrels; but all the reconciliations were hollow and of short duration. Meanwhile, in constant pursuit of an elusive goal she had neglected the Montmorency, that vital centre group whose firm loyalty to the Crown made it the essential basis of a King's party. The way was thus free for Guise and the Constable Montmorency, dropping their long and traditional rivalry, to draw together. Both were now opposed to the Bourbons; both felt their Catholic faith threatened by the Queen-Mother's policy.

The result of this tragic neglect was seen when in April 1561, the Constable Montmorency, the Duke of Guise, and another nobleman formed what was known as the Triumvirate — a Catholic party or league. It marks a turning point in our story. For now a party existed, menacing in its power, whose object was to defend the Catholic faith, apart from the King and if need be against him.

The Crown was thus isolated between two parties of passion — Catholic and Huguenot — with all the Court factions on one side or the other. It was unable to control events or prevent the outbreak of civil war: indeed, by flirting with heresy and so fanning the flames of religious strife, Catherine de Medici had unwittingly hastened the day when the calamity of civil war would fall on France.

III

THE MASSACRE OF
ST BARTHOLOMEW

WE have seen how dangerously short-sighted was Catherine de Medici's policy of appeasement. With an optimism as striking as it was foolish she had set out to succeed where the Emperor Charles V had failed — to effect a compromise in religious doctrines between Catholic and Protestant. She handled the Colloquy of Poissy in August and September 1561 like a Court intrigue; and inevitably failed. She merely stimulated the growth and insolence of the Huguenot party, enraged the Catholics by the favour shown to heretics, and thus intensified the religious passions of the country. France emerged from the Colloquy a long step nearer civil war.

At the same time she had made a fatal blunder in the way she tackled the problem of Court faction. Here she had been so busy keeping Guise and Bourbon in artificial friendship that she had entirely neglected the middle party upon which the independence of the monarchy ought to have been based in a crisis — the party of the Constable Montmorency. The consequence of this neglect was that Guise and Montmorency drew together and formed an alliance in defence of Catholicism. The Crown was left to manœuvre without any real strength of its own between two parties of passion.

But manœuvring was the very genius of this well-meaning woman; and in the autumn and winter of 1561–2 she was feverishly busy with it. She pursued her policy of a peaceful settlement with all the obstinacy and assurance of which her remarkable vitality was capable.

There seems little doubt that at this time she was

overestimating the strength of the Huguenot party, and thought it irresistible; as, indeed, by her own misguided encouragement she was doing her best to make it. She kept the Genevan leader Beza and the Admiral Coligny at Court, hoping with their co-operation to restrain the excesses of the Huguenots throughout the country and to work out an immediate policy, which, while satisfying the Huguenots by its extended toleration, would yet avoid clashes with the Catholics. That policy was embodied in the famous edict of January 1562; and, such was Catherine's adroitness, she managed to get the edict passed as the advice of a special, enforced Council. It gave official recognition to the Huguenot Church by permitting worship in the suburbs outside towns, and in the country, though assemblies within towns, where they were likely to provoke Catholic attacks, were forbidden. Even Huguenot synods and consistories were allowed to meet, with the permission of the magistrates, a permission they were told to grant.

Catherine's tactical skill at this time was really astounding. Although in October the Papal Nuncio had been writing to the Pope urging him to form a league with Spain and the other Catholic princes to aid the French Catholics against the Queen-Mother and the Huguenots, now in January Catherine actually succeeded in persuading the Papacy to look favourably on her Edict of Toleration as a necessary concession to avoid greater concessions. She even revived doctrinal talks between Catholic theologians at Court and the Calvinists; and — astonishing spectacle — the Papal representative was seen listening to a Protestant sermon and psalm-singing. At the same time, through Beza and Coligny, Catherine persuaded the Huguenots to acquiesce in the restrictions of her Edict.

But behind this façade of success was an alarming and well-nigh desperate situation. The more hot-headed of the Catholic nobility had watched with increasing hostility Catherine's relations with the Huguenot leaders. She had succumbed to the charm both of Beza and Coligny and turned more and more to the latter for advice. It seemed as if government policy were passing into the control of Coligny and the Protestant party, and so well were things going with the Huguenots at Court that Protestant worship there was quite open and many were either converted to the new faith or toyed with it. When a bishop announced his conversion, the evil effect of Catherine's conduct could no longer be ignored.

To retain the leading Catholics at Court in such a situation was impossible. The Duke of Guise left in October 1561, and there was a general exodus of Catholic nobility that month. They had already been discussing the possibility of taking up arms against the Protestants, and the Nuncio had made his suggestion to the Papacy of a Catholic league. In mid-November all Europe was talking of the possibility of armed intervention by the Catholic powers.

And then came the final blow. For some months the despicable Anthony of Navarre — Julian the Apostate, as the Huguenots were to call him — had been preparing to rat once more. In December he finally went over to the Catholic Triumvirate, who were plotting to use him in the same way that Calvin had intended just a year before; that is to say, they proposed to support his constitutional right to the regency and depose Catherine de Medici. One noble lord exclaimed that that woman ought to be thrown into the Seine.

In face of this menace, Catherine lost her head. Thinking that the Catholics were about to rise and invite an invasion of France by other sovereigns, she turned to the Huguenot nobles and asked them to discover what forces the Huguenot churches could raise in defence of the monarchy. Coligny sent a circular letter to the various provincial synods and through them to the consistories, and soon was able to tell Catherine that two thousand one hundred and fifty churches and more offered their persons and services at their own expense.

Again Catherine had blundered; blundered seriously, for her action encouraged the Huguenots to complete their military organization, with the result that the direction of their policy passed from the more cautious ministers, schooled in the Calvinist doctrine of passive obedience, to the captains and nobles who were their military leaders. Moreover, when war did at last come, her action presented the Huguenots with the invaluable argument that they were really fighting for the King.

Catherine had now placed herself in the position of manœuvring, not between two political and religious parties, but between two hostile armies.

Her difficulties were multiplying. The Edict of January, granting toleration to the Huguenots, had to be registered in the various *parlements* or high courts of justice, and, though she was able to browbeat the provincial *parlements* when they resisted and thus without much difficulty get her way, coercion was not so successful with the *Parlement de Paris*. This body did not capitulate before March, and by then its resistance had stirred up the religious passions of the city. At Court, Anthony of Navarre created trouble by demanding the dismissal of Coligny and his family. Perhaps it would have been wiser if Coligny had defied the King of Navarre and stayed at Court. Instead, he withdrew, leaving the Huguenot cause in the hands of a woman — Catherine — who was notoriously variable, and of the Prince of Condé, who was hot-headed and irresponsible; and Catherine disliked Condé.

In this situation a spark was enough to cause an explosion; and on March 1st, 1562, there occurred the affray known as the Massacre of Vassy. While passing through his territories, the Duke of Guise came across a Huguenot assembly worshipping in the town of Vassy, contrary to the Edict of January. In the course of the squabble that followed his men killed thirty of the congregation and wounded one hundred and twenty or thirty. During the last year or so there had been plenty of massacres on both sides; but coming at this inflammatory moment and being the work of the Duke of Guise, it was the incident that precipitated war. Condé was at Paris, free from the restraining advice of Coligny, and he sent out a call to arms to the Huguenot churches.

Catherine tried to stop the outbreak of hostilities. She ordered the Duke of Guise, who was marching on Paris with a large armed following, to leave his followers and come to Court. Instead, he joined the Constable and the third Triumvir and together they entered Paris with two to three thousand men. Then Catherine wrote to Condé urging him to come to Court and protect her children, herself, and the Kingdom; an invitation which might have prevented war if it had been accepted, but not being accepted, simply lent additional speciousness to the Huguenot claim that they were taking up arms to protect the King. Finally, she appealed to Coligny; but he too failed to rise to the occasion, and so the Triumvirs were able to march on the Court, leaving Catherine no option but to submit with as good grace as possible to the Catholic army. The Catholics were thus able to enter on war with the person and authority of the King on their side; and soon Catherine's enforced submission was transformed into willing co-operation when Condé, with singular lack of decency, or indeed of fore-sight, published her confidential appeal to him to help.

Both sides rather drifted into war than entered it suddenly. But in fact the country was already in plain revolution. In April a mob at the city of Sens had fallen on a congregation of Huguenots worshipping, as they had the legal right to do, outside the city walls, and slaughtered all but a few hidden by Catholic friends. Afterwards they slew the captain or guard of the congregation and his men, who happened to be away from the city at the time of the massacre. The passions aroused everywhere may be illustrated by the action of the children on this occasion, who tied a rope about the captain's feet and dragged his body through the streets for hours, crying, 'Bring out your swine, here is the swineherd.'

In this first of the Religious Wars both sides appealed for outside help, the Catholics and Catherine asking for aid from

Spain and Savoy and the Huguenots from German Protestants and Elizabeth of England. It was a sign of that tendency, present right through this period—a tendency of more than academic interest to us today—for a general European war to break out over conflicting ideologies. Nor is it without interest to notice how far *Realpolitik* and not mere community of creed determined the action of princes, even of Philip II.

At any rate, there can be no illusion about Queen Elizabeth's realism. Her ambassador in France, who to give him his due was a hot-gospeller and crusader, put the inducement this way: France was about to be carved up by Spain and Savoy and other powers, and Elizabeth had better be in at the game and get her share. Elizabeth gave her help—restricted help—on terms: the Huguenots were to give her Havre at once, and at the end of the war she would exchange it for Calais. Condé's agreement to these terms was a measure of his folly as well as his desperation: he made himself infamous as a Frenchman.

The war went excellently for Catherine de Medici: it eliminated all her generals! Anthony of Navarre was killed—a marvellous stroke of luck for her, and good riddance from almost every point of view; one of the Triumvirs was killed; the Duke of Guise, another of the Triumvirs, was assassinated; and the third Triumvir, the Constable Montmorency, was captured. On the Huguenot side Condé was captured. One might say that Catherine had had the devil's own luck. All she had to do to end the war was to let the two captives, Montmorency and Condé, negotiate the terms; and being captives, they were good peacemakers.

From the point of view of the Huguenot ministers, Condé in these peace negotiations sold the pass. The Pacification of Amboise, in March 1563, conceded liberty of conscience, but in the vital matter of liberty of worship it imposed severe restrictions, from which, however, Condé's own class, the high nobility, was exempted. Lesser folk were permitted to hold Protestant worship only in Huguenot towns or in the suburbs of one town in each bailiwick, while in the Paris region there were to be no Huguenot assemblies.

After securing peace between Frenchmen, Catherine turned the united country—with Condé trying sheepishly to excuse his conduct to Elizabeth—on the English, and drove them out of Havre.

But was it peace? In one sense, yes; because four years were to elapse before war broke out again, and that is not a negligible length of time. On the other hand, no prophetic gifts were needed to see trouble ahead.

In the first place, the assassination of the Duke of Guise in the late war was a crime which was ultimately expiated in the Massacre of St Bartholomew. The assassin was a young Huguenot nobleman, who was captured and, before being torn in pieces by four horses, accused Coligny of having employed him to do the deed. He alternately maintained and retracted his accusation. Coligny published a reply denying the accusation, and there seems no reason to doubt his word; but with rather unfortunate honesty he went on to declare that he was glad Guise was dead, as he was an enemy of God and the King. Neither he nor Beza had a single word of condemnation for the crime; and extreme Huguenots celebrated the death of the tyrant Guise and bemoaned the execution of the martyr-assassin in floods of poetry, hailing the latter as 'the happy man chosen of God', 'the tenth Paladin, the liberator of France'. Is it any wonder that the widow and son of Guise regarded Coligny as his murderer? or that assassination—a crime hitherto despised in France as a pestiferous Italian custom—rapidly found its way into French life?

Moreover, there emerged from the first Religious War the significant fact that the major part of the nation was Catholic. Catholicism had begun to stir itself and pay more attention to its spiritual duties; and on the Huguenot side recourse to arms had been a mistake. 'If it had not been for the war', wrote the Venetian ambassador, 'France would be at present Huguenot, because the people were so rapidly changing their faith and the ministers had acquired such credit among them that they persuaded them whatever they wished. But when they passed from words to arms and commenced to rob, ruin, or kill ... the people began to say, "What sort of a religion is this?"'

Catherine de Medici had been prone—as the Venetian ambassador had obviously been—to over-estimate, and over-estimate seriously, the strength of the Huguenots. The war broke that spell for her; and though she was still intent on her policy of moderation, and, through the death of the Catholic leaders in the late war, was far better placed to make concessions, her new grasp of realities was shown by her determination not to extend the peace settlement of Amboise but rather to apply it strictly. The result was an undercurrent of Huguenot dissatisfaction, for not only did many find it difficult to worship except by travelling some distance, but the restrictions also erected a serious obstacle in the way of their propaganda.

Real peace in France was not achieved. Religious passion and mob violence continued; and the situation in many places can be suggested by the following reminiscence of a Huguenot gentleman: 'I have often heard my mother say that, just before I was born, she several times had the greatest difficulty to save herself from being drowned like others of all ages and sexes by a great lord of the country, a persecutor of religion. He had them thrown into a river close by his house, saying that he would make them drink out of his big saucer.'

In 1564 Catherine began a tour of France to show the King to his people, a tour which lasted till the beginning of 1566 and included the famous meeting with the Spanish Court at Bayonne in June and July 1565. One might easily leave the Bayonne meeting out of Catherine's story if it were not for its legendary importance and its effect on future events. Catherine's main object in going to Bayonne was to meet her favourite daughter Elizabeth, who had been married to Philip II as part of the peace settlement of Cateau-Cambrésis in 1559. She hoped to persuade Philip II himself to be present, and to bring off a double marriage for her children with his family.

The notion that Catherine at this time was harbouring any sinister and far-reaching plan against Protestantism may certainly be dismissed as false. But fiction no less than fact has its role in human affairs; and it is not difficult to understand why this particular misconception took root. Calvinist propaganda had spread from France into the Spanish Netherlands, and was threatening to create as much trouble there as in France. Hence a meeting between the rulers of Spain and France quite naturally gave rise to rumours that a united front was forming against Protestantism; what we today should describe as a Madrid-Paris axis. Philip II no doubt would have liked this. But its one-sided character was too obvious: it would merely have saddled the French with the terrible task of trying to suppress their own Huguenots in order to save Spain in the Netherlands. And, in point of fact, the French government would have rejoiced to see Spanish power in the Netherlands break.

Philip II did not go to Bayonne. His place was taken by the Duke of Alva. The problem of heresy was discussed, and there was mention of a league between France, Spain, and the Emperor. But it is certain that no league was made. All the same, the Huguenots suspected the worst, as democratic Europe, with more reason, suspected the worst from a meeting of Hitler and Mussolini in pre-war days. Ardent Protestants throughout western Europe expressed their fears; and the nightmare of a Catholic league against Protestantism, which began to haunt even Englishmen, found its reputed origin in the interview at Bayonne. When the Massacre of St Bartholomew occurred seven years later, it was immediately said to have been planned at this nefarious, but in fact quite innocuous, interview.

By the year 1567 affairs were again going badly at the French Court; the nobility full of quarrels, and Catherine de Medici once more engendering deep distrust. She was being too clever by half, promising Philip II to suppress the Huguenots, and telling the Huguenot leaders the opposite. To the Huguenots the limitations on freedom of worship remained a constant source of discontent, and when, in this year 1567, the Duke of Alva took a large army from Spain to the Netherlands and began his rule of terror there, French Calvinists followed the fortunes of their Netherland brethren with much the same passionate interest and fear that many of our own contemporaries were displaying a few years ago, when democratic principles were being overthrown on the Continent; wondering when their turn would come. In reality, so far was Catherine from welcoming Alva's plans, that she refused permission for his army to march through France, and watched the growth of his military power in the Netherlands with anxiety. But the Huguenots could not know this. They had no faith in her, and when the news reached them that Alva had treacherously seized two of the Netherland leaders, Egmont and Horn, the French Huguenot leaders feared that Catherine intended to play the same trick on them. It was a desire to get their own blow in first, rather than anything else, which led them to revolt and attempt to seize the King by surprise at Meaux in September 1567.

In this way began the second Religious War; surely an indication that in the circumstances of the time civil war was endemic. The war did not last long. It was over by March 1568, and only one battle was fought in which the old Constable Montmorency — he was seventy-five — was mortally wounded.

But it was a truce rather than a peace. Killings and drownings went on unofficially, and more people are said to have been murdered after the publication of the peace than were killed in the war. Nor is this surprising, for a significant reaction had set in, and everywhere Catholics were forming themselves into local leagues, pledged and armed to withstand the Huguenots. A definite change had also come over Catherine de Medici. Every instinct — of maternal jealousy and of royalty — had been shocked by the Huguenot attempt to seize the King; and she was now convinced that they were aiming not so much at religious appeasement as at a political revolution. She abandoned her policy of moderation, dismissed the Chancellor with whose name it was associated, and in her new temper did indeed plan to seize the Huguenot leaders, Condé and Coligny, as Alva had seized Egmont and Horn. However, secrets were not easily kept at Court: news of the plan reached its intended victims, and the third Religious War broke out in consequence in August to September 1568.

This was the longest of the wars hitherto, and the most cruel. 'We fought the first war like angels,' said a Huguenot leader, 'the second like men, and the third like devils.' Whether or not 'angels' was the appropriate word for the first war, 'devils' certainly was for the third. They slaughtered women and children, and wreaked particular vengeance on Catholic priests. They took an abbey and compelled the monks to hang each other. They put garrisons to death in spite of the terms of capitulation, and in cases of direct reprisal showed absolutely no mercy. One city, guilty of the merciless sacking of a Huguenot city, was stormed, its soldiers and inhabitants put to the sword, and the city burnt.

On the Catholic side there was equal or greater savagery. At Orleans, where the Provost of the city had interned the Huguenots in the prisons, the Catholic mob was roused by its preachers; some ran to one of the prisons and put everyone there to death, while others went to a second prison and, being unable to break down the door, set fire to it. Many were burnt to death; others, after throwing their children from the walls in the hope of saving them and seeing them caught on pikes or cut to pieces, jumped themselves and were slaughtered in the same way. Two hundred Huguenots were said to have been killed in this outbreak of mob violence. At Auxerre the mob killed a hundred and fifty Huguenots, stripped their bodies, dragged them through the streets and threw them into the river or into the

61

sewers. Catholic soldiers often showed a similar fury. On one occasion, at the storming of a château, they dragged the Marquis from his sick-bed and threw him into an oven, while on other occasions they made captives jump to their death from the highest tower of a castle. Some commanders tried to stop these bestial cruelties, but others, like the Catholic Monluc, who boasted of his deeds in his Memoirs, employed terrorism as a general policy.

In the first important battle of the war Condé was killed: he was shot in the back after being wounded and after the battle was over. If anything, his death was a gain for his side, since the leadership now passed to the Admiral Coligny. With his ambition and his factious inclinations, Condé had been the evil genius of the Huguenot movement, and he more than anybody had been responsible for the supremacy of its military and disorderly elements.

The manner of Condé's death was yet another sign of that moral anarchy which was soon to culminate in the Massacre of St Bartholomew. And appropriately enough, there were some remarks made by Catherine de Medici at this time which furnish us with a glimpse into the unprincipled mind from which that infamous act was to spring. On one occasion she told the Spanish ambassador that she proposed to offer a free pardon and fifty thousand crowns to anyone who killed Coligny, with smaller rewards for the murder of his brother and another leader; and in fact, a reward for Coligny's murder was officially proclaimed. On a later occasion she told the ambassador that he would soon see 'a service to God and this King so remarkable that Philip II and the world will rejoice over it'. And when peace came, she assured the Papal Nuncio that it was merely a device to lure Coligny and his followers to Court in order to lay hands on them. Seen in retrospect, these statements might appear to have a sinister bearing on the events of Bartholomew's Eve, 1572. But their real and only significance is psychological: they reveal the unscrupulous, Italianate mind of that woman. Her remark to the Nuncio, for example, was probably just any old tale to keep her stocks high in Papal circles.

Peace came at last; the Peace of St Germain in August 1570. There had been a growing desire for it, shared by both sides and accentuated by the misery of the country and the appalling state of government finance. Moreover, the influence of the Guise party at Court had been waning. The war had naturally brought the Guise back to power, and the Cardinal of Lorraine had come to rule the roost at Court. His overbearing nature and his insolence to Catherine de Medici and others had turned them against him. There was also a general revulsion, which Catherine shared, against Spanish influence at Court. In fact, a new party was arising; a party known as the Politiques — in contrast with the *dévots* or *religieux* — moderate Catholics, liberal in their tendencies, who thought first of the good of the State and 'preferred the repose of the Kingdom and their own homes to the salvation of their souls; who would rather that the Kingdom remained at peace without God than at war for Him'. The chief nobleman of this party was Francis de Montmorency, the eldest son and heir of the old Constable Montmorency, killed in 1567. His Politique outlook enabled the age-long feud of Montmorency and Guise to break out again; and the fall of the Guise party at Court was his opportunity.

Catherine, too, was switching over to a politique outlook — to a policy of holding the balance between the parties. And, as she so often did, she was associating her new policy with matrimonial projects. She proposed to marry her daughter, Margaret, to Henry of Navarre, the young heir of Anthony and titular head of the Huguenot party. This would bring another crown into the family. And she was also planning to marry her second son to Elizabeth of England — yet another prospective crown.

Obviously, these matrimonial projects, involving in each instance union with a Protestant, called for the support both of the Politiques and the Huguenots, and it is therefore not surprising that the Peace of St Germain brought these two parties into power in place of the Guise. Nor is it surprising that the Huguenots were granted a measure of toleration which went somewhat further than ever before. Under Politique and moderate Huguenot leadership the new policy marched. True, wooing Queen Elizabeth was a discouraging, though hardly dreary business; but in May 1572, Catherine obtained from England — not a wedding, but what seemed a far from unsatisfactory substitute, a defensive alliance against Spain, known as the Treaty of Blois. It needed time to show that Elizabeth's diplomatic *finesse* could outmatch even that of Catherine.

But though the situation might seem promising, it was not free from danger. The Politiques believed, as did Coligny, that the way to ensure internal peace was to follow a policy of religious toleration at home and sink domestic differences in a national war against the country's great rival, Spain. There was a sound instinct in this, for though the treaty of Cateau-Cambrésis in 1559 had put an end to Franco-Spanish hostility over Italy, geographical facts inexorably drove the two countries to enmity. Spain and its outlying territories held France like a nut in a pair of nutcrackers, with the Spanish Netherlands in the north, Luxemburg and Franche-Comté in the east, then northern Italy, and finally a salient — Roussillon — into south-western France. It was vital to French interests to break this encirclement, but equally vital to Spain to maintain it, for the artery of the Spanish Empire in Europe — the line of communications between Spain and her invaluable Netherland possessions — ran through the territories to the east of France.

The Revolt of the Netherlands offered France the chance of weakening her rival and possibly of securing lands in a natural area for French territorial expansion. And when in April 1572 a new and hopeful phase of the Revolt started with the capture of Brille by the Sea-Beggars, the time for seizing that chance seemed to have arrived. So, at least, thought the Politiques;

and so, of course, did the Huguenots, especially the Admiral Coligny. What is more, the King, Charles IX, shared their enthusiasm.

This last is the significant fact; the fact from which begins the story of St Bartholomew. Something extraordinary had happened: for the first — and the last — time in his life Charles IX had thrown off his mother's tutelage. Coligny had come to Court, captured the affection of the young King, and drawn him enthusiastically into his war plans, even to the point of allowing an army of Huguenots to march secretly against the Spaniards. And this had been done without Catherine's approval or knowledge.

As the Queen-Mother saw the situation, it was perilous in the extreme. Coligny had stolen her son from her: the crime of crimes in her jealous eyes. He was also leading France to her destruction, for his policy meant war with Spain —a war which France would have to fight alone. Catherine was quite right in believing that no support could be expected from England. In fact, English interests and Elizabeth's policy were firmly opposed to France encroaching on the Netherlands seaboard: Elizabeth infinitely preferred to see the Spaniards there, and in the event of war she would at best have maintained an unfriendly neutrality. Not less disturbing to Catherine was the realization that a war policy could only have the effect of confirming Coligny's influence over the King.

These thoughts pointed to one conclusion—the elimination of Coligny; and neither her own unprincipled mind, which had already, in the late war, contemplated such a deed, nor the increasing lawlessness of the times, was likely to cause Catherine any qualms about murdering the Huguenot leader. Her instrument and her opportunity were both at hand. Her instrument was Henry, Duke of Guise, whose father, the late Duke Francis, had been murdered in the first Religious War. The Guise family, as we have seen, firmly believed that Coligny had employed the assassin to do that deed. Nothing could shake their belief nor placate their desire for vengeance; blood called for blood. The new Duke had demanded from the King the right to exact reparation by a duel, but had been refused. Assassination remained the only way.

Catherine's opportunity was the marriage of her daughter Margaret to Henry of Navarre, which took place on August 18th, 1572, and along with the rest of the great nobles, brought practically the whole Huguenot high nobility to Paris to honour their leader's marriage. Catherine was a fool to choose a highly explosive occasion like this, when the nobility of both factions were in town, to exact her revenge on one man; and she ought to have foreseen what would happen. However, choose the occasion she did. There can be very little doubt that she authorized the Guise family to carry out their blood feud and assassinate Coligny.

On August 22nd, as Coligny was returning home from the Court, an arquebus was fired at him from the window of a house, but instead of killing, it merely smashed a finger and wounded him in the arm. With sure instinct the Huguenot nobles at once fixed the blame on the Duke of Guise, angrily demanded justice, and swore that if they did not get it from the King they would execute it themselves. The King, for his part, was genuinely indignant at the attempt on the Admiral's life, and promised an inquiry into the deed.

Catherine found herself in a dreadful quandary. Responsibility for the assault was bound to be traced to the Duke of Guise, and with equal certainty he would insist on her sharing it. And so, if no worse happened, the devil's game of civil war would start again. In such situations people are thrown back on their deeper promptings, and in her desperation Catherine seized on an idea that was then in the air. Her daughter's marriage, by bringing the leading Huguenot noblemen from all over the country to Court, had presented a unique opportunity of getting rid of them all at a blow; an opportunity which a generation that knew its classical history and recalled the story of Tarquin and the poppies could not fail and had not failed to perceive. It was this idea that Catherine seized upon. In other words, a frantic woman determined to save herself and rescue France from its deadly plague of religious strife by the wholesale murder of the Huguenot leaders in Paris.

On the night of August 23rd —the day after the attack on Coligny, and St Bartholomew's Eve —Catherine told her son, the King, of her share in the attack and played on this neurotic boy's feelings until she had persuaded him to consent to a general slaughter of the Huguenots.

In the early morning of August 24th the order was given; the tocsin —the signal for the citizens of Paris to rise —was rung, and the massacre began. The Duke of Guise had charge of the murder of Coligny and of the Huguenot leaders, lists of whom were prepared so that not a single person should escape; while the King himself gave the order which drove the Huguenot gentlemen in the royal palace of the Louvre into the arms of the assassins. Lesser folk were left to be slaughtered by the citizens. Our nerves today, when similar passions have inflicted on the the world so many and such appalling bestialities, are perhaps too numb to register all the horror that many generations have felt at the scenes of the Bartholomew Massacre. But it was a dreadful, inhuman affair. Neither age nor sex was spared, and many a brute seized the chance to murder an old enemy, whether Huguenot or not. The slaughter went on for several days. One or two of the Huguenot leaders had the good fortune to get away, though every effort was made to catch and kill them. Apart from the two young princes of the blood, Henry of Navarre and the Prince of Condé, not a single Huguenot leader was to have been allowed to escape.

From Paris the news spread to the provinces and royal orders were verbally given to kill the Huguenot leaders there. True, these orders were cancelled by later instructions; true, also, it scarcely needed orders to provoke massacres in those provinces —rather less than half in number —where they occurred. Nor of course was the slaughter confined to the leaders of the Huguenots.

Estimates vary as to the number of victims. Probably three to four thousand were killed in Paris, and as many more in the provinces. One Parisian, a butcher by trade, boasted that he himself had killed four hundred on Bartholomew Day.

The news of the Massacre was received in other countries in varying moods, according to the religious sympathies of rulers and people. Philip II wrote to Catherine that the punishment 'given to the Admiral and his sect was indeed of such value and prudence and of such service, glory, and honour to God and universal benefit to all Christendom that to hear of it was for me the best and most cheerful news which at present could come to me'. The Venetian Senate voted its congratulations; the Duke of Tuscany acted similarly. At Rome the Pope assembled all the cardinals, told them the news, and went with them to chant a *Te Deum*. He had a medal struck in honour of the event and frescoes painted at the Vatican. And in her communications with Catholic rulers, Catherine took full credit for a clever and meritorious, not to say holy deed.

But in the Protestant world there was horror and indignation; and Catherine was by no means inclined to cut herself adrift from the alliance with England or her useful relations with the German princes and Swiss cantons. She therefore invented one tale after another in her search for an explanation of the Massacre that Protestant rulers, for diplomacy's sake, could swallow.

In both Catholic and Protestant circles, in France as well as abroad, there were many people who believed that the Massacre was a long-premeditated plan. Many Protestants were convinced that it had originated at the famous interview at Bayonne in 1565. The question has been one of the favourite controversies of history; and although historians have long been almost unanimous in rejecting the idea of premeditation, they still feel that it is a problem which must be discussed in any book on the period. It would not be difficult to do as Lord Acton did in a well-known essay written in 1869, and marshal evidence for the older verdict that seems very weighty. And on finding the Papal Nuncio, after the event, writing that Catherine thought 'no one ought now to doubt that these things had happened in accordance with a long-thought-out plan of which she had spoken to me before at Blois', one's first instinct might very well be to convict her out of her own mouth. But the truth is that this woman, an adept at diplomatic prevarication, was weaving such a web of conflicting lies round the Massacre that it behoves us to avoid falling into the trap of believing anything that she said. Most scholars today are agreed that in a desperate situation she seized on a desperate plan — a plan which had been talked of by many people beforehand, and must have been there, ready to assert itself in her mind. Had Coligny been killed instead of being merely wounded, in all likelihood there would have been no Massacre of St Bartholomew. Equally, if the Massacre had really been premeditated, it is extremely unlikely that the efficient execution of the plan would have been jeopardized by a preliminary and isolated attempt on Coligny's life.

It remains to add that there is no evidence to suggest that Catherine ever felt any remorse for her deed.

IV

THE CLOSE OF THE RELIGIOUS WARS

CATHERINE DE MEDICI hoped that the Massacre of St Bartholomew meant the final destruction of the Huguenots as a militant party. Coligny was dead; and indeed his loss was irreparable. Nobody in the future bridged the two elements of the Huguenot movement — the nobility and the churches — as he had done. Most of the other leaders were also dead. The two titular heads of the party, the young princes of the blood, Henry of Navarre and Henry, Prince of Condé, were virtually prisoners at Court; and, terrified by the Massacre, they announced their conversion to Catholicism. When Catherine saw them at their first Mass she laughed in triumph.

Appearances seemed to justify her, for in addition to the loss to the movement by slaughter, a large number of Huguenots, especially among substantial bourgeois, recanted in terror. But though the Bartholomew Massacre stripped the Huguenot movement of its fringe of members who lacked the stomach to face adversity, and robbed it, for the time being, of its leaders among the high nobility, the ministers were ready to assume leadership, and the common people, especially in Huguenot cities like La Rochelle, remained faithful. In the new period leadership by the high nobility was to be more or less absent until, as we shall see, the Politiques linked up with the Huguenots; and even then ministers and people were more prominent than in pre-Bartholomew years.

Thus Catherine's policy of annihilation was a failure. She laughed too soon. When the King sent a governor to take over control of La Rochelle in September 1572, the ministers and people refused to admit him, and the King was obliged to dispatch an army to capture the city. Its resistance was heroic, and at last in July 1573 the government was forced to admit failure and make a peace granting to La Rochelle, and to other towns which had also revolted, liberty both of conscience and worship. Huguenots elsewhere were granted liberty of conscience only.

The restarting of civil war was not the only effect of the Massacre of St Bartholomew. In the sphere of political theory Huguenot apologists had hitherto been careful to maintain their loyalty to the King, and to square their actions with the theory of the divine right of kings, to which school of political thought Calvin belonged. Loath to claim any right of resistance, they had been careful to argue that they were in fact fighting for the King, to free him from the control of the Guise party. Their argument may seem to us a mere pretext; but the change which took place in their attitude after August 1572 shows it was more than that. In the Massacre of St Bartholomew the Crown had perpetrated an impious act, for which there could be no forgiveness; and Huguenot writers now deliberately attacked the monarchy, making use of the distinction between a king and a tyrant and plundering the Old Testament and classical history for examples of tyrannicide and liberators. Brutus appeared in their text alongside Judith, and Tarquin of course was there as an example of a tyrant. They were concerned with expounding the rights of subjects against tyrants — *vindiciae contra tyrannos*, to quote the title of their most famous post-Bartholomew tract.

Nor did the Huguenots stop at theory. Their movement, as we have seen, was strong in the south of France, in the Midi and Languedoc. Here, as in La Rochelle, they rose in revolt after Bartholomew, and found strong support among the nobility. They ignored the peace of July 1573, remained in arms, and proceeded to frame a rebel government. Languedoc was divided into two governments, centred at Nîmes and Montauban, each with a Count at the head controlled by an elected council or estates, which in important matters consulted the estates of each diocese. The two supreme councils were given control of finance, and money was obtained by levying taxes on towns and villages, whether they were Huguenot or Catholic. During subsequent years this organization and its powers were extended. Here indeed was a state within a state, a separate republic which had virtually displaced the King and sent representatives to him, demanding the free exercise of religion throughout the realm and other sweeping concessions, which the King dared not grant and yet dared not refuse outright.

Still another grave danger threatened the government as the result of the Massacre. It came from the Politique party, whose anger had been aroused only in less degree than that of the Huguenots. The Massacre had involved the eclipse of their policy and their annihilation as a party of power, while many of their number, as enemies of the Guise, had narrowly escaped slaughter, and though escaping themselves, had seen their relatives killed. Coligny, for example, was cousin to the dead Constable Montmorency's several sons: his murder added to the vendetta between the two factions. After Bartholomew the Politiques were a party longing for vengeance on the Guise and for the overthrow of that intolerable woman, Catherine de Medici, along with her foreign favourites. In other words, Court faction was once more linking itself with religious discontent. The old and sordid tragedy was to be played anew.

The Politiques wanted a leader, a new Condé. They could not get Henry of Navarre or the young Condé, since both were virtually prisoners at Court. They therefore aimed at securing Catherine's third surviving son, the Duke of Alençon, that engaging young reprobate whose dashing courtship of Queen Elizabeth provides one of the best comedies of her reign. Alençon was a restless, ambitious young man, jealous of his elder brother, and a great friend of the murdered Coligny. He was quite willing to play the game of the Politiques, provided they could smuggle him away from Court; and during the years 1573 and 1574 there were constant plots for his escape.

Retribution for the appalling crime of St Bartholomew was obviously approaching; and if this present age had been congenial to the reflection, we might be drawing the comforting conclusion that there are liberties with the moral order which cannot be taken without dire consequences.

On May 30th, 1574, Charles IX died, the second of Catherine's sons to die prematurely. He was barely twenty-four, a nervous and weak youth. Huguenot writers told gruesome stories of the terrors that haunted him in his last days: they point a moral and adorn a tale — no more. At the time of his death his brother and successor, Henry III, was away in Poland playing at being king in that bankrupt and anarchic kingdom; for Catherine de Medici, with her foolish desire to set a crown on all her children's heads, had secured his election to the Polish throne in 1573 and had sent him off, much against his will, into a distant and uncongenial exile. Strange to say, it was because she loved him so much. And that love — he was her favourite son — was now engaging her, with all her accustomed vigour, in securing his French kingdom for him.

A month before Charles IX's death, when his health was clearly giving way, a fresh plot to get Alençon from Court had given Catherine the excuse to strike at the Politiques. She clapped their two leaders — one of them Francis de Montmorency, now head of that House — in the Bastille and made Alençon a prisoner, thus ensuring that no one could prevent her from holding the regency of the kingdom until Henry III got back from Poland, and that no attempt would be made to place Alençon on his brother's throne.

It was smart policy — as St Bartholomew had been; and retribution followed the one as the other. In fact, Catherine had got her son, Henry III, into a paralysing situation by her action. When she arrested Montmorency she thought that his younger brother, Damville, governor of Languedoc, who was

far and away the ablest of the Montmorency-Politique group
had fallen into a net set to catch him. Had he done so, she would
doubtless have executed her Bastille prisoners. But Damville
was too clever. He escaped the net and saved his brother's life
by the surest method — by uniting with the Huguenot organization of Languedoc and erecting an independent republic that
Catherine simply dared not defy.

Thus Catherine's subtlety had merely driven the most
powerful Politique into the Huguenot ranks. All France south
of the Loire was in due course proclaimed to be under Damville
as governor and general chief, while he in turn acknowledged
the supremacy of the Prince of Condé, who had escaped from
Court and was safe in Germany. A veritable republican
government was elaborated, with a Council of State to advise
Damville, an Assembly of Deputies, Provincial Councils, offices
of Justice and Finance, four Law Courts, and a financial
division of the whole area. Customs duties and taxes were levied,
and this revolutionary organization ran its own police, schools,
and hospitals. Condé and Damville were assigned specified
salaries, and money and authority were provided to levy troops
abroad.

France seemed to be breaking in two. And to make matters
worse, the royal Treasury was empty. Charles IX's funeral had
cost a great deal of money, still more had been sent to the new
King to pay the expenses of his journey back to France; and
when Catherine tried to raise loans at Venice and Florence, she
failed. Still more significant, she could not raise a loan at Lyons,
even at fifteen per cent interest, for three of the chief financial
houses of that city had gone bankrupt, and Lyons, like Antwerp,
the chief financial capital of Europe, was saying farewell to its
departing financial greatness. Catherine had no money to pay
her troops, and in the next year the Crown was to make a
partial default in its dividends on the *rentes*, the first ripple of
that state bankruptcy which came in 1580.

There was little or no hope of Henry III being able to face

Damville and his combination of southern moderate Catholics and Huguenots. And when in September 1575 Alençon at last succeeded in escaping from Court and joined the revolt, to be followed in February 1576 by Henry of Navarre, capitulation was the sole option left to the Crown. Capitulation is the only suitable description for the Peace of Monsieur which Henry III made in May 1576. Official regrets were expressed for the Massacre of St Bartholomew, and concessions were made to the Huguenots amounting to practically complete religious liberty, with devices to ensure their being carried out. The terrorism of St Bartholomew was thus written down as a failure.

But permanent appeasement had not yet arrived. It was indeed unattainable without a strong monarchy to enforce it; and the monarchy under Henry III was disastrously weak, not only financially but also in the character of the King. Henry III was a case for the Freudian psychologist. He was subject to bursts of energy, and then would let everything go hang. Here is a contemporary's description of him when he arrived at Lyons to face the appalling political problems that I have just described. 'The King goes every night to balls and does nothing but dance. During four whole days he was dressed in mulberry satin with stockings, doublet, and cloak of the same colour. The cloak was very much slashed in the body and had all its folds set with buttons and adorned with ribbons, white and scarlet and mulberry, and he wore bracelets of coral on his arm.' He had spells of gay and dissolute life, and then would join bands of flagellants, wandering about the streets, disguised and with their faces covered and sometimes in bare feet, chanting psalms and scourging each other. When he was in these religious moods, or when he felt disinclined for business, nothing would induce him to attend to affairs of state; at other times he would brook no interference with his authority, not even from his mother. He was the one child of Catherine de Medici who, so far from being dependent on her, actually made her fear him. She continued to play a leading part in the government of the country, as active as ever in the bewildering turns of policy, and apparently almost as powerful; but from now on it was a regime of intermittent dyarchy.

Henry soon began to gather round him a set of young courtiers who were contemptuously called *mignons*: men who dressed and behaved like dandies, wearing their hair long, 'crimped and recrimped in the most artificial way', their heads sitting on their ruffs 'like the head of John the Baptist on a platter'. They spent their time gambling, swearing, fighting, and dancing; and their conduct gave rise to unspeakable satires. 'Princes of Sodom' was how a satirist described the members of a new order of chivalry founded by the King. It was madness; but there was a dash of statecraft in it. For these *mignons* were the sons of lesser nobility, owing their whole fortune to the King; men from whom Henry might fashion a new aristocracy by heaping wealth, honour, and high office on them. They were reliable courtiers, fearing and honouring their master 'more than God'; and they were courageous and daring.

Some years later the King developed a passion for lap-poodles, lavished huge sums of money on them and took scores of them wherever he travelled, with a whole retinue of attendants to look after them. How could the monarchy be strong or respected in such a person? The House of Valois was certainly heaping contempt on itself before dying out. And yet it would be unfair to think only of the ridiculous side of Henry III. As one sees him in the dispatches of the English ambassador, he often appears as the able man he was, and as a clever and liberal-minded statesman. But this was not the impression that he made on French noblemen; and the psychological twist in his personality was fatal for the prospects of France.

A King who was always shocking the Court with his pranks, who, in the midst of financial chaos, lavished money on his pleasures and questionable amusements and was incapable of sustained effort in anything, would have been unable, even if he had wished, to reconcile the Guise party and ardent Catholics to the drastic concessions made to heretics by the Peace of Monsieur. As a matter of fact, Henry himself felt the humiliation of the Peace and was determined to find a way of release from the oath binding him to observe it. Action, however, was taken out of his hands, for Catholics in various parts of the country, under the leadership of Henry, Duke of Guise, and with encouragement from Spain, began to band themselves together into a Catholic League.

Here was the old situation of the time of the Triumvirate being re-created — two organized and armed parties of passion, with the monarchy, helpless, between. Henry III met the danger by placing himself at the head of the League and sending orders to the governors of the provinces to recruit members for it, thus forming an army against heresy, but an army under the King, not Guise, and at very little cost to the Crown. The future was to show how dangerous a Catholic League could be when separate from the Crown, and therefore how clever Henry III's manœuvre was. But of course he could only carry it out at the cost of renewed war with the Huguenots. Fortunately for Henry, the Huguenots in this war lacked the assistance of either Alençon or Damville. They were defeated, and in September 1577 were forced to accept a much more limited freedom of worship.

At this point, I think the historian who tries to maintain any significance and simplicity in his narrative and carry the interest of his readers with him, must surrender to the confusion of the whole story and jump, with only a hint or two of what was happening, to the year 1584, when the welter of petty, anarchic, and unedifying detail suddenly shapes itself into a clear pattern.

In the interval between 1577 and 1584 the country became more and more unsettled, despite the unflagging endeavours of Catherine de Medici, who spent sixteen months in an exhausting perambulation of the provinces, coping with universal discontent; at Court the *mignons* continued to provoke hatred and strife; there was ever-deepening financial gloom, accompanied by increased taxation and suffering almost beyond endurance among peasants and gentry; and of course there was another religious war — if indeed so grave a name should be given to a revolt which was brief, involved only a fraction of the Huguenot party under Henry of Navarre, and seemed so obscure in its origins that legend has given it the frivolous title of The Lovers' War. The Duke of Alençon, during these years, turned his restless ambition into two external adventures: intervention in the Netherlands on behalf of the rebels there, and his final, breath-taking courtship of Queen Elizabeth. In both enterprises — even that of the Netherlands, which might well have plunged France into the final calamity of war with Spain — he secured support from the King, for the relations between these two remaining sons of Catherine de Medici had long been so bitter, and their quarrels, for all their mother could do, so constant and even scandalous, that Henry III was thankful, at any price, to be rid of a domestic nuisance and danger. He both hated and feared his brother.

In June 1584 fever put an end to Alençon's adventures and started the last phase of Henry III's troubles. Alençon's death had a dramatic effect on the whole situation in France, for it left the country with a prospect that no keen Catholic could face with equanimity — the prospect of a heretic king. Henry III was the last of the Valois. It was obvious that he would die childless. And the heir to the throne was the leader of the Huguenot party, Henry of Navarre.

The Guise family and the Catholic leaders acted rapidly. In September 1584 — Alençon had died in June — they banded themselves together, and some three months later made a treaty with Spain constituting a Holy League, an offensive and defensive alliance for the extirpation of heresy in France and the Netherlands; and in place of Henry of Navarre they recognized his aged and colourless uncle, the Cardinal Bourbon, as successor to the French throne. The League spread rapidly.

In Paris a similar organization had come into being independently. At first secret, its founders had divided up the city into sections, each with a leader, and adherents were gained one by one. Then, preachers were set to work to play on the passions of the people; pamphlets were written; and Paris was in process of being whipped up by Catholic demagogues to play the role that its mob played in the Revolution of 1789.

Once more the Crown found itself isolated between the parties. Henry III and Catherine tried to persuade Henry of Navarre to turn Catholic. In all likelihood, he already foresaw that conversion would one day be inevitable, but he refused to take the step now. Wisely; for he would have surrendered the support of his party and placed himself without resources in the hands of the Guise party and the untrustworthy Henry III.

The League did not wait on events. With Spanish money it set about raising armed forces, including foreign mercenaries, and then confronted the King with the necessity of making his choice of sides. Catherine de Medici, intent as usual on appeasement, set off to see the Duke of Guise and try to prevent war. She was old, suffering torments from gout and a multitude of other ailments, and had frequently to negotiate from her bed. The effort was magnificent, but fruitless; Guise negotiated with an army behind him and an ultimatum as his argument. The King had no alternative but to surrender; and at the dictation of the League he was forced in July 1585 to issue an edict revoking all past edicts of pacification, banning heresy, exiling all Protestant ministers, and giving their adherents the alternative of conversion to Catholicism or exile. Henry of Navarre declared that one half of his moustache turned white when he was told of the edict.

I have said that the King had no alternative. He did indeed have the heroic one of refusing to put the stamp of royal authority on a body that was allied to Spain — the national enemy of France — and was precipitating a war in which Spain would have the excuse to intervene. Had Catherine been more nationally minded or Henry III more courageous, anything might have seemed better than surrender. Henry's position was in truth desperate; and no better proof could be cited than the state of his financial credit. In the autumn of 1586 merchants were demanding fifty per cent interest for loans to him.

The edict proscribing Protestantism led to war — the war known as the War of the Three Henries; Henry III, Henry Duke of Guise, and Henry of Navarre. During its course Henry of Navarre gave an indication of the fine military qualities he possessed by winning a brilliant victory in a pitched battle. But the war dragged on. More and more it became evident that the King was an unwilling partner and that he and his mother were doing their rather futile best to bring about peace, while more and more Guise and his adherents showed their contempt for the person and authority of the King and their determination to pursue their own ends in defiance of him.

The League devised a new oath for its members, binding them to obey the King only so long as he proved himself a Catholic and did not favour the heretics. And on the invitation of the Paris leaguers, city after city linked itself by contract with the capital. The situation at Paris was rapidly deteriorating into rebellion against the King. Priests, acting as demagogues, were inflaming passions and attacking the orthodoxy, morality, and policy of the King, while Madame de Montpensier, sister of the Duke of Guise, a redoubtable and fearless woman who harboured a mortal hatred of Henry III and swayed the mob with her fanaticism, was there to urge on and direct the pulpit propaganda. It accomplished more, she declared, than her brothers' armies. The execution of Mary Queen of Scots in England in February 1587 was a heaven-sent opportunity to this vixen; and it was at her suggestion that one of the Paris priests posted in a cemetery a huge picture, showing, in a series of harrowing scenes, all the agonies and tortures to the final bloody spectacle of the traitor's death, through which Catholics were made to pass in Protestant England. The moral for France — that this was the fate awaiting Catholics if the Huguenot Henry of Navarre succeeded to the throne — was obvious, and was brought home to the crowds of excitable Parisians who flocked to the cemetery.

For rather more than a fortnight Henry III dared not do anything. Then he had the poster taken down at night, and two months later arrested three of the leading priestly agitators. Parisians sounded the tocsin and rose in revolt. The trouble died down; but the League had discovered its strength. France was passing into confusion, from which a wavering King was unable to save it.

The critical moment in this final struggle of authority against insolence could not be far off. It came in the famous Day of Barricades at Paris in May 1588. The League had urged the Duke of Guise to come to Paris: the King ordered him not to enter the city. He arrived on the 9th of May with nine companions only; and soon a crowd of thirty thousand was following him in triumphal procession through the streets. Making his way to Catherine de Medici's lodging, and then, with her, to the Louvre, he bowed to the King, explained that he had disobeyed the royal command and come to Paris to justify himself, and finally withdrew unmolested to his own house. Pope Sixtus V, whose wise and penetrating remarks on the ability of Queen Elizabeth and the naval strength of England have an arresting frankness, made the apt comment on this occasion: 'Guise', he said, 'was a reckless fool to put himself in the hands of a King whom he was insulting; the King was a coward to let him go untouched.'

Guise had defied his sovereign; and Henry III had now to choose whether he would resume his authority by overthrowing the citizens, or surrender, or flee from his own capital. He tried the first: the people of Paris, organized and equipped by their leaders, threw up barricades, isolated the King's forces in small bands, and having surrounded them, compelled them to lay down their arms. Then, while his mother pretended to negotiate with Guise, Henry slipped out of Paris and escaped. Guise was left 'King of Paris'.

Henry III had fled from Paris; but not to fight. He had left his mother temporizing with the Duke of Guise, and negotiations went on while the Duke replaced loyal officials in Paris with out-and-out Leaguers, sent to stir up the Leaguers in other cities, writing of the King with disdainful insolence, and — to put it briefly — built up an impregnable position for himself. The terms which the King was forced to concede in the Edict of Union in July 1588 were those of complete surrender. He placed almost absolute authority in the hands of the Duke of Guise, and in foreign as well as domestic policy granted practically everything that the League demanded. Guise was received at Court and made Lieutenant-General of France.

Humiliations continued to descend on the wretched King. The Duke of Savoy, a petty princeling, thinking that France was disintegrating, had the impudence to invade a part of French territory and seize it. Then when the Estates General met at Blois in October, instead of finding that assembly loyal, Henry discovered that the League had 'made' the elections and that still further humiliations were to be inflicted upon him.

But the end of the King's patience had been reached. The defeat of the Spanish Armada by the English in July–August had freed him from any fear of Spanish intervention, and in September he had summarily dismissed those of his ministers who were the creatures of his mother, thus breaking from Catherine de Medici's control and from her policy of appeasement. He turned to those noblemen whose interests were likely to suffer most from Guise ambition. A feeling of approaching catastrophe was in the air. A Tuscan diplomat had written home to say that 'the day of the dagger will come'; and on all sides the Duke of Guise was being warned of a plot against his life, and urged, but in vain, to leave the Court.

Henry and his little circle of new advisers discussed the

82

possibility of trying the Duke for treason. But he was too powerful for legal action to be taken against him. The dagger was the only way. On December 23rd at 7.30 in the morning Guise came to a Council meeting at the Château of Blois, to which the King had summoned him. When he and his brother, the Cardinal of Guise, had arrived, mounting the famous outside staircase that led to the Council Chamber, the doors were closed behind them and a solid body of guards filled the staircase. The meeting began; the King, waiting in a cabinet off the adjoining royal bedchamber, sent for the Duke. As he approached, the door through which he came was locked, the King's bodyguard of gentlemen formed up behind him and then fell on him and murdered him. The Cardinal of Guise was seized, imprisoned, and the next day, as he in turn went to answer the royal summons, was struck down and murdered. Others were imprisoned, including the leaders of the League in the Estates General; but bloodshed stopped with the slaughter of the two chiefs.

The King had carried out this drastic coup without consulting his mother. Afterwards, he broke the news to her. She was lying ill in bed, and less than three weeks later died, bemoaning —so it was said and may be believed —the fate that she saw would befall the last and best beloved of her sons.

Like Catherine de Medici when she perpetrated the Massacre of St Bartholomew, Henry III believed that his bloody purge would put an end to the troubles of France; that the League would collapse. He failed, as Catherine had failed, to appreciate that behind political ambition and intrigue there was genuine and deep religious feeling and popular fanaticism. At Paris the priests preached revolt and the citizens responded, while the Sorbonne, following the example of Huguenot writers after August 1572, placed its moral and intellectual authority on the doctrine that it was lawful to take up arms against tyrants. Children marched through the streets of Paris, led by their curés and others, all carrying torches, which from time to time they dashed to the ground, crying 'So may God quench the race of Valois.'

It was war, not peace, that the King gave to France. The League took the field, while Henry III allied himself with the King of Navarre and the Huguenots. The war went in favour of the two Kings. They laid siege to Paris, and it seemed as if the city, for all its fanatical ardour, was lost, when the inevitable happened. In the mood created by the murder of the Guise, even the blackest of all crimes, regicide, took on the semblance of a noble action. On August 1st, 1589, a young Dominican friar, Jacques Clément, whose fanatical purpose seems to have been aided by Madame de Montpensier and others, made his way into Henry III's presence and mortally wounded him with a knife. Thus perished the last of the Valois kings. He was thirty-eight years of age. When the people of Paris heard the news, they placed tables in the streets, drank, feasted, sang, and danced.

Henry III had survived his mother by only seven months. The Age of Catherine de Medici was ended.

Though the future course of the Religious Wars lies outside the scope of our subject, we must briefly round off the story. The new King, Henry of Navarre — Henry IV, as he now was — had to begin the reconquest of the country all over again. Some of the royalist nobility who had followed Henry III placed their loyalty to France before too ardent a pursuit of religious aims, and were content with the prospect that the new King would in due time turn Catholic; but others withdrew, so that the army sank to half its numbers and Henry IV had to retire on Normandy and begin his campaign from there.

It was a long, long task. But though fortunes waxed and waned and years passed by, the ultimate odds were all in Henry IV's favour. In the first place, France at last had got what it needed most, a strong man as King. Henry IV had his shortcomings, but they were essentially Gallican; part of a personality that the French loved. On the manly side, his courage, his ability to face hardship, his capacity for leadership, and his *bonhomie*, all were qualities that he possessed in a remarkable degree. He was a great and a charming man. And one fact is certain: had France possessed such a King in 1559, or even later, its history would have been startingly different.

As for the League, in the long run its strength was its weakness. Paris, under the leadership of fanatical demagogues, played a supremely heroic and dramatic part in the resistance to Henry IV. But the fanaticism of its leaders led to excesses, suggestive of the Terror during the French Revolution, which alienated moderate people, stimulated the growth of a Politique section of the League, and at last so wore out the nerves of the citizens that reaction set in. The ardour of their welcome to peace and a legitimate King, when they arrived, surprised everyone.

The foreign support which the League received, while time and again its salvation, proved an embarrassment in the end, and aided Henry IV. The League had no obvious rival to proclaim King when the fainéant Cardinal of Bourbon died, a captive, in May 1590. The King of Spain aimed at securing the throne for his daughter; the Duke of Savoy — another foreign ally of the League — coveted the throne, or, at any rate, a section of south-east France; and members of the House of Lorraine harboured conflicting aspirations. It was a monstrous situation, against which the national sentiment of France was ultimately bound to revolt.

At long last, in July 1593, the time was ripe for the proper solution of the problem, one that Henry IV had foreseen for years: he allowed himself to be converted to Catholicism. And in March 1594 he reaped his reward by entering Paris amid the plaudits of the people. He was quite cynical in his readiness to buy off the self-seeking, recalcitrant Catholic leaders still arrayed against him; and gradually the troubles dwindled into a war against Spain only. Even this ended in May 1598.

A month before — in April — Henry had finally liquidated the religious problem of France by the Edict of Nantes. It established toleration — liberty of conscience and liberty of worship — on a liberal but not quite complete scale, and granted full civil rights to the Huguenots, instituting special law courts to secure them justice. It also conceded certain political guarantees which left the Huguenots something of a state within a state, thus recognizing that the Edict was not merely a concession to a section of the community, but a treaty between two warring powers. Such was the cleavage in the French nation effected by thirty-five years of intermittent strife. In the next century Richelieu abolished the political guarantees in the name of national unity, and Louis XIV, in the name of religious unity, revoked the edict of toleration. France returned to One King, One Faith, and that Faith, inevitably, the Catholic Faith.

*   *   *

As we look back on this dismal story of the French Religious Wars, what are our reflections? What, in particular, are we to think of Catherine de Medici, on whom, if there was any personal responsibility for events, that responsibility must in the main rest? How far was her policy at fault? How far were the qualities and defects of her character involved? How far was she the victim of uncontrollable circumstances? Should we, perhaps, echo the indulgent verdict of Henry IV, who said, 'What more could one poor woman, with a handful of children, do?'

Undoubtedly, the root of the trouble was the weakness of the monarchy. It was a calamity for France that the crisis of its religious problem coincided with the successive accession to the throne of two children and a period of thirty years of incompetent kingship. Even if there had been no Queen-Mother, with a lust to rule, and if the premier prince of the blood had been an able man, it is doubtful whether he could have saved the country from civil war.

Quite irrespective of her ability, Catherine de Medici was

deplorably handicapped. Her sex, her birth, her foreign origin were all chinks in the armour of her prestige. John Knox had blown the Blast of sixteenth-century mankind against the Monstrous Regiment of Women. 'I am assured', he wrote, 'that God hath revealed to some in this our age that it is more than a monster in nature that a woman should reign and bear empire above man.' Women, he declared, were painted forth by nature to be weak, frail, impatient, feeble, and foolish; they were the port and gate of the Devil; their covetousness, like the gulf of Hell, was insatiable. For the weak to nourish the strong, the foolish to govern the discreet, in brief, for women to rule men, was contumely to God and the subversion of good order and justice. The Bible, the Fathers, Aristotle, and the Classical world were at one on the subject; and men, he thought, were less than the beasts to permit such an inversion of God's order. Knox blew his blast against the regency of a Queen-Mother, Mary of Guise, in Scotland, and the rule of a woman, Mary Tudor, as Queen of England. The stridency of his trumpet may have been peculiar to himself, but the tune it played was acceptable to most men of his day. As a noble author of Henry VIII's reign wrote: 'Indeed, God did not create this kind — women — unto rule and to have governance, and therefore they never reign prosperously.' It was a fundamental assumption, incalculable in its effects. A foreign ambassador summed up Catherine de Medici's difficulties in the following sentence: 'It is sufficient to say that she is a woman, a foreigner, and a Florentine to boot, born of a simple house, altogether beneath the dignity of the Kingdom of France.' There were few of the many attacks on Catherine which did not drive home one or other, or all, of these points.

The second half of the sixteenth century was prolific in women-rulers: Mary Tudor, Mary of Guise, Elizabeth, Mary Queen of Scots, Margaret of Parma, and Catherine de Medici herself. With one exception — Queen Elizabeth — they must ultimately be written off as failures. But the fact that there is one exception makes us ask how far qualities of character combined with sex to spell success or failure.

Both Catherine de Medici and Elizabeth were essentially feminine in their opportunism, their tendency to see things in a personal rather than an impersonal way, and — dare one add? or would it be wiser to attribute this to the Renaissance? — their unscrupulousness. But, having noted these similarities of character, we are immediately struck by very strong contrasts. It may be put this way: we can, without too gross a caricature, keep within the characteristics of opportunism, personal bias, and unscrupulousness in describing Catherine. It is impossible to be bound by them in describing Elizabeth.

Elizabeth was a woman of much finer sensibility; she was essentially merciful. It would be quite incongruous to think of her planning a Massacre of St Bartholomew, and the dagger as a political expedient — save when she grasped at the suggestion, as an alternative to the public execution of Mary Queen of Scots in 1587 — was alien to her. Perhaps it would be unfair to cite her successful assertion of authority, since she was a queen-regnant and Catherine was not. But a question of character also enters here. Elizabeth was a true daughter of Henry VIII; she was to the manner born, and had the reserve of character to carry off her regal supremacy, in spite of her sex: contrast, as French contemporaries did, her handling of the Essex rebellion with Henry III's handling of its French precedent, the Day of Barricades.

Moreover, Elizabeth had a trained intellect. Behind her bewildering opportunism there was a firm grasp of principle. She was a statesman, and Burghley in his old age paid tribute to her greatness as such. Catherine may have been, indeed she was, a woman of practical intelligence, but hers was not a trained mind; she never understood that abstract ideas could even exist, nor that there are occasions when compromise and conciliation are politically as well as morally ruinous. She was completely lacking in the qualities of a statesman.

But the contrast which perhaps mattered most of all — the fundamental distinction between the two women — is that Elizabeth loved her country with the consuming passion that few but women can experience. In her England was personified. Catherine de Medici did not know what patriotism meant. She was always a foreigner; she had no country. Her passion was her children, not France; she was the mother, not the Queen.

I think it needs little reflection to realize that one of the most significant facts in Elizabethan history is England's escape from religious wars; and we may be helped in our final appraisal of Catherine de Medici if we ask how far this immunity was due to better fortune or better policy. Better fortune there certainly was. I have already mentioned one advantage, namely, that Elizabeth was a queen-regnant. But this alone, without the necessary qualities of character to assert her authority and counteract the grave disadvantages of sex, would not have saved England from civil strife. Mary Queen of Scots would probably have failed in Elizabeth's place, and so too would a woman with Catherine de Medici's foreign outlook — this was Mary Tudor's tragedy — her lack of principle, and her matrimonial inclinations. Catherine, in Elizabeth's place, would have married a great prince; therefore a foreigner and a Catholic. And then the fat would certainly have been in the fire.

Again, England had inestimably better fortune in the lack of any princes of the blood, and in the relative weakness of feudal ties and propensities among the nobility. But it is also true that France — at any rate before 1584 — was not exposed to the appalling danger of having a rival claimant to the throne, present for nearly twenty years in the country and posing, as did Mary Queen of Scots, as the leader of the opposite faith. The Northern Rebellion in 1569 might well have been the first of the English religious wars.

England was also fortunate in its insular isolation, which constituted against Catholic missionaries a sanitary cordon that France lacked against Geneva and the German Protestant cities; but of course there is — or perhaps we should say, there was — no really effective cordon against the spread of ideas, and given a weak monarch and mistaken policy England would have drifted into religious wars just as certainly as France.

Perhaps France could not have escaped her fate: with child-kings, for which accident and not Catherine de Medici was responsible, the probability of trouble may have been equivalent to practical certainty. All the same, we have in the course of this narrative noted blunder after blunder in Catherine's policy, and these, coupled with her shortcomings of character and intellect, undoubtedly affected the nature and duration of France's thirty-odd years of disaster.

A final, if brief, comment must be made on the economic effects of the wars. At the beginning of the sixteenth century France was developing its commerce and industry with great rapidity: England in comparison was a backwater. But it was in Elizabethan and Jacobean England that the first industrial revolution — to use a phrase now being applied to this period by economic historians — forged ahead. No doubt there are other reasons than the incidence or absence of war to explain this profoundly important contrast in the economic fortunes of the two countries. In England, unlike France, the legal and constitutional framework of society favoured individualism; there were no *rentes* through which the Crown, under the guise of investment, could divert the savings of the people from economic enterprise into the prodigal ways of royal expenditure; and parliament exercised a control over taxation to which there was no parallel in France. But if the political structure of a society affects its economic structure, the reverse is also true, and it is best to centre one's attention on the two fundamental and interrelated factors in English economic development: the possession by individuals of capital to invest in commercial and industrial projects, and the existence of orderly, peaceful conditions to foster their growth. In France, the financial drain of the Italian Wars had already by 1559 partially exhausted the wealth of the country. The long period of civil strife which followed, with its chronic and continuous state of disorder, its human and material losses, and its costliness, was fatal to economic enterprise: even river and road communications fell into disrepair.

Modern large-scale industry, as the examples of England and the Netherlands demonstrated, could only develop freely at the expense of the old medieval gild system, with its rigid and obstructive control of craftsmen. But sixteenth-century France, instead of witnessing the decay of the craft gilds, saw something approaching a universal extension of this form of constraint, under the authority of the State; and the period of religious wars, with the reconstruction that followed under Henry IV — reconstruction inspired and planned, as was inevitable, by the Crown — clamped State regimentation on the industrial life of France until the eighteenth century. Such large-scale industry as developed was organized, controlled, and in part financed by the Crown, and, instead of being concentrated on the heavy industries and labour-saving devices as in England, was mainly confined to luxury trades and the fine arts, such as silks and tapestries. In England individual initiative broke down gild regulations, waged successful war on the Crown's proclamations and letters patent, and even drove blithely through obstructive statutes. If, like England, France had enjoyed peace and orderly government in the sixteenth century, if wealth had been allowed to accumulate in the hands of individuals, and if a sufficient financial margin had remained with poorer folk to create a market for large-scale industry in goods other than luxuries, who can doubt that individual enterprise would have broken through restraint in that country also, though with less rapidity because the obstacles were tougher? And then, instead of *étatisme* in the political sphere stifling individualism in the economic, we might have seen the opposite process at work in sixteenth- and seventeenth-century France. That, after all, is what happened in the eighteenth century.

Rural life in France suffered terribly from the Wars of Religion. The professional soldiers of the time, whether foreign or native, generally lived on the country and were a curse to friend and foe, pillaging and ravaging almost as a matter of course. Intervals of peace were too often that in name only; disorder bred brigandage, and even the Crown, in its desperate need for money, preyed on the wretched peasants and helped to complete their ruin. 'The length and scale of the war has so desolated the provinces of our Kingdom', wrote Henry IV in 1595, 'that most of the land is deserted and uncultivated.' But if the fate of agriculture was the most spectacular economic disaster of all, it was the least enduring. Fields remain even when they are deserted, and a new generation soon comes along to replace the lost one.

> My father lived at Blenheim then,
> Yon little stream hard by;
> They burnt his dwelling to the ground,
> And he was forced to fly:
> So with his wife and child he fled,
> Nor had he where to rest his head.
>
> With fire and sword the country round
> Was wasted far and wide,
> And many a childing mother then
> And newborn baby died.

It was the same poignant story in sixteenth-century France; but you will remember that Old Kaspar was soon at work again on his father's lands and telling his grandchild Wilhelmine of man's fatuous ways.

ESSAYS IN
ELIZABETHAN HISTORY

NOVEMBER 17TH

OVER the years I have written many short historical studies in articles, lectures and reviews. Most of them served an immediate purpose and are best left unresurrected; some were on themes that I have subsequently traversed in my books. A few, however, escape these two vetoes and I hope that I have not erred in deciding to make them available to a wider public.

I do not know how long a certain diffidence about reliving my past would have delayed the appearance of this volume, had it not been for the approach of a date which this country of ours has good reason to salute. I refer to November 17th, 1958, the fourth centenary of Queen Elizabeth I's accession to the throne: a day now forgotten, but once celebrated by generations of Englishmen. When I was young, I cherished the thought of one day writing the posthumous history of Good Queen Bess, tracing through the centuries a legend which became part of our folklore and which is not yet dead, though much of its vitality has ebbed away. Time and temperament have quietly disposed of my youthful ambition, and in consequence the posthumous history of Queen Elizabeth must remain a subject in search of an author: a fascinating and far from insignificant subject.

Had I written my dream-book, a central thread, running through most of the story, would have been that day, November 17th, whose fourth centenary this volume is meant to commemorate. For Protestant Englishmen who saw the first Elizabethan Accession Day, it had much of the quality of Bastille Day for Frenchmen or November 7th for present-day Russians. It was a Thursday, and they called the day before, when rumour spread that Mary Tudor was dying, Hope Wednesday. As its first and later anniversaries came round, many minds must have recalled the event and hearts warmed in

95

devout thankfulness. But it was not then the custom to mark the years of a monarch's reign by special celebrations: after all, in Catholic England there had been saints' days galore to provide the people with Holy Days and fortify parish bell-ringers with practice, refreshment and fees. Protestant England cut down the number of saints and thereby deprived the people and their bell-ringers of much traditional festivity.

The diminution in saints' days, we may presume, produced favourable conditions for the more or less spontaneous appearance of a new type of Holy Day — a holiday as Protestant as the compulsory fish-day instituted by Parliament in 1563 and dubbed by the Papists 'Cecil's Fast'. At any rate, the inspiration that made a national Holyday of November 17th — the Queen's Day, Accession Day, or, as it was often erroneously called, Coronation Day — was the revolutionary spirit of November 1558, revived by Catholic threats at home and abroad and personified in a Queen, whose life, to ardent Protestants, was the most precious thing on earth. The contemporary historian, William Camden, tells us: 'The twelfth year of the reign of Queen Elizabeth being now happily expired, wherein some credulous Papists expected, according to the prediction of certain wizards, their Golden day — as they termed it — all good men through England joyfully triumphed, and with thanksgivings, sermons in churches, multiplied prayers, joyful ringing of bells, running at tilt, and festival mirth began to celebrate the seventeenth day of November, being the anniversary day of the beginning of her reign; which, in testimony of their affectionate love towards her, they never ceased to observe as long as she lived.' Camden was perhaps a year or two late in his dating. In some places church bells seem to have been rung as early as 1568; but the general celebration of Accession Day probably followed the successful weathering of the first great crisis of the reign — the Rebellion of the North in November and December 1569, and the promulgation, just after, of the Papal Bull deposing Elizabeth.

As the pattern of this annual festival became settled, its central attraction was at Court, where in the tiltyard at Westminster courtiers displayed their prowess, and, aided by professional writers, let fantasy riot in more and more elaborate and costly devices, pageantry and masking. At Cambridge, and presumably at Oxford, there were orations in College halls and bonfires in the quadrangles, while, throughout the land, in village and town, all the church bells were rung. In churchwardens' and borough-chamberlains' accounts we can still see recorded the cost of repairing the bells in preparation for the day and the rewards given to the bell-ringers. At Bridgnorth, for example, there is the following entry in 1585: '3s. 4d. to the clerk of the Castle church for ringing of the Queen's Holiday; 7s. to the clerk of St Leonard's church for ringing at the same time.' In 1601 the cost is noted of felling, preparing and carting wood for the bonfire customarily lit on that day. Bells and bonfires: they were long to remain features of popular rejoicing on November 17th.

A search of local records would probably reveal many pleasing variations in the celebration of this day. At Ipswich in 1583 the town's schoolmaster presented 'certain pageants in joy of the Queen's coronation', and was paid forty shillings 'for his pains and charges'; while in 1594 the authorities purchased twelve bushels of rye, 'which was baked in bread at the town's charge and given to the poor of this town the day before the coronation day'. In 1584, the London parish of St Andrew, Holborn, began a new practice by converting into a sort of Maundy occasion each of 'the two memorable feasts of our gracious sovereign lady, Queen Elizabeth' — her birthday on September 7th, and her 'coronation day' on November 17th. On the birthday, 'fifty-two old women of the greatest age in the parish' received at a maid's hands a spice cake, a draft of wine and twopence in money, the total cost being 17s. On 'coronation day' — the Queen then entering the twenty-seventh year of her reign — twenty-seven of the parish's most aged women were

97

assembled in the church, this time with twenty-seven 'young
maiden children' attendant. 'After public prayers earnestly
made for her Majesty's long and prosperous reign over us', the
maids and churchwardens distributed to the old women a spice
cake, a draft of burnt claret wine and threepence apiece,
while the children received a cake, a draft of claret wine and one
penny apiece: superior largesse to that of the birthday. 'And so',
adds the worthy churchwarden, who entered this charming
note in his account book, 'after prayer and thanksgiving again
zealously made for her Majesty, with joyful hearts and thankful
and devout minds, they all departed in God's praise home to
their houses, expecting (if it so please God) the continuance of
so good an exercise, to the glory of God, the parish's credit and
their relief; that by this means many prayers and thanksgiving
unto God may be continually made of many, for the continuance of His manifold and great blessings, many years to endure,
upon His church, our Queen and Realm.'[1]

Writing to Dudley Carleton in 1602, John Chamberlain,
the letter writer, described the celebrations in the capital on the
last Accession Day of the reign: 'Her day passed with the
ordinary solemnity of preaching, singing, shooting, ringing
and running. The bishop of Limerick ... made a dull sermon at
Paul's Cross. At the tilt were many young runners.' Carleton's
fool, Garret, he added, 'had good audience of her Majesty and
made her very merry'.

By 1576 the Church had added the day to its select rota of
Holy Days, and in that year the royal printer issued 'A Form
of Prayer with Thanks Giving, to be used every year, the 17th
of November, being the day of the Queen's Majesty's entry
to her reign'. To that biblically-minded generation, God
seemed to be working in Elizabethan England with the
same sure purpose revealed by the scriptures in Israel; and
the psalms and lessons for the day were chosen with striking
appropriateness:

[1] I am indebted for this item to Mr H. G. Owen, a research student of mine.

Lord, thou hast granted to thy land
The favours we implor'd
And faithful Jacob's captive race
Hast graciously restor'd.

Many a puritan heart, as these opening words of the 85th
psalm were intoned, must have been stirred by thoughts of
Catholic Mary's days and the miraculous preservation and
triumph of her sister, Elizabeth. That is how John Foxe in his
Book of Martyrs saw the working of Providence; how Holinshed
the chronicler and many a speaker in the House of Commons
saw it too. For the first lesson, officiating clergymen were
offered a choice of passages from the Old Testament, recalling
the godly rulers of Israel — Jehoshaphat, Hezekiah and Josiah,
men who 'did that which is right in the sight of the Lord', and
whose enemies God confounded. For the second lesson, the
thirteenth chapter of St Paul's Epistle to the Romans was pre-
scribed, opening with that famous verse, which was the familiar
bulwark of monarchy in those days: 'Let every soul be subject
unto the higher power. For there is no power but of God. The
powers that be are ordained of God.'

Two years later there were special metrical thanksgivings
available in print, to be sung as psalms:

Sound out the trump courageously,
Blow as on solemn days:
Both high and low, come fill the sky
    with sweet resounding praise.
For why? when we were bound in thrall,
    and eke in grief did stand,
The Lord did set us free from all
    by this his servant's hand.

As the cult of the Queen spread and mellowed, ballad-writers
were to add other such simple verses to the music of the day.

And so, each year, the people fêted their Eliza, whose boast it was that 'though God hath raised me high, yet this I count the glory of my crown, that I have reigned with your loves' The like had never before been known in this land, and perhaps has only been repeated since in the unique hold on English men's affections won by Sir Winston Churchill during the late war.

On the Queen's death, her successor, James I, transferred the Accession Day celebrations to his own date, March 24th. The courtly pageantry of the Westminster tiltyard was held on that day; and apparently the villagers rang their bells. But the old spontaneity, rooted in popular affection, could not be sustained. Very soon, the glory of England, which for Elizabethans had been in the present, slipped into the past, and the ghost of Good Queen Bess returned to possess a nation's heart. Bishop Goodman, in his *Memoirs of the Court of King James* relates that 'after a few years, when we had experience of the Scottish government, then — in disparagement of the Scots and in hate and detestation of them — the Queen [Elizabeth] did seem to revive. Then was her memory much magnified — such ringing of bells, such public joy and sermons in commemoration of her, the picture of her tomb painted in many churches; and in effect, more solemnity and joy in memory of her coronation than was for the coming in of King James.' The posthumous history of Elizabeth I had begun.

To put a precise year or time to the revival seems difficult, but on November 17th, 1620, John Chamberlain indited a letter to his friend, Dudley Carleton: 'From London this 17th of November, the happiest day that ever England had to my remembrance.' He was not the only eminent Englishman to think nostalgically of the past. In a speech in the House of Commons on November 27th, 1621, when Queen Elizabeth's Accession Day was probably in his mind, the unpoetic Sir Edward Coke was moved to say that 'she was the flower of Queens, as the rose [is the] queen of flowers'. And in April 1623 John Chamberlain reported that the St Paul's sermon of a young Magdalen preacher was liked the better because 'he was not long nor immoderate in commendation of the [present] time, but gave Queen Elizabeth her due': a comment that virtually paraphrases a similar appreciation of a Paul's Cross sermon in 1617. Francis Osborne, who wrote his *Traditional Memoirs of the Reign of Queen Elizabeth* in the middle of the century — they were published in 1658, the first centenary of Accession Day — referred to the felicity of her reign, which, he says, 'was never since matched, nor have we had yet any cause to hope it will be'. He mentions 'the bonfires and loud acclamations used still by the people upon the day of her inauguration'.

Discontent and despondency — disgust with the government, dislike of the Scots, fear of Catholicism: these had led Englishmen to recall the memory of Good Queen Bess and honour her day. The fear of Catholicism was to continue for a very long time; and when under Charles II and James II the Protestant faith seemed once more to be in danger, old passions were revived and, in London at least, Queen Elizabeth's Accession Day — now apt to be called her Birthday — acquired something of the significance it possessed in her own lifetime.

A new chapter of our story begins with Titus Oates and the exploitation of his Popish Plot for party ends. For London prentices and the London mob, November 17th became henceforward a second Guy Fawkes day. In 1678, the first November of the Plot years, 'great solemnities' were planned for 'the birthday of Queen Elizabeth', and we are told that 'a constable brought one lately before a Justice of the Peace for speaking treason against Queen Elizabeth'. The following year, during the agitation over the Exclusion Bill — directed against the succession of James to the throne — London's celebration of November 17th was staged with unparalleled elaboration. Great sums of money are said to have been spent on wine and spirits for 'incredible multitudes' of people and on the tableaux for a fantastic procession: tableaux that included the Pope, with the Devil in attendance as his privy counsellor, Cardinals and Jesuits, and Sir Edmund Berry Godfrey, the people's martyr and Papists' victim. That morning the bells started ringing at 3 a.m. and at 5 a.m. the procession started on its way from Moorgate to Temple Bar, where, before the statue of Queen Elizabeth — adorned for the occasion with a crown of gilded laurel and a golden shield bearing the legend, 'The Protestant Religion and Magna Charta' — the Pope, in all his grandeur, was toppled on to a huge bonfire. Afterwards, this grotesque show, with the doggerel verses written for it, was commemorated in a descriptive pamphlet, entitled *London's Defiance to Rome*.

There were similar celebrations in following years, and when in 1682, at the desire of the Lord Mayor — who feared a tumult — King and Council intervened to prohibit the factious people from burning the Pope, 'they drowned him' instead. In November 1688 William of Orange had just landed in England; and a correspondent then wrote that James II, fearing the London prentices, who were daily committing disorders, deemed it prudent to defer his departure from the city till after 'Queen Elizabeth's birthday'.

In Queen Anne's reign, the celebration of Accession Day once again became an instrument of party politics. 'This being Queen Elizabeth's birthday', wrote Swift in his *Journal to Stella*, on November 17th, 1711, 'we have the d—— and all to do among us.' The Whigs designed to have a mighty torchlight procession at midnight, with effigies of the Pope, the Devil, Cardinals, the high-churchman Sacheverell, etc., which were to be thrown on the bonfire. However, by order of the Secretary of State the effigies were seized, and the public had to be content with a broadside account of the intended mock procession, along with verses written for the occasion:

> Let us sing to the memory of glorious Queen Bess,
> Who long did the hearts of her subjects possess,

And whose mighty actions did to us secure
Those many great blessings which now do endure:
For then she did lay that solid foundation
On which our religion is fixed in this nation.

It was ironic, and yet it was also apt, to use the name and day and fame of Queen Elizabeth for the crude passions of a Protestant mob. Ironic, because she herself had been high Anglican in outlook and the inflexible opponent of fanaticism and intolerance. Apt, because fate had made her the instrument of revolution, and her accession day, which its commemorators loved to call the Birthday of the Gospel, had indeed been that. She had been engaged in mortal conflict with Catholicism for close on half a century, her own life and the ethos of her country at stake. She boasted of being 'mere English', and, as the Virgin Queen, identified herself with patriotism and the people to the exclusion of all other earthly attachments. She was, she rejoiced to be, England's Eliza; and if her devotees committed many solecisms in her name, she can scarcely be blamed.

The annual salute to Queen Bess's fame continued. When in 1713 Pope Pius V — author of the famous bull of 1570 deposing her — was canonized, there came a counterblast in a tract entitled *A Protestant Memorial for the Seventeenth of November, being the Inauguration Day of Queen Elizabeth*. The author remarks: 'In a grateful remembrance of God's mercy in raising up, continuing, and prospering this most illustrious benefactor of England, the good Protestants of this nation (those especially of London and Westminster) have annually taken notice (and not without some degree of decent and orderly solemnity) of the 17th of November, being the day on which her Majesty Queen Elizabeth began her happy reign. And', continues the author, 'such decent and orderly observation of it seems to me not only warranted by former motives, but also enforced by a new and extraordinary argument', namely, the canonization of Pius V. A volume of *Miscellanies*, published in George I's reign and containing 'Merry Observations' on remarkable days throughout the year, also mentions this day: a day, the author affirms, which 'will prove another protestant Holiday, dedicated to the pious memory of that antipapistical Princess and virgin preserver of the reformed Churches, Queen Elizabeth. This night', he adds, 'will be a great promoter of the tallow-chandler's welfare; for marvellous illuminations will be set forth in every window, as emblems of her shining virtues; and will be stuck in clay, to put the world in mind that grace, wisdom, beauty and virginity were unable to preserve the best of women from mortality.'

In 1718 a periodical, giving an account of public spectacles, linked the ancient and laudable custom of burning the Pope on November 5th with that of commemorating Queen Elizabeth on the 17th; but — and this is the point to note — the author was conscious that decline had set in. 'I am sorry', he comments, 'to see this ceremony is not performed of late years with the usual pomp and triumph.' A few more traces of the day remain. Newbury in Berkshire, we are told, rang its bells every November 17th for Queen Elizabeth's accession, down to 1739. Then, in 1760, a correspondent of the *Gentleman's Magazine* wrote to say that, 'this being the anniversary of Queen Elizabeth's accession', he was reminded of the celebration in 1679. Evidently, the festival had become, or was becoming, little more than a memory. By 1803 even the memory was fading. In that year another correspondent of the *Gentleman's Magazine* quoted a couplet from one of the satires of John Oldham, the late-seventeenth-century poet:

> Louder than on Queen Bess's day the rout
> For Anti-Christ burnt in effigy shout.

He proceeded to ask: When is Queen Bess's day; why was it so called; and when was it discontinued?

The day has its place in John Brand's *Observations on Popular Antiquities*, as re-edited by Sir Henry Ellis in 1813 and often re-published in the nineteenth century; but it is as a defunct anniversary — except that Ellis noted (as he also did in another publication in 1827) that the day was still kept as a holiday at the Exchequer and at Westminster and Merchant Taylors' schools.

Times had changed. The raw emotional appeal of 'the Birthday of the Gospel' could not survive the Age of Reason and the French Revolution. Catholic emancipation was on its way, and England no longer needed her Eliza. In any case, romantic notions about monarchy were out of date. There was little credence in a great Queen, nor was there much sympathy with a Queen who was something of a blue-stocking. Harris Nicolas, writing a biography of Lady Jane Grey in 1825 and listing her linguistic accomplishments, remarked — and presumably would have said much the same of Elizabeth: 'She possessed acquirements now properly deemed neither requisite nor useful in female education.' If William Cobbett had lived a few generations earlier, the odds are that he would have shouted with the lustiest for 'the best of women', on November 17th; but to him Elizabeth was 'Bloody Queen Bess', and by perversity Mary 'Good Queen Mary'. And in the sentimental, civilized age of Victoria, how could the murderer of Mary Queen of Scots be good? Except in folklore, where scores of apocryphal stories about her kept on circulating, the posthumous history of England's Eliza was ended. When the three-hundredth anniversary of Accession Day arrived on November 17th, 1858, neither heart nor mind responded. The leading article in *The Times* that day was on manure.

If today we are inclined to salute an ancient Holyday, it is not because bygone passions have revived. Our historical perspective has changed and our knowledge advanced. We recognize the Elizabethan period as an age strangely like ou own, and, understanding its problems, see in the Queen a leade meet for the times: one endowed with wisdom, courage and tolerance, able to inspire the nation, save it from its perils, and conjure immortal glory from its aspirations.

THE ELIZABETHAN AGE[1]

IT could hardly have been expected of me that I should choose any other subject for this occasion than my Elizabethan period; and the name of Bishop Creighton, whose work as a historian we commemorate, was also an injunction to keep to my last, for, as you all know, Creighton was one of Queen Elizabeth's biographers. There is, or there was, a tradition that this lecture should be broad in its scope (though not necessarily in its chronology); that it should proceed more obviously from reflection than from research. Seeking for a theme in this vein, it occurred to me that I might try to answer the question, What made the Elizabethan period a great age? Can the historian by his process of analysis answer, or at least throw some light on, so subtle and difficult a question? If he can, then he may exceed the purely antiquarian purpose of satisfying man's curiosity about the past, and, in this bewildering, changing society of our own day, may proffer that modicum of understanding which is to be found in historical analogy. The supreme privilege of human beings among God's creatures is that they can garner experience; and history is man's storehouse.

No one is likely to accuse me of begging the question by assuming the greatness of the Elizabethan age. Its own people grew to be conscious of it. The ballad-writers, the chroniclers, the playwrights — in short, the literary voice of Elizabethan England, and voices abroad also, including Pope Sixtus V — proclaimed it. The apocalyptic mood of Mr Churchill's great words — 'This was their finest hour' — possessed many Elizabethans. And after the Queen was dead and the age become a

[1] The Creighton Lecture, University of London, 1950; published by the Athlone Press, 1951.

107

memory, after the novelty of possessing a male sovereign in
the person of James I had worn off — and how quickly this
happened! — Englishmen grasped with instinctive certainty
that that indeed had been their finest hour. So the tradition
remained in this land of ours. While personal monarchy lasted
or religion suffused politics the greatness of the age was personified in Elizabeth — 'the Queen whose feast the factious rabble
keep', as Dryden wrote.

> Fixt in our hearts thy fame shall live;
> And maugre all the popish spite,
> To honour thee our youth shall strive,
> And yearly celebrate this night.

So ran some verses written in 1679 to celebrate the anniversary
of Elizabeth's accession to the throne — 'the Birthday of the
Gospel', as it was called.[1] And when such passions died down
and personal monarchy went out of fashion, still the age was
acclaimed great, though the credit might be transferred from
the sovereign to her ministers. In our own lifetime, even the
cynics, in the years of disillusion after the first world war,
however they bespattered personalities left the tradition about
the age free from denigration.

Thus, with the consensus of the centuries behind us, we may
proceed with our inquiry: Why did England achieve greatness
in this age? If we try to generalize the question and apply it
first to the individual, we might agree that in addition to
the capacity for greatness there must be the will to achieve it
and the opportunity. Many a potential genius must have died
after a commonplace life through the lack of a chance to live
otherwise; and all of us who have passed our youth must
realize that opportunity may be there but ability alone is no
guarantee that it will be seized. The same considerations surely
hold in a nation's life. The thesis is implied in the passage of

[1] C. H. Firth, 'The Ballad History of the Reigns of the Later Tudors', in *Trans.
Royal Hist. Soc.*, 3rd ser. iii, 117–18; E. K. Wilson, *England's Eliza*, p. 73.

Mr Churchill's from which I have already quoted. When the stream moves quietly and satisfactorily along, how tempting it is for a nation to rest on its oars!

In the Elizabethan period the waters were far from quiet. That, indeed, may partly explain why Elizabethan history has so manifest an appeal to readers today. Then, as now, Europe was concerned with the clash of two faiths inextricably mingled with politics. Then, as now, the devotees of both sides felt that the truth which was in them was a cause transcending all others. Do not be surprised that I compare the struggle of Catholicism and Protestantism in those days with that of our rival ideologies today. Time has detached religion from politics and emptied it of the old passion and intolerance: but sixteenth-century zealots viewed the rival faith with all the detestation and fear that we see in our world today; and the connection of religion with the state confused international and national politics.

On its doctrinal side the English Reformation may be described as a partisan story down to the accession of Elizabeth. In pre-Nazi and pre-Communist days scholars were prone to make calculations about the number of Catholics in England in 1558 or at later dates. Doubtless there was virtue, although there could be little accuracy, in their labours. Nowadays, however, they strike me as in some ways irrelevant or even naive: irrelevant and naive in the sense that similar calculations about Hitler's Germany or Czechoslovakia would be. Revolutions are not explained by statistics, but by leadership, organization, intensity of conviction, passion and purpose.

The conditions for revolution existed at the end of Mary Tudor's reign: two rival ideologies, one in opposition, with several hundred of its leaders abroad, ready to return and overthrow their opponents. The Protestants possessed certain advantages. They had the sympathy of London and other influential parts of the country. No less important, Mary's reign, by its association of Catholicism with a foreign king and a disastrous pro-Spanish foreign policy, and by the hatred its religious persecution engendered, tended to make patriots anti-Catholic and generally weaken the Catholic cause. We might compare the situation with the Weimar regime in Germany vis-à-vis the nascent party of Hitler.

If a Catholic sovereign had succeeded Mary, the forces of that party would have controlled the machine of government and England would have continued Catholic. Trouble, however, would have come from London and other centres, from Parliament also, perhaps; and the country might well have drifted into civil war. At any rate, the internal stresses of such times must surely have checked the ebullient spirit of the nation. As it was, Elizabeth, a Protestant, came to the throne and, helped by the political bankruptcy of the recent past, was able to make Protestantism the symbol of England. The English Reformation ceased to be a partisan story: it became a national one.

> Come over the bo[u]rn, Bessy.

In these words the England of the ballad-writer apostrophized the new Queen in 'A Songe betwene the Quenes Majestie and Englande', published in 1559.

> Lady, this long space
> Have I loved thy grace,
> More than I durste well saye;
> Hoping, at the last,
> When all stormes were past,
> For to see this joyfull daye.[1]

London's welcome of Elizabeth on her accession was an anticipation of revolution. What is more, our latest interpretation of her religious settlement is a study in the tactics of revolution.[2] The Elizabethan Prayer Book and Act of Uni-

---

[1] Firth, op. cit. p. 71.
[2] Cf. my article, 'The Elizabethan Acts of Supremacy and Uniformity', *Eng. Hist. Rev.* lxv, 304-32.

formity were extorted by the pressure of the Marian exiles, backed by a House of Commons under the leadership of radical Protestant devotees. How misleading, one reflects, is that hackneyed phrase of our text-books which describes the settlement as a *via media*, and starts off the reign on such a note. Valid it may still be in part, but it empties passion from the story and gets the perspective wrong. The Elizabethan age opened with a striking victory for the Protestant revolution; and the subsequent events of the reign — the consolidation of the Catholic Church at the Council of Trent; the French Religious Wars with the infamous blood-bath of the Massacre of St Bartholomew; the flight of Mary Queen of Scots to England, there to become the focus for religious and political discontent, leading almost immediately to the Rebellion of the North; the Papal Bull, releasing Englishmen from their allegiance to the Queen; the Papal plan of an 'Enterprise' against Protestant England; the infiltration of Catholic missionaries from the continent, preparing, as it were, a 'Fifth Column' for the day when the 'Enterprise' would be launched; the recurrent plots against the Queen's throne and life; the unfolding of English policy as anti-Spanish and anti-Catholic — all these happenings, and more, determining the domestic and foreign climate of the next forty years, kept the spirit of revolution constantly alive, and as often as not at white-hot intensity.

Here we must note a paradox. The Queen herself had an instinctive hatred of revolution and its votaries. She did not want to proceed as rapidly as she was forced to do at the beginning of the reign; she modified the revolutionary Protestant programme and injected conservative elements into the service and policy of the Anglican Church; throughout her reign she was the effective obstacle to Puritan activities; and time and again, with her caution and prudence and delays, she was the despair of her statesmen, carried away by the exuberance of the times. Nevertheless, even to the hot-heads — indeed, to the hot-heads most of all — she was the personification of their cause. She was their Judith, their Deborah, their 'Fayre Elisa, Queene of Shepheardes All', their Diana, their Laura, their 'Cynthia, the Ladie of the Sea', their Gloriana and Belphoebe. These were not random extravagances, fashioned by Court sycophants. They voiced a national cult. An American scholar has made a meticulous study of the literature of the age and filled a substantial volume with extracts on such themes.[1] Nor was literature the only expression of the mood. Running through the parliamentary debates of the reign, and reaching lyrical pitch during the period of plots and danger to Elizabeth's throne and life, is the same note. 'If it might prolong her Majesty's life but for one year', said a Member in 1585, 'I protest I would be content to suffer death with the most exquisite torments that might be devised.' 'It makes my heart leap for joy to think we have such a jewel', said another M.P.; 'it makes my joints to tremble for fear, when I consider the loss of such a jewel.'[2] Both rhapsodists belonged to that large Puritan element in the House of Commons which managed to worship the Queen and yet be a never-ending source of trouble.

> Ring out your bels!
> What should yow doe els?
> Stricke up your Drums for joy!
> The Noblest Queene
> that ever was seene
> In England doth Raigne this day.

The quotation is from a ditty, whose title is expressive of its refrain: 'A pleasant newe Ballad, of the most blessed and prosperous Raigne of her Majestye for the space of two and fortye yeeres, and now entring into the three and fortith to the great joy and comfort of all her Ma[jestye's] faythfull subjects.'[3]

[1] E. K. Wilson, *England's Eliza* (Harvard Univ. Press, 1939).
[2] B.M. Lansdowne MS. 43, fols. 168b, 173b.
[3] Wilson, op. cit. p. 52.

Once more let us turn to our contemporary world as a stimulus to imagination. In Italy, Germany, and Russia we have seen a body of doctrine — the *mystique* of a people — linked to the simpler emotions of patriotism and hero-worship. So it was in Elizabethan England. Protestantism was the *mystique*. It fed and was fed by nationalism. The patriotic note runs through the ballads of the reign. It is implicit in the striking development of historical writing and reading: 'an exercise' — Elizabethans held — 'second only to a study of Holy Writ in its power to induce good morality and shape the individual into a worthy member of society'.[1] There was founded in this period the first Society of Antiquaries, to which John Stow and William Camden and many others interested in the antiquities of England belonged. History as the hand-maiden to patriotism: that, too, is familiar in our day.

The cult of Elizabeth has its analogies with the cult of Mussolini, Hitler, and Stalin. It is interesting to reflect that nowadays the revolutionary *mystique* has had to find its personification in an individual, the head of the state, who in varying degrees has been deified by its votaries. There are, however, profound differences to note, as well as analogies. The modern dictator finds the principal psychological basis of power in the cult of himself. He must be the high priest of the *mystique*. In the sixteenth century personal monarchy provided the framework for leadership: power rested in the office of monarch, and therefore it was possible for the Queen to personify the emotion of the nation without necessarily being doctrinaire. Hence the paradox of revolution with moderation at the helm.

Rare personal qualities, great art, and good fortune were needed for the role. It is said that no man can be a hero to his valet; but in this instance those about the sovereign had to be schooled into an instinctive recognition of leadership. A contemptuous, rotten, or merely blasé Court, though it attempted

[1] L. B. Wright, *Middle Class Culture in Elizabethan England*, p. 297. Cf. L. C. Knights, *Drama and Society in the Age of Jonson*, p. 244.

in its own sordid interests to sustain an artificial comedy, would have ruined the play. And there had to be the artistic capacity to draw out and respond to the emotion of the country at large. Elizabeth possessed these qualities *in excelsis*. But, as I have said, she was no revolutionary: she was not, as her sister, Mary Tudor, had been, a *dévote*. Good fortune — which was partly policy — also enters into the argument. If Elizabeth had had a husband and family, the chances are that the ardours of English Puritans would have found a rival focus and their discontents have been directed against the sovereign, thus destroying the spell over the community. In quite another way than that usually thought of, a Virgin Queen may have been essential to the Elizabethan tradition.

Elizabethan England should be regarded as a revolutionary age: that is the point I am anxious to make. Hitler claimed that a nation so inspired is irresistible, except by a like faith. And though Hitler's Germany was overwhelmed, this was accomplished by an opposing faith, stronger for being detached from fanaticism. Indeed, the boast was not an empty one. Inspiration, a sense of purpose, faith, and enthusiasm: though we may sometimes think them misplaced, devilish, or what you will, are they not ingredients of greatness? And surely they are qualities which we perceive in many aspects of the Elizabethan age. They were present in a strange blend of lust for easy riches, piratical impulse, patriotism, and fervid Protestant zeal in the voyages of Elizabethan seamen. 'The too familiar compound of avarice, self-righteousness, and hypocrisy': that is how a finely sensitive and imaginative scholar described these characteristics in 1905.[1] They are words that we too might have used in pre-Hitler days. But we now know the type; and we should not think 'hypocrisy' apt. Listen to the mystical note in the writing of John Davys, the Elizabethan navigator:

[1] Walter Raleigh, 'The English Voyages of the Sixteenth Century', in *R. Hakluyt's Principal Navigations* (Hakluyt Soc. 1905), xii, 32 n. 1.

THE ELIZABETHAN AGE

There is no doubt but that we of England are this saved people, by the eternal and infallible presence of the Lord predestinated to be sent into these Gentiles in the sea, to those Isles and famous Kingdoms, there to preach the peace of the Lord: for are not we only set upon Mount Zion to give light to all the rest of the world? Have not we the true handmaid of the Lord to rule us, unto whom the eternal majesty of God hath revealed his truth and supreme power of Excellency?... It is only we, therefore, that must be these shining messengers of the Lord, and none but we.[1]

Change the doctrinal and national medium, and such exaltation finds echoes in our own days. 'God's Englishman' was an Elizabethan. As a Tragedy of the 1590s declared:

> Mighty Jove the supreme king of heaven,
> That guides the concourse of the meteors
> And rules the motions of the azure sky,
> Fights always for the Briton's safety.[2]

But behind this *mystique* what was there? Certainly not a propaganda machine, nor a police state. There was a society which politically, socially, and economically had many reasons, if not every reason, to be buoyant. This was the culminating period or phase of a civilization, in which conservative elements from the past were still a vigorous reality, while new forces, having overcome an initial extravagance, had not yet developed their inner weaknesses to the point of gross abuse and social collapse.

In his essay *The Elizabethan World Picture* Dr Tillyard has demonstrated how in its view of the universe and of society the Elizabethan age preserved the medieval idea of order and degree.

[1] Raleigh, op. cit. p. 31.
[2] *The Lamentable Tragedy of Locrine* (*c.* 1591, by Peele?), quoted by Knights, op. cit. p. 245.

The heavens themselves, the planets, and this centre
Observe degree, priority, and place.

.   .   .   .

O! when degree is shak'd,
Which is the ladder to all high designs,
The enterprise is sick. How could communities,
Degrees in schools, and brotherhoods in cities,
Peaceful commerce from dividable shores,
The primogenitive and due of birth,
Prerogative of age, crowns, sceptres, laurels,
But by degree, stand in authentic place?
Take but degree away, untune that string,
And, hark! what discord follows ...[1]

If this philosophy had been too rigidly applied, it might have imposed the paralysis of caste upon society. If it had been utterly ignored, 'the enterprise' would indeed have been sick. Vulgarity, not quality, would have marked the age; and for its gospel we might have had the familiar lines:

The rich man in his castle, the poor man at his gate,
God made them high and lowly, and ordered their estate.

Not unlike the Elizabethan in sentiment, you will note, but how different in implication as well as diction!

In a sense, it is strange to find a philosophy of degree still vigorous in the second half of the sixteenth century, for the Reformation, through the dissolution of the monasteries and chantries and the sale of their vast estates, had threatened social upheaval. It created a prolonged and unprecedented market in land, comparable with a period of great industrial expansion in more modern times: the opportunity for speculators, for new fortunes and new men. Speculators there were:

[1] Shakespeare, *Troilus and Cressida*, Act i, sc. 3.

new fortunes and new men as well — in the peerage, the King's Council and elsewhere. The voice of rebellion — of the conservative Pilgrims of Grace — protested against this trend in Henry VIII's reign; and in the brief, unhappy reign of Edward VI discord, as the philosophy prognosticated, did indeed afflict the country. It was the long reign of Elizabeth which ensured that change should proceed in an orderly way and a conservative setting. For all her popular arts, the Queen, both in temperament and policy, was essentially aristocratic. Under her father, the peerage had received a strong and needed injection of new blood. Elizabeth remained satisfied with this and created very few new peers, though aspirants to that dignity were many and clamorous in her later years. Thus by stinting honour she kept it precious, and by insisting on deference to rank she strengthened social stability.

Like the word 'nobleman', 'gentleman' was a term of art in the Elizabethan age, set in the prevailing order of 'degree, priority, and place'. The official view is clearly stated in a commission to Norroy King of Arms: 'no sheriffs, commissaries, archdeacons, officials, scriveners, clerks, writers or others shall call or write in courts and open places or use in writing the addition of esquire or gentleman, unless they can justify the same by the law of arms and the laws of the realm, or ascertain the same in writing from Norroy or his deputies'.[1] Such a theory of nomenclature might seem to indicate a system approaching the social rigidity of France at that time.

However, economic facts, and among them the active land-market, were too strong for an inflexible system. As the purchasers of ecclesiastical estates, like speculators on the modern stock market, sold out and took their profits, ultimate holders of the land benefited from the additional source of wealth. There was prolonged and severe monetary inflation in the second half of the sixteenth century; but — subject to the vagaries of the English climate — rising prices, coupled with

[1] *Cal. Patent Rolls, Eliz.* ii, 92.

an expanding market, brought great prosperity to those land-holders who were fortunately situated as regards rent and showed enterprise and ability. This — to borrow the title of Professor Tawney's classical article[1] — was the age which saw the rise of the gentry. Not only did their wealth increase: they were better educated. They sent their sons to the universities, which as a result both of the Reformation and what we call the Renaissance, ceased to be primarily ecclesiastical seminaries. In increasing numbers they also sent them to the Inns of Court to obtain a non-professional knowledge of the law. They invaded the borough seats in parliament and monopolized the House of Commons for their class, as they already dominated local government through the office of Justice of the Peace.[2]

But it was not only the gentleman-born who enjoyed increased wealth and education. Lower classes in the landed hierarchy, and especially yeomen, were beneficiaries. The social distinction between gentleman and yeoman was sharp in theory, and to some extent in practice; but it was not difficult to stride across the barrier. Neither the university student nor the law student had to be *bene natus*. True, a conservative planner at the beginning of Elizabeth's reign, disturbed, like Colonel Blimp, at the prospect of England going to the dogs, wished to impose this restriction on legal training.[3] Like Colonel Blimp he remained a voice ineffective. Though they might be yeomen's sons and be scornfully known as 'gentlemen of the first head', students were by courtesy regarded as gentlemen. Moreover, as Sir Thomas Smith remarked, anyone able and willing to 'bear the port, charge, and countenance of a gentleman' could readily — if at a price — raise himself to that status. Many a yeoman preferred to remain as he was:

[1] *Economic Hist. Rev.* xi, 1-38.
[2] Cf. my *Elizabethan House of Commons*.
[3] *Hist. MSS. Com., Hatfield MSS.* i. 163.

Then let me live and die a yeoman still.
So was my father, so must live his son.[1]

But the socially ambitious could climb the ladder; and with class distinction fluid, intermarriage was common. Thus, in agriculture, the chief economic activity of Elizabethan England, there was incentive — plenty of it, social and monetary.

Commerce and trade, for which this was also a period of great expansion, brought similar, and, to a few, much greater rewards. Thomas Wilson, a shrewd social observer, writing about 1600, declared that in his time he had known twenty-four aldermen of the city of Norwich who were esteemed to be worth £20,000 apiece — some much more, and the better sort of citizens the half. 'But', he went on, 'if we should speak of London and some other maritime places, we should find it much exceeding this rate. It is well known that at this time there are in London some merchants worth £100,000; and he is not accounted rich that cannot reach to £50,000 or near it.'[2] If correct, such sums would be most impressive fortunes when translated into present-day values. Wealthy citizens could, and did, buy landed estates for themselves, and, like ambitious yeomen, establish themselves as 'gentlemen'. Moreover, riches were attractive and flexible conventions made intermarriage with the gentry easy. Nor was the flow one way. By the system of primogeniture younger sons of the gentry were driven out to seek a livelihood, and many of them moved into the towns to engage as citizens in trade and commerce. No prejudice existed against this, as in France. There can be no doubt that economically Elizabethan England — especially before the war years — was prosperous. The emphasis was on enterprise and the individual. In the industrial sphere the effect of this was

[1] From the play, *George a Green*, quoted by Knights, op. cit. p. 248 n. 2. For the yeoman, see Mildred Campbell, *The English Yeoman under Elizabeth and the Early Stuarts* (1942).
[2] 'The state of England ...', ed. F. J. Fisher, in *Camden Miscellany*, xvi, 20-1.

so marked that economic historians have found themselves describing an early industrial revolution.[1]

The diffusion of wealth and education and the quickening tempo of economic life had their effect upon the arts and literature. In architecture the home took the place formerly held by the church. It was an age of much building. In contrast with France, where Catherine de Medici spent prodigal sums on palaces, the Queen of England, growing poorer as the nation grew richer, was content with what she inherited. But her courtiers made up for her inactivity, while very many of the gentry and the better-off yeomen rebuilt their homes. 'If ever curious building did flourish in England, it is in these our days', wrote William Harrison in Holinshed's *Chronicles*. And as early as 1562, a bishop remarked: 'Englishmen indulge in pleasures as if they were to die tomorrow, and build as if they were to live for ever.'[2] The furnishings and equipment of the home told of new standards of life. So did personal splendour. The growth of London as a social centre, rivalry at Court, foreign travel, and the goods which merchants, with an eye to business, imported into England — not to mention the example of a Queen whose love for variety in dress was notorious — led, among courtiers and those who aped them, to an emphasis on clothes that was startling: an 'exotic and ostentatious display' such as 'never before nor since has occurred in the history of English costume'.[3] When 'green-headed youths, covered with feathers, and gold and silver lace'[4] bore 'their birth rights proudly on their backs', and an Earl of Oxford helped to bankrupt himself with his finery, the moralist might sharpen his barbs, but charity reflects that the zest of youth leads to much folly.

I do not know whether anyone has attempted to calculate, in the rough manner which alone would be possible, the number

[1] Cf. J. U. Nef, *Industry and Government in France and England, 1540-1640* (1940).
[2] *Zurich Letters* (Parker Soc.), i, 108 (app., p. 64).
[3] Iris Brooke in *Life under the Tudors* (1950), p. 212.
[4] T. Birch, *Memoirs of Queen Elizabeth*, ii, 15.

of books, pamphlets, etc., which were published in the several decades of the Elizabethan period and the decades that went before. The increase, I imagine, would be most striking. And so, in many respects, was the advance in quality. From the early Elizabethan play *Gorboduc* — itself a landmark — to the plays of Shakespeare, what a development! And a point relevant to our argument: the more scholars explore such documents as the records of the Court of Star Chamber, where the behaviour and speech of ordinary Elizabethans are preserved for us, the more Shakespeare becomes understandable as a part of his own age. As for prose: ignoring the euphuistic fashion — which afflicted the Queen, though it had its merits in royal utterances — a good deal of the writing, in historical documents no less than printed books, kept near to the vigour and directness of everyday speech. Metaphors and similes were not limp and lifeless through long and indiscriminate usage. They were freshly invented or gathered in the taverns and the street; and, apart from the natural raciness of an unsophisticated, lively people, we must remember that the ordinary man heard in church each week the verbal music of the Prayer Book. Nowadays, literary critics are becoming enthusiastic about Elizabethan prose: about the primitive muscularity of Nashe, for example, and the vivid invective of Martin Marprelate.[1] In a measure this is due to that change in taste which the best American writing of our generation has done so much to produce. And, incidentally, it seems to me that one might not go far wrong in drawing comparisons between the vitality of American life and that of Elizabethan England.

Within forty years of Elizabeth's death, after almost as many years of increasing political, religious, and social discontent, England was rent by civil war. The political machine had broken down. That fact alone would prompt us to ask how intimate was the connection between the greatness of the age

[1] Cf. Knights, op. cit. pp. 301 seqq.

that was past and its system of government. The answer will be clearer if we first draw a moral or two from the Stuart tragedy. When Elizabeth died, the Tudor political system was doomed. Those economic, educational, and social changes to which I have alluded, made certain of that. The only question was whether there would be imaginative and peaceful adaptation to a new age or whether incompetent leadership would allow the old system to fester and collapse. James I succeeded to an impoverished crown: he cannot be blamed on that count. He was weak in character, and did not know when to say 'No': these are fatal defects in any leader. He subjected Court and government to favourites, and between them they allowed the mercenary instincts of individuals free play. Corruption was rampant, honour cheapened by the sale of peerages and lesser dignities. The political and social evils, evident in the England of 1603, grew like deadly weeds; and, as the dramatists of the time perceived, the decencies of the old order were violated. Charles I completed the disaster. He turned the Puritans and the House of Commons, who had been the most ardent of Queen Elizabeth's votaries, into dangerous critics of the monarchy. Instead of personifying a nation, he led a party.

Control was what the nation needed, and what it got in the reign of Elizabeth; control which, while encouraging the energies of the people and sustaining their gaiety, restrained the cruder promptings of individualism. Government was paternal; and in the economic sphere I fancy we should understand it better if we compared it with the present-day regulated State with its emphasis on the public good. Everything depended from the centre. All aspects of life, from the personal behaviour of individuals to high matters of state came before either the Crown or the Council, or both. And never before and never again was the Privy Council so efficient. Elizabeth kept it small, balancing extremely able commoners with aristocrats; and even the aristocrats were converted by hard work and good training into tolerable and sometimes highly effective statesmen. Unlike James I, she did not blur the distinction between the two elements by rewarding the commoners with peerages. William Cecil was the signal exception to this policy, which maintained the professional outlook of the abler administrators.

But the sovereign was even more important than the Council in determining the quality of government. Under personal monarchy the machinery of government was the ruler's. In theory it was intimately linked with the royal prerogative, while in practice there was a flexibility which permitted and even demanded constant intervention from the centre. If we cast our thoughts back to Hitler's Germany, where the personal influence of the leader and his court in the normal functioning of government shocked our liberal minds, we shall obtain some idea of the picture. Or there is another, and in some respects better, parallel in the peculiar position held by Mr Churchill while England was at war. Those who have read his *Second World War* will remember the appendices of minutes and memoranda which, as a journalist said, 'he fired off unremittingly in all directions'. Though, as this journalist added, the picture is incomplete without the 'come-backs' to some of his 'peremptory rockets', the general effect, one concludes, must have been to keep officials on their toes — as undoubtedly, but by other devices, he kept the nation on its toes. We can readily imagine the effect in the sixteenth century of a Queen, with not a few of Mr Churchill's qualities, on the Whitehall of her day, and beyond that on the country at large. Elizabeth was perfunctory about nothing. Or to be precise, her officials could never rely upon her being perfunctory: which had much the same result. They could never be sure of obtaining her signature to a document without an inquisition, followed sometimes by biting criticism and a stormy refusal. She might interfere in anything. *Mutatis mutandis*, Mr Churchill's notes on the tattered Admiralty flag and on the growing habit among civil servants of addressing each other by their Christian names might have come from the Queen. 'I would to God', wrote Walsingham on one occasion, when she criticized the phrasing and latinity of the commission to try Mary Queen of Scots, 'her Majesty could be content to refer these things to them that can best judge of them, as other princes do.'[1] Perhaps some of our wartime officials, receiving their Churchillian 'rockets', echoed Sir Francis Walsingham's sentiments!

The effect of such a person in such a position was to keep faction, corruption, and other abuses in check, and to maintain that order of 'degree, priority, and place' which was the fragrant essence of society. The able men she chose as her statesmen, and particularly William Cecil, by their vigilance and hard work helped to make a success of paternal government.

It was the Queen herself who kept the nation charged with emotion. The citizens of London and the multitude of visitors there were thrilled by their frequent sight of her. In later life Bishop Goodman described how when a boy in the year 1588, on a dark December evening, they were suddenly told that the Queen was gone to council, 'and if you will see the Queen you must come quickly'. They ran to Whitehall and were admitted to the courtyard, which, lighted by torches, was soon full. After an hour's wait, they saw Elizabeth emerge, 'in great state'.

> Then we cried 'God save your Majesty! God save your Majesty!' Then the Queen turned unto us and said, 'God bless you all, my good people!' Then we cried again 'God save your Majesty! God save your Majesty!' Then the Queen said again unto us, 'You may well have a greater prince, but you shall never have a more loving prince'. And so, looking one upon another awhile, the Queen departed. This wrought such an impression upon us, for shows and pageants are ever best seen by torch-light, that all the way long we did nothing but talk what an admirable queen she

[1] Conyers Read, *Sir Francis Walsingham*, iii, 52 n. 4.

was, and how we would adventure our lives to do her service.[1]

The countryside was given a taste of Londoners' ecstasy in the Queen's annual progresses.

Or take an illustration of the personal touch in quite different style: her treatment of Drake when, at a most delicate and threatening moment in Anglo-Spanish relations, he returned from his voyage round the world. His plunder had to be sequestered in case Elizabeth was compelled to return it; but she sent word that he was to be allowed, in utmost secrecy, to abstract ten thousand pounds' worth of it. She received him at Court, listened with delight to his story, and made her celebrated visit to Deptford to knight him aboard the *Golden Hind*. One might say that she had cocked a snook at Philip of Spain. At such a critical time it was impudent bravura; but it was also political art. As for her skill in handling Parliament — her supreme achievement in patriotic romance — that is a story which would be credible only if fully told.

And now, perhaps, we can assemble our argument. The Elizabethan age was one of rapidly expanding horizons, economic, cultural, and geographical; an age to stir the imagination and incite the energies of the people. At Court, the structure of politics, based on faction and emulation, kept life intense and vigorous.[2] Though sordid in many of its details, it was transformed into romance by the personality of the Queen and disciplined by her masterful character, backed by an acute and highly trained intelligence. In the country the day of the gentry had arrived. It was not simply a matter of inheriting and maintaining old standards of wealth and comfort. Life was in flux: a challenge to enterprise and ability. As at Court, faction and rivalry stirred and invigorated county society. At times and places they revealed their evil

[1] Quoted by Firth, op. cit. p. 106.
[2] On this, cf. my essay, 'The Elizabethan Political Scene', included below.

side, but they were kept within bounds by the aristocratic structure of society — the doctrine of 'degree, priority, and place' — and by the vigilant authority of the Privy Council. In the towns, Fortune could be wooed, and for the ambitious apprentice there were success-stories, such as that of Jack of Newbury, which sober life did not render incredible:[1] stories which might be likened to the proverbial marshal's baton for the Napoleonic soldier, or 'From Log Cabin to White House' for the American of half a century or more ago. Court, county, and town — even London, which, though already a Wen, was still a community — were intimate societies and could respond easily to a prevalent mood. If opportunity beckoned, the will to achieve was quickly diffused; and, with London a national Mecca whose royal and legal courts brought constant pilgrimage from the local communities, the blood coursed through the whole body when the heart of the kingdom throbbed.

Consider the impact on such a society of those voyages whose narratives Hakluyt collected, with their stories and fables of new-found lands and peoples. To a youthful and responsive age, sure of the verbal inspiration of the Bible, conscious of divine intervention in the triumphs and afflictions of everyday life, and believing the many tales of monstrous births and miraculous happenings which honest John Stow recorded in his *Chronicles* and ballad-makers sometimes commemorated in verse — to such an age stories from afar were merely an extension of the wonders in an illimitable world. 'All things became possible; credulity was wiser than experience.' In this mood the poet Spenser rebukes the disbeliever in his 'happy land of Faery':

> But let that man with better sence advize,
> That of the world least part to us is red:
> And dayly how through hardy enterprize,
> Many great Regions are discovered,

[1] Cf. *The Works of Thomas Deloney*, ed. F. O. Mann.

Which to late age were never mentioned.
Who ever heard of th' Indian Peru?
Or who in venturous vessell measured
The Amazons huge river now found trew?
Or fruitfullest Virginia who did ever vew?

Yet all these were, when no man did them know;
Yet have from wisest ages hidden beene:
And later times things more unknowne shall show.
Why then should witlesse man so much misweene
That nothing is, but that which he hath seene?
What if within the Moones faire shining spheare?
What if in every other starre unseene
Of other worldes he happily should heare?
He wonder would much more: yet such to some appeare.[1]

And Marlowe's dying Tamburlaine:

Give me a map; then let me see how much
Is left for me to conquer all the world,
That these, my boys, may finish all my wants.

Reinforcing these reasons for an exuberant national spirit
was the dynamic of Protestantism in mortal conflict with the
powers of darkness. In his recent volume of *Unpopular Essays*
Bertrand Russell has a comforting and, one hopes, a pers-
picacious passage on the struggle between liberals and fanatics,
exposing the inherent weaknesses of a society possessed by
what I have called a *mystique*. Now, if Sir Francis Walsingham
and his fellow-Puritans — who incidentally dominated nearly
every parliament of Elizabeth's reign — had had their way,
doubtless we should have been pointing Bertrand Russell's
moral with an Elizabethan example. But the secret of that age

[1] *Faerie Queene*, bk. ii, introduction, stanzas 2-3. Cf. Raleigh, op. cit. pp. 101 seqq.

is the unfanatical nature of the Queen. Through her control of foreign and domestic policy England enjoyed the advantages of the liberals coupled with the dynamic of the fanatics.

Government, I am convinced, was a principal, if not the principal, ingredient of national greatness. Would all that energy have been released if the political setting had been different? Professor Nef has written a book to demonstrate the radically different development of industry in contemporary France, due to governmental factors;[1] and I should be inclined to strengthen his thesis with further arguments. Then, it is obvious that the story of voyage and exploration would have been different if Mary Tudor had lived to old age and Philip of Spain remained King of England. Supposing, however, that there had been a regime, similar to the Elizabethan in religious and constitutional complexion but less efficient and less inspiring. What then? Political, religious, and social discontent would have emerged sooner; and even if the friction thus created had not hindered the growth of wealth and enterprise, it would have emptied national life of its spirit. Instead of living in the present, men might have looked to the past — to the days of Bluff King Hal, as Jacobeans looked to the days of Good Queen Bess. Instead of 'a literature of youth and hope', there might have been 'a literature of regret and memory'. England was a small community — four to five millions, knit together socially in many ways, some of which I have described. What wireless has done for our generation, the size, homogeneity, and cohesion of Elizabethan society did for those days. It made romantic leadership of the nation possible. If, in sober historical documents no less than in the literature of the age, the emotional tie of sovereign and people is abundantly clear, then surely it is no illusion to imagine that such leadership enabled the nation to achieve its 'finest hour'. After all, we have lived through a similar period ourselves.

[1] Nef, op. cit.

THE ELIZABETHAN AGE

Of course there were greed and folly, poverty, cruelty, petty tyranny, and injustice in Elizabethan England. And it is right that we should occasionally weep over Jerusalem. But the quality of a society is not to be judged by microscopic examinations here and there, nor assessed without relation to its times. Compared with contemporary France or Spain, or other western countries, the purely social merits of Elizabethan England shine bright. Here, for example, is the comment of a German nobleman, visiting this country in 1584-5.

> It is a very fertile country, producing all sorts of corn ... There are plenty of sheep, cows, and various kinds of meat. The peasants and citizens are on the average rich people, not to speak of the gentlemen and noblemen. They are fond of pomp and splendour, both high and low ... I have seen peasants presenting themselves statelier in manner, and keeping a more sumptuous table than some noblemen do in Germany. That is a poor peasant who has no silver-gilt salt-cellars, silver cups, and spoons.[1]

Professor Tawney has described the Elizabethan age as 'a balanced society'. It was in harmony, politically and socially, with the prevailing philosophy: 'concord within the realm amongst the several members of the same',[2] 'hospitality' as the duty of the gentry. There were individual grievances, but not grievances against the system — at least, to any serious extent. In such circumstances a sense of freedom and social well-being can exist. A civilization attains balance; and if — as was then the situation — political, cultural, social, and economic factors are such as to call for high endeavour on the part of the individual, and the community is knit together by enthusiasm and inspiring leadership, it may achieve great-

[1] G. von Bülow, 'Journey through England and Scotland made by Liupold von Wedel', in *Trans. Royal Hist. Soc.*, 2nd ser. ix, 268.
[2] G. de Malynes, *Saint George for England* (1601), quoted by Knights, op. cit. p. 143.

ness. The balance did not last long; and one may doubt whether it could have done so. It was not there in November 1558 when Elizabeth came to the throne, and it was in jeopardy in March 1603 when she died. Like other societies, the Elizabethan age contained the seeds of its own decay.

THE ACCESSION OF
QUEEN ELIZABETH I[1]

THERE are occasions in history when the thoughtful student suspects that much more was going on behind the scene than he is allowed to know. The accession of Elizabeth I is such an occasion. Outwardly everything was peaceable and orderly. It seemed as inevitable and natural a succession as that, say, of Henry VIII after his father, Henry VII. But if we reflect that Elizabeth's Protestant predilections were known to everyone, and that religious differences had been one of the powerful motives in the attempt to supplant Mary Tudor by Lady Jane Grey in 1553, we are prompted to ask why there was no resistance to Elizabeth's accession. Was the sinister precedent of 1553 a cautionary tale, and no more? Another question poses itself: since a change of religion in those days threatened as profound a revolution as the ideological movements in our own time, how was the revolution accomplished? Merely to ask the question is to set the evidence in a new perspective.

Throughout Mary Tudor's reign Elizabeth had been the hope of all Protestants and of the growing body of the discontented. The many plots and intrigues of those years were focused upon her, and sometimes involved those about her. It was a perilous position to be in. It had placed her in danger of death at the time of Wyatt's rebellion and remained a constant threat to her safety. She could not prevent the irresponsible use of her name, nor could she betray any secrets that came to her ears: indeed, her future — if she was to have any — depended on retaining that popular support which might at any time involve her ruin. This trying experience furnished her

[1] Published in *History Today* (Coronation issue), May 1953.

with indelible lessons in statecraft. It may very well explain her extraordinary lenity to Mary Queen of Scots, when in her own reign the presence of this princess in England created, though in reverse, a similar situation. It certainly influenced her in her essentially personal policy of refusing to determine the succession to the throne. In 1566, when the House of Commons was pressing her relentlessly on this subject, she retorted that none of them had been 'a second person' and 'tasted of the practices against her sister'. Some who had then tried to involve her in plots were, she added, in that very Parliament: 'were it not for my honour, their knavery should be known'. 'I stood in danger of my life: my sister was so incensed against me ... So shall never be my successor.'

Mary Tudor, a religious *dévote*, could not bring herself, until very near the end, to acquiesce in the succession of her sister. As late as March 30th, 1558, this pathetic Queen made a will, 'thinking myself to be with child': the child she so ardently desired to guarantee the future of her ideological revolution. On October 28th, when the perils not of childbirth but of disease forced her hand, she added a codicil that referred to her 'next heir and successor by the laws and statutes of this realm'; and some ten days later she yielded to the pressure of her Council, agreeing to send Elizabeth a message that she was content for her to succeed to the crown. She asked her — and how little authority her first request carried, those about Mary must have realized, if she did not — to maintain the old religion and pay her debts.

On November 9th, a special envoy, the Count de Feria, arrived, sent over from the continent by the absent King, Philip. His ostensible purpose was to console the Queen. He found her a dying woman, given up by all her doctors, both English and Spanish. His deeper purpose was to extend Philip's sway over England from the closing to the new reign; and he assembled the Privy Council to tell them how much his King desired the succession of Elizabeth, relying on her friends then present to tell her of this *démarche*. The Councillors, who were already wondering how they would fare under the new dispensation, received him 'as if he brought them the bulls of a dead Pope'.

On November 10th, Feria visited Elizabeth in the country. She had been sweet and agreeable to Philip's ordinary representative, but when the proud Feria started patronizing her and explained that she would owe her throne, not to the Council but to the King, his master, she replied that 'the people' and no one else 'had placed her where she now is'. 'She is very attached to the people', he commented 'and very confident that they take her part: which', he added, 'is true.' Clearly, she was determined to be the puppet of no party and no person, especially no foreign sovereign: she was to be England's Queen. 'She is a woman of much vanity and acumen', Feria remarked; and he noted her admiration for her father, Henry VIII's method of government — a comment of considerable significance.[1]

In thus asserting from the start her personal independence, Elizabeth proved herself profoundly wise and also acutely aware of the way events had played into her hands. Her prospects and latent power sprang from the unpopular character of Mary's rule; and the climax of that unpopularity had come with the national humiliation of losing Calais to the French at the opening of the year 1558. 'I never saw ... England weaker in strength, men, money and riches', wrote the scholar-statesman, Sir Thomas Smith, criticizing this reign in 1560. 'As much affectionate as you note me to be to my country and countrymen, I assure you I was then ashamed of both.' 'They went to the wars hanging down their looks. They came from thence as men dismayed and forlorn. They went about their matters as men amazed, that wist not where to begin or end. And what marvel was it? ... Here [in England] was nothing but fining, heading, hanging, quartering, and burning; taxing,

[1] Kervyn de Lettenhove, *Relations Politiques des Pays-Bas et de l'Angleterre*, i, 279-82.

levying and pulling down of bulwarks at home, and beggaring and losing our strongholds abroad. A few priests, men in white rochets, ruled all; who, with setting up of six-foot roods and rebuilding of rood-lofts, thought to make all cock-sure.' A prejudiced statement, no doubt; but that of a moderate Protestant, not a fanatic, and few Englishmen would have reversed the picture.[1]

No wonder the dying Mary was compelled to acquiesce in the inevitable; no wonder her Councillors and hundreds of others were anxious to salute the rising sun, hastening to Hatfield, where Elizabeth and future fortune lay. But, however propitious the signs, the success of a revolution cannot be taken for granted. At home, the incalculable factor was the action of rabid Catholic leaders. No one could foretell that Cardinal Pole — Archbishop of Canterbury, a man with royal blood in his veins, and a potential focus for resistance — would be stricken with fever and die a few hours after the Queen; nor that four more Catholic bishops would die in the next month or so, and the number of episcopal vacancies thus rise to the debilitating proportion of ten out of a total of twenty-six. Nor, abroad, could the reaction of the irascible Pope Paul IV to Elizabeth's accession be foretold; and certainly it could not be anticipated that his quarrel with Cardinal Pole and Mary Tudor would induce friendly feelings towards Anne Boleyn's daughter. Then, again, England was in a formal state of war with France and Scotland, and the nearest Catholic claimant to the throne, Mary Queen of Scots, had recently married the Dauphin of France. Philip of Spain, zealous Catholic though he was, could not permit the union of France, Scotland and England: that might have been guessed, but it must have been very much in the minds of Elizabeth and her advisers that there was plenty of fuel about if anybody set light to the Catholic tinder at home.

Stray bits of evidence indicate that Elizabeth was taking

[1] Strype, *Life of Sir Thomas Smith*, pp. 249-50.

precautions during Mary's last illness. An original letter of hers survives, dated from Brockett Hall, Hertfordshire, on October 28th, 1558, thanking someone — who for obvious reasons is unnamed — for his readiness 'to do unto us all the pleasure ye can': an offer, she assured him, that she would not forget, 'whensoever time and power may serve'.[1] We may guess that the person concerned was some powerful nobleman. Again, at Longleat there are three letters from her Cofferer, Thomas Parry — an intimate servant — written to Sir John Thynne in October and November, from which we may infer that Thynne, the builder of Longleat, was in close touch with the Princess and Parry, and was acting in her interests, gathering support for her in Wiltshire. The message which Elizabeth willed Parry to send — Blessed is the servant to whom the master, when he comes home, may say, 'I have found thee a faithful and good servant' — conveyed its meaning clearly enough in those weeks when Mary lay dying.[2] Finally, in 1592, in a paper meant to be shown to the Queen, a certain Thomas Markham reminded her that during Mary Tudor's last illness — he being then in charge of a band of three hundred footmen at Berwick — she, through her Cofferer, Mr Parry, signified that with all convenient speed he should repair to Brockett Hall, 'leaving his own band with such other captains as he could trust to be in readiness with their bands likewise to serve for the maintenance of her royal state, title and dignity'. This he did, arriving with signed undertakings from the captains to adventure their lives in Elizabeth's service, along with ten thousand men.[3] If this late reminiscence be substantially correct — and the odds are that it is — then we can assume that in October to November 1558 Elizabeth was organized and ready to fight for her throne, if need arose.

Nor was she without friends in Mary's Privy Council.

[1] B.M. Cotton MS. Vespasian F. III, fol. 27.
[2] Thynne Papers, vol. iii, fols. 21, 23, 24. I owe this information to Professor S. T. Bindoff.
[3] *Hatfield MSS.* iv, 189.

It may have been with the calculated purpose of splitting Catholic ranks, or perhaps out of mutual respect, or even a blend of both: whatever the motive, particular attention seems to have been paid to Nicholas Heath, Archbishop of York and Mary's Lord Chancellor. He was a moderate man, who had been happy under the Henrician Reformation, though unable to accept the Edwardian. Mary's reign, as events were to show, had won him back immovably to Papal Supremacy, but he remained Henrician in his loyalty to the Tudor dynasty. With such a man in such a position, it would have been hard to engineer a Catholic revolt against Elizabeth's accession. From a letter which Heath wrote to Cecil in 1573 it is evident that there were negotiations between him and Elizabeth's representatives when the end of Mary's reign was foreseen. In this letter he recalls inviting Cecil to his house three or four days before Mary's death, when he discussed affairs of state and the subject of religion. He remembers that he begged Cecil to persuade his mistress not to continue him as Lord Chancellor — an office he disliked, but which, judging from Elizabeth's 'gracious and favourable mind' towards him, he was afraid would again be imposed on him. When, on Mary's death, he delivered up the great seal to the new Queen, she spoke so appreciatively of him that his fears were revived.[1] In fact, Elizabeth kept Heath for a month or two on her Council; and it may well be that his last attendance, on January 5th, 1559, represents the critical moment when the Queen allowed the whole Council to know that she intended to break the tie with Rome and he decided that the parting of the ways had come. Heath's loyalty and Cardinal Pole's death were great blessings of fortune.

The nervous atmosphere of the time can also be seen in a document which has recently come to light.[2] It is a long memorandum of advice sent to Elizabeth by her able and

[1] Cotton MS. Vespasian F. XIII, fol. 287.
[2] Printed by me in *Eng. Hist. Rev.* lxv, 91-8.

devoted follower, Sir Nicholas Throckmorton, when rumour reached him that Mary was dead or dying. Perhaps it was written on November 17th, the day of Mary's death; perhaps the day before — 'Hope Wednesday', as it was called[1] — when her death was hourly expected. The news or rumour seems to have caught him when he was in the country; but he was in London by November 18th, acting as Elizabeth's agent and ready to take action on his own initiative. In his memorandum he offered his mistress advice about her first steps as Queen, and included a long list of persons whom she might consider for posts in her government. Throckmorton was a keen Protestant, and it was symptomatic both of the dangers he foresaw and of his faith in Archbishop Heath that this Catholic name headed his list of those 'meet' to be Lord Chancellor. Throckmorton counselled Elizabeth to walk warily: to keep Mary's Privy Council in being for the moment, and not to let those she intended to displace know their fate. Neither 'the old or new should wholly understand what you mean'. It was policy in which Elizabeth needed no instruction; or, at any rate, policy which she carried out with a *finesse* surpassing that of her adviser. 'To succeed happily through a discreet beginning' was the burden of the memorandum. Caution, subtlety, secrecy were required.

The precedent of Lady Jane Grey found no echo at Elizabeth's accession. By sheer good fortune there was no similar person to act as a focus for resistance. No one in his senses would have turned to Mary Queen of Scots, then the enemy of England. Mary Tudor's Council acted unhesitatingly; and two or three hours after the Queen's death, Nicholas Heath, presiding in the upper house of Parliament, addressed the assembled Lords and Commons. 'God this present morning hath called to His mercy our late Sovereign Lady, Queen Mary; which hap, as it is most heavy and grievous unto us, so have we no less cause another way to rejoice with praise to Almighty

---

[1] Cf. John Foxe, *Acts and Monuments*, ed. Pratt and Stoughton, viii, 677.

God, for that he hath left unto us a true, lawful and right inheritress to the Crown ... which is the Lady Elizabeth ... of whose most lawful right and title ... we need not to doubt.' From Parliament the Lords proceeded to the door of Westminster Hall, where Elizabeth was proclaimed Queen, and from there to the Cross in Cheapside, where, in the presence of the Lord Mayor and Aldermen in their scarlet gowns, the proclamation was repeated. That afternoon, as a simple diarist records, all the church bells of London 'did ring', while at night the citizens 'did make bonfires and set tables in the street, and did eat and drink and make merry for the new Queen, Elizabeth, Queen Mary's sister'. Alas! poor Mary.[1]

Elizabeth herself was at Hatfield: far enough removed from London to be surrounded by her followers and on the defence against any untoward happening. It was there that a delegation of Mary's Council came to announce her accession. Six days of discreet activity followed, and then, on November 23rd, accompanied by a thousand and more lords, knights and gentlemen, ladies and gentlewomen, she came to Lord North's residence, the Charterhouse, outside the walls of London. On the 28th she made a triumphal state entry into the City, and with trumpets blowing rode through crowded streets to the Tower, stopping to hear children make their speeches and waits their music. She was welcomed by citizens, who declared 'their inward rejoicings by gesture, words and countenance'; and 'there was such shooting of guns as never was heard afore'.

It was her first wooing, as Queen, of 'the people', on whose rapturous support and devotion her instinct as an artist, and her experience in the dangerous days now over, led her to rely: as it were, a rehearsal for that matchless Londoners' day, some six weeks later, when once more she came to the Tower in order to pass through the City, now prodigally organized for splendour, pageants, speeches and music, on the way to

[1] Holinshed, *Chronicles*; *Machyn's Diary* (Camden Soc.), p. 178.

her Coronation — the occasion, indeed, for consummate romance and dazzling statecraft.

Lucky Londoners! They saw so much of their heroine. A diarist notes an evening in the following April, when, after supping at Baynard's Castle with the Earl of Pembroke, 'the Queen's Grace rowed up and down Thames, and a hundred boats about her Grace, with trumpets and drums and flutes and guns and squibs [fireworks] hurling on high, to and fro till ten at night ere her Grace departed'. The waterside was thronged with a thousand people. And at the beginning of July the London authorities took their citizens to Greenwich and held their musters there and fought mimic battles before the Queen and the Court, to the blowing of trumpets, banging of drums, and shooting of guns. Elizabeth thanked them heartily, whereupon 'there was the greatest shout that ever was heard, and hurling up of caps'. We are told that above a thousand spectators watched that show.[1]

The pageants and speeches which Londoners prepared for Elizabeth's Coronation progress through the City left no doubt of the role they had cast for her. She was to be their Protestant saviour, their Deborah, to rescue the land from darkness and despair. In that age, when the hand of God was seen in any striking occurrence, her survival from the perils of Mary's reign was assumed to be part of the divine dispensation. John Foxe appended to his story of the martyrs an account of 'the miraculous preservation of the Lady Elizabeth'; and Holinshed borrowed it as a suitable ending to his chronicle of Mary Tudor. The same theme had been in the broadsides of 1559. Thomas Brice published in that year a doggerel 'Register of the Martyrs' from 1555 to 1558, to the refrain 'We wished for our ELIZABETH':

> When raging reign of tyrants stout,
> Causeless, did cruelly conspire

[1] *Machyn's Diary*, pp. 180, 196, 202-3.

To rend and root the Simple out,
With furious force of sword and fire;
When man and wife were put to death:
We wished for our Queen ELIZABETH.[1]

In addition to the Protestant populace of London and other home zealots, there were the Marian *émigrés*, who had fled to Strasburg and the towns of Switzerland, where they had lived a godly life and been actively engaged in propaganda against Mary's regime; longing for the day when they could turn their steps homeward and restore the Gospel to England in the radical simplicity to which they had become accustomed in exile. That day had come. They had received 'the joyful tidings of God's favour and grace, restored unto us'. Now was 'the time for the walls of Jerusalem to be built again in that kingdom, that the blood of the martyrs, so largely shed, may not be in vain'. Among the *émigrés* were the most eminent Protestant divines. They expected the English Church to be handed over to them.

The new Queen was therefore confronted with a revolutionary movement, skilled in the arts of propaganda and organization. By her birth and her role during the troublous reign now ended, as well as by the expectation of thousands at home and hundreds from abroad, she was marked out as its titular head. Her instinct for romantic leadership prompted her to respond to the mood. She desired to lift the nation from dull despair to a glowing pride in the present; 'to do some act' — as she confessed — 'that would make her fame spread abroad in her lifetime, and, after, occasion memorial for ever'. In this instinct of hers lies a clue to the greatness of the new age. But the question which posed itself in 1558-9, and which was to retain its force through the critical decades that followed, was whether she would rule a country or lead a party. Could

[1] *Tudor Tracts*, ed. A. F. Pollard (Arber's *English Garner*), p. 270; cf. E. K. Wilson, *England's Eliza*, chap. 1.

she exploit the enthusiasm of revolution without succumbing to its philosophy and its extreme courses? Unlike her sister she was no *dévote*: she rejoiced in her own description of herself as 'mere English'.

In the early weeks of the reign, her watchword was caution. With France nominally at war — peace was not concluded until March–April 1559 — and the latent but by no means negligible threat to the throne represented by the Dauphin's wife, Mary Queen of Scots, there was reason to be prudent. To sober down the clash of creeds, Elizabeth issued a proclamation forbidding preaching and religious innovations; but she gave her Protestant followers a sign when on Christmas Day she instructed the bishop celebrating Mass before her not to elevate the Host — symbol of the Catholic doctrine of a real presence in the sacrament — and, on his refusal, left the service before this was done. There was no doubt which way she intended to go, but what would be her destination and how fast she would travel remained uncertain.

In this situation, and urged on by the popular demonstration at her Coronation procession on January 14th, Elizabeth met her first Parliament on January 25th. She had now to declare her hand. In many ways this was the crucial occasion of the reign. Certainly it set the pattern for the future; and we should never forget that the Queen, whose personal part in the story, though it must be largely inferred, was obviously vital, was a young woman of twenty-five. It is a lasting wonder that in so masculine a society, a woman, and one so young, managed to formulate policy and dominate those about her.

The House of Commons proved to be, like the citizens of London, overwhelmingly radical in its religious sympathies. Outside the House, remaining purposefully in London, were gathered the eminent divines, back from exile. Along with their friends in Parliament, they acted as a pressure group, whose programme was the instant overthrow of Catholicism and a wholesale conversion of the country to an extreme form of Protestantism.

The Queen, for her part, was beset by advice and pressure from all parties. There was no obligation on her to consult her Council: she may not even have asked for a formal lead, preferring to sound them individually and frame the policy herself. Her will was supreme. Amidst the babel of tongues about her, she seems to have been swayed by two lines of thought: profound respect for her father's statesmanship, and a desire to obtain as comprehensive and tolerant a settlement as possible. Even Protestants — those who were realists — stressed the perils, from abroad as well as at home. Move slowly seemed to be the most cogent advice in January 1559: it was certainly what Elizabeth's instinct prompted her to do.

When government policy declared itself, it was confined to an Act of Supremacy, with a clause conceding the cup as well as the bread to communicants. The Reformation — the Revolution as Protestant zealots thought of it — was in its initial stage to be a milk-and-water affair, confined to severance from Rome. The Catholic order of Church service was to continue until time and a second Parliament produced the propitious conditions for a Protestant Prayer Book. In this way Elizabeth hoped to stay any Catholic *démarche* from abroad, avoid trouble at home, and wean the more moderate leaders of the Marian Church from their Catholicism. If she could do the last, then she would be less dependent for staffing her Church on radical *émigrés*, and a conservative settlement might be feasible. She wanted revolution without tears.

The policy failed. First, the Marian bishops would not co-operate. Then, the Protestant divines and their agents in the House of Commons took the bit between their teeth. They altered the government bill and inserted the minimum programme they were inclined to accept. This involved the restoration of the second and more radical Prayer Book of Edward VI's reign. Elizabeth's reply was to get the House of Lords to strike out their amendments. She was still clinging tenaciously to her policy and her lone, strange Supremacy Bill; still clinging to these, when suddenly, within a few hours of dissolving the Parliament, she changed her mind and adjourned the assembly over Easter, instead of dissolving it. News had arrived that peace had been concluded with France, and with that news the last imperative reason for delaying a full Protestant settlement disappeared.

The true revolutionary character of the situation had asserted itself; and, with the Catholic leaders refusing to follow the moderate lead from the Government, it looked as if control of affairs would pass to the *émigrés*. They attempted to impose their own settlement: a more radical Protestant regime than that achieved by the end of Edward VI's reign. Elizabeth resisted them. The ultimate destination which she had set herself went no farther than the first, very conservative Prayer Book of 1549: one that the Catholic bishop, Stephen Gardiner, in those days had not found impossibly obnoxious. The final struggle between the revolutionary leaders and their Queen was obstinate: so obstinate that her officials contemplated the possibility of a deadlock. But Elizabeth was forced to compromise. So were the radicals; and our Prayer Book to this day retains the results. The decorous character of the Anglican Church is perhaps the most distinctive element in Elizabeth's personal, if limited, triumph.

The Queen had put the reins on revolution, and for nearly half a century she kept a firm grip on them. It was to her advantage — indeed, it was her triumph — to drive that restive steed. Throughout the rest of her days she had to cope with the effects of the disappointment that she inflicted in 1559. The revolutionary spirit did not die down: rather, it spread and intensified. Yet, to the zealots, she, whose firmness alone kept them in check, remained their Deborah and Judith. Her Accession Day — November 17th — became known, and was known in this land for nearly two centuries, as the Birthday of the Gospel. For this remarkable achievement her own consummate art as a ruler and leader of the nation was largely responsible; but it also rested on the stark fact that her votaries had no alternative person to worship. To be 'England's Eliza' she had also to be England's Virgin Queen.

THE ELIZABETHAN POLITICAL SCENE[1]

A STUDENT of Elizabethan history, delivering the Raleigh Lecture, might be expected to centre his attention on the great Elizabethan whose fame he commemorates. No doubt there are fresh things to be said about Raleigh's career, puzzling incidents to be set in better perspective. But man does not live in a vacuum, and on occasions it profits more to describe an environment than to write another biography. Though Raleigh's name finds only a casual place in my narrative, let us bear in mind that he was a figure, if a less conspicuous one, in the political scene that I have chosen as my theme.

The pattern of government in Elizabethan England looks relatively simple to the casual eye: Queen, Privy Council, Councils in the North and the Marches of Wales, Exchequer, Parliament, law courts, the organs of local government. It is all familiar enough in our constitutional histories. And if we wish to fill in the administrative framework, we may turn to a well-known table of 'Queen Elizabeth's annual expense, civil and military', which contains a list of all officials in the Queen's pay, with the amounts of their salaries and allowances.[2]

This traditional approach to the subject gives us the façade, but it is no sure guide to what lay behind. Consider the administrative framework. Our list of officials in the Queen's pay is precisely what it purports to be. Nevertheless, it is misleading — astonishingly so — about the income that officials received, and far from complete as a list of those in the administrative service.

---

[1] The British Academy Raleigh Lecture, 1948; published in the *Proceedings* of the Academy for that year.

[2] Peck, *Desiderata Curiosa*, i, 51 seqq.; *Ordinances for the Royal Household* (1790), pp. 241 seqq.

Official salaries had taken little account of the passage of time or monetary inflation, and in some instances were scarcely more than token payments. Obviously, there had to be compensation somewhere. It was found in payments by people using an official's services, whether as clients or suitors. Such payments were of two kinds: 'fees', which conformed to a tariff; and 'gratuities', which occasionally became fixed and figured as new fees, though normally they remained flexible and might, with unscrupulous givers and receivers, merge into what even that insensitive age termed bribery. No wonder that a correspondent, calculating the earnings of certain great officials at Court, made a triple estimate, according as the official wished for Heaven or Purgatory as his ultimate destination or was indifferent about his soul's welfare. The Lord Keeper of the Great Seal, for example, received from the Crown, in fees and annuities, £919 per annum, the Lord High Admiral £200, and the Principal Secretary £100.[1] Yet John Manningham noted in his diary in 1601 that the Lord Keeper's office was 'better worth than £3000 per annum', the Lord Admiral's 'more', and the Secretary's 'little less'.[2] He was certainly not taking a gloomy view of their after-life.

Similarly with the number of officials. In addition to those appearing in our list because they were on the Queen's pay-roll, there was a host of minor officials who received no salary from the Crown and are therefore not mentioned. These men were paid out of the fees and gratuities of suitors and litigants. Originally they had often been servants, aiding their masters in the labours of office; and a trace of private service still survived in their appointment, which was generally in the gift of the higher officials, not the Crown, and, incidentally, was a source of profit. The transition from servant to official was still proceeding, as new items appeared in the scale of fees confronting suitors. It was the way the civil service grew.

[1] Peck, op. cit. i, 51, 58, 61.
[2] *Manningham's Diary* (Camden Soc.), p. 19.

Clearly, the administration looks very different when approached in this way. Perhaps a similar emphasis on the realities of life at Court will throw fresh light on the nature of personal monarchy. If we can penetrate its secrets of power, reveal the stresses and strains to which it was subject, and uncover its inherent weaknesses, we may do more than write a chapter in Elizabethan history. We may revive past experience as a warning of the dangers to which a particular type of government is exposed.

We must begin by focusing attention on the two extremes of the picture; and first on the Queen, whose personal decisions controlled a wide range of governmental and administrative activity, and whose will or whim could both make and unmake careers and fortunes. A vast amount of patronage was at her disposal. There were hundreds of offices in her gift, and others which could be diverted to her use by the device of recommendatory letters or verbal orders, sometimes amiable in tone, sometimes hectoring, but at all times difficult, if not dangerous, to resist. There were also royal lands to be leased or sold, or to be granted as reward for services; a source of great wealth, and most eagerly solicited. Finally, there were all those grants by letters patent, whether charters, licences, monopolies, or whatever they were, which conferred some benefit on the recipient.

At the other extreme were the customers in this colossal business — the suitors, who thronged the Court (thus, incidentally, guaranteeing a large 'presence' by which the reputation of monarchy was sustained) or alternatively pursued their petitions more precariously from a distance. Competition was bound to be keen. It was intensified by the custom of primogeniture, which forced out the younger sons of the landed gentry to seek their own fortunes.

Between monarch and suitors were interposed members of the inner ring of the Court; broadly, those with access to the privy chamber, more specifically, those officials and courtiers — not excluding the ladies of the Court — whose place or friendship gave them the Queen's ear. Of necessity these were the intermediaries whom very many suitors had to employ to press on the sovereign their requests for office or favour, and pilot their suits through treacherous currents to the safe harbour of the royal signature. As Spenser feelingly wrote,[1]

> Full little knowest thou that hast not tried
> What Hell it is in suing long to bide;
> To lose good days that might be better spent;
> To waste long nights in pensive discontent;
> To speed today, to be put back tomorrow;
> To feed on hope, to pine with fear and sorrow;
> To have thy Prince's grace, yet want her Peer's;
> To have thy asking, yet wait many years;
> To fret thy soul with crosses and with cares;
> To eat thy heart through comfortless despairs;
> To fawn, to crouch, to wait, to ride, to run,
> To spend, to give, to want, to be undone.

Unalloyed friendship might occasionally procure a suitor the support he needed, but usually support was purchased. Bribery we should call it; and bribery it sometimes deserved to be called. However, it was not so immoral as we might think. Ministers and courtiers were compelled to sell their influence, for even if the Queen had jumped the centuries in her thoughts and seen the wisdom of paying servants adequately, her revenues would not have permitted it. Nor, indeed, was the practice strange in a society based on the principle that anyone seeking a service paid for it. It was analogous to our custom of 'tips', except that 'tips' were not restricted to menials. Everyone, from the Lord Treasurer or a countess down, accepted them. 'I ever took it that a man may with honesty accept a gratuity given', said an official whose actions were under scrutiny in 1597.[2]

---

[1] *Mother Hubberd's Tale*, ll. 895 seqq. As *pièce justificatif*, cf. *Hatfield MSS.* vii, 393.
[2] *Hatfield MSS.* vii, 363.

In the nature of things, evidence about gratuities is fitful. But, whether pursued openly or surreptitiously, the practice was generally recognized. One of his mother's chaplains, making suit through Robert Cecil for a prebend at Windsor in 1594, declared: 'As I cannot promise rewards after the custom of the world, so I unfeignedly promise my poor prayers for your Honour and yours.'[1] As early as 1559 we find Lord North acting as intermediary for a man who sought Sir William Cecil's support for his device to reform the coinage. He 'will give you 500 marks for your pains', North wrote to Cecil, 'and offers me 500 marks to dispose at my pleasure. I am desirous to bestow unto yourself 200 marks, unto Mr Treasurer 200 marks, and to take the rest myself'.[2] The suit was unsuccessful. So far as one can judge, Burghley was not open to crude bribery, nor did he let his advice to the Queen be deflected by prospects of monetary gain. Herein lay one reason for Elizabeth's unique reliance on him. But do not let us imagine that he was a stranger to gratuities.[3] If we attempted to construct a budget of his income and expenditure, we should undoubtedly become aware of the gap that they filled;[4] and certainly in the Mastership of the Court of Wards he possessed a constant source of such income. He 'grew rich' by means of this office, 'and ofttimes gratified his friends and servants that depended and waited on him', wrote one of two panegyrists, members of his household; though it is fair to add that the second writer stressed his moderation.[5] In 1582 a second Lord North wrote to tell him of a wardship: 'Forgo not this occasion. I have known but few such fall in my time. Get her into your possession.'[6]

[1] Ibid. iv, 527.

[2] Ibid. i, 154-5.

[3] e.g. in 1587 the representative of the merchant adventurers with Drake was authorized 'to promise and assure to pay or deliver to your use ... the full sum of £1000', 'for the obtaining of our portions in those goods brought home' by Drake (ibid. iii, 281-2).

[4] Some idea of his expenditure can be obtained from Peck, op. cit. i, 22-3.

[5] B.M. Additional MS. 22925, fol. 28b; Peck, op. cit. i, 20-1.

[6] *Hatfield MSS.* xiii, 208.

Burghley may or may not have profited from this particular wardship; but after his death someone compiled what I think must be interpreted as a list of gratuities that he received between January 1596 and August 1598 for granting wardships. It is endorsed, 'This note to be burned.' There are eleven items, totalling £3103 6s. 8d. One is a gratuity of £1000 paid by Attorney-General Coke for Walter Aston, an exceedingly rich heir, aged thirteen, who afterwards became the poet Drayton's patron. And a very good bargain it was — for Coke and Burghley, though not for the Queen. Officially, the lands — which a century later were said to be worth £10,000 a year — were assessed at £256 6s. 8d. per annum, and the wardship of the body, which carried the right of marriage, at a capital sum of £300 — payments which went to the Crown and were distinct from the gratuity to Burghley. Aston later compounded for his marriage by paying Coke £4000.[1]

Our minds will now be attuned to a letter from that shameless if reverend place-seeker, Tobie Matthew, who rose to be Archbishop of York and once provoked a tart comment from the Queen by oft-repeated reference in a sermon to rewards for the deserving.[2] On his appointment to the bishopric of Durham he wrote to Burghley, acknowledging that he owed his promotion to him. Not having a suitable office to bestow, he sent him £100 in gold by the bearer. Of course, the gift may have been returned, but as the bishop a few weeks earlier had declared that he would express his thankfulness in deeds as well as words, we may reasonably doubt if it was.[3]

[1] S.P. Dom. Eliz. 268, no. 41; P.R.O. Wards Misc. 348; B. H. Newdigate, *Michael Drayton and his Circle*, pp. 146-8. I am indebted to my former pupil, Mr J. Hurstfield, for the manuscript information, and for much of my knowledge about wards.

[2] T. Birch, *Memoirs of Queen Elizabeth*, i, 48. 'Well, whosoever have missed their rewards, you have not lost your labour.'

[3] B.M. Lansdowne MSS. 78, fol. 40; 79, no. 40. In 1597 the new Bishop of Chester wrote to Robert Cecil: 'Having received so great a benefit by your means, I ... will further express my thankfulness by some special gratification' (*Hatfield MSS.* vii, 351).

Offices were bought and sold. Burghley once denounced the practice as insufferable, to which it was retorted that 'the the same fault ... is winked at, and the mart kept within the Court'.[1] Perhaps his denunciation was directed less against gratuities than against officials bargaining to surrender their patents of office to particular purchasers, who then set about securing their own appointment — a practice with obvious dangers. All the same, in the later part of the reign there was often little distinction between gratuities and plain sales. For example, there were several candidates in 1594 for the vacant Receivership of the Court of Wards — a royal appointment carrying a fee of 100 marks plus £70 diet and allowance. One aspirant offered Burghley and Robert Cecil £1000; another offered £1000 to Robert Cecil along with £100 for his wife 'to buy her four coach horses', and on learning from him that the Queen intended to let one of her ladies, Lady Edmunds, enjoy the patronage, promptly offered to pay her the £1000. Someone else got the post, and presumably Lady Edmunds netted at least £1000.[2] This same lady — who with the Countess of Warwick appears to have dabbled in many suits — when offered £100 to intervene with the Queen over a Chancery case, treated the offer as too small.[3] 'As a man is friended, so the law is ended' was a contemporary aphorism. Incidents in Judge Manwood's career show that it had point.[4]

The accident of evidence has centred our attention on the Cecils. Others were in the game, much more deeply in relation to their opportunities than Burghley, no doubt. When Sir

[1] *Cal. S.P. Dom. Add. 1566-79*, p. 46. Nevertheless, Burghley advised Heneage about buying an office for his brother (*Hist. MSS. Com., Finch MSS.*, p. 6).

[2] *Hatfield MSS.* iv, 497, 529, 531-2, 534, 537.

[3] Birch, op. cit. i, 354.

[4] Cf. *D.N.B.*; Lansdowne MS. 104, fols. 76-9; Harleian MS. 6995, fol. 49. John Wynn's lawyer wrote: 'Mr Wynn, I am wearied to see the tumbling and tossing of law and conscience, for both are ended, as the proverb is, as a man is friended.' Incidentally, he paid tribute to Sir Christopher Hatton's probity: 'The old Chancellor is gone that esteemed neither letters nor would be carried with means or rewards' (N.L.W., Wynn of Gwydir Papers, Panton group, 9051 E, no. 135).

John Carey, a relative of the Queen, heard that she was critical of his wife for selling petty places in the garrison at Berwick, he commented: 'If her Majesty would search into takers so narrowly ... she might find takers of another kind nearer hand, such as take more in one day than she — Lady Carey — hath done in all her life.... It is not the use in any place where she hath been, to do good turns *gratis*.'[1] Unfortunately, we know very little about this aspect of the Earl of Leicester's career, and it is not satisfactory to quote from so gross and malevolent a libel as *Leicester's Commonwealth*. All the same there is some interest, whatever degree of truth there may be, in the writer's accusation that 'no suit can prevail in Court (be it never so mean) except he be first made acquainted, and receive not only the thanks, but also be admitted unto a great part of the gain and commodity thereof'.[2] Sir Thomas Heneage was another statesman of baser metal than Burghley. In 1592 the Earl of Essex wrote to his friend and follower, Sir Henry Unton, reporting that he had spoken about some suit to Heneage, who 'gave me his word to do his best, and the more for my sake. But', he added, 'I think your best friend unto him will be your £1000'.[3] Once, as we know, Heneage was paid £60 to subscribe a bill for a minor duchy official.[4]

Statesmen and courtiers were not the only ones on whom the refreshing rain of gratuities descended. They, too, were remote, and as a rule had to be approached through intermediaries — very often their secretaries. Michael Hicks, one of Burghley's secretaries in his later years, in a letter to a friend, casually referred to certain minor appointments with which, as occasion offered, he could demonstrate his affection — 'as welcome and acceptable to you as twenty fair angels laid in

[1] *Cal. Border Papers*, ii, 787. Cf. Spenser's lines (*Mother Hubberd's Tale*, ll. 515-16):
For nothing there is done without a fee:
The Courtier needs must recompensed be.
[2] *Secret Memoirs of Robert Dudley*, ed. Drake (1706), p. 53. Cf. Collins, *Sydney Papers*, i, 297.
[3] *Hatfield MSS*. iv, 276.
[4] Ibid. xiv, 29.

the hands of us poor bribers here in Court'.[1] If a suit involved attendance on the patron — and we read of Burghley and Essex overwhelmed with suitors[2] — there were more menial servants to be tipped. A suggestive glimpse of the process is offered by the city of Exeter's bill for a suit before the Privy Council in Mary Tudor's reign. 'For remembering' their masters and 'preferring our suit', the secretaries or servants of the Lord Treasurer, the Earl of Pembroke, the Lord Chancellor, the Secretary, and the Lord Admiral were paid varying, not unappreciable, sums; the Lord Treasurer's porter was tipped 'for letting us in, and other his pains'; and the three clerks of the Council, in addition to their legitimate fee, were given two and a half times this sum as a gratuity.[3]

'The gentlemanly profession of serving men' was a common career for younger sons of the gentry, and the vast households of Court magnates offered attractive prospects. The pressure to enter some great man's service, or place a protégé, was constant. Burghley declared that 'it was his disease ... to have too many servants', but he could do little about it:[4] the Earl of Essex, youthful, exuberant, ill-disciplined, kept adding to his retinue. Such men could no more pay their servants adequately than the Queen could hers. Defending himself — on an odd, whimpering note — against the charge of being a councillor that abused his credit to his private gain, Burghley once declared — with questionable accuracy — that, unlike many others, he kept no servants 'to whom I pay not wages and give liveries'.[5] If we were to infer from this that his servants did not depend on gratuities, we should be egregiously wrong. The most revealing evidence about the bribery of those days comes from the correspondence of his secretary, Michael Hicks; and

---

[1] Lansdowne MS. 107, fol. 162.
[2] Cf. T. Wright, *Queen Elizabeth and her Times*, ii, 427; Birch, op. cit. i, 168.
[3] *Hist. MSS. Com., Exeter MSS.* pp. 362-3.
[4] *Hatfield MSS.* v, 293.
[5] Lansdowne MS. 103, fol. 46 (printed Strype, *Annals*, III, ii, 379-83); Conyers Read, *Sir Francis Walsingham*, iii, 119.

long before the time of Hicks, John Wynn of Gwydir, who in 1572 had a letter for this statesman, told his father that it would be handed to one or other of Burghley's chamber, 'who will look for a reward, which should be measured in accordance with his speeding much or little or none at all'.[1]

Burghley's statement that some people did not pay wages to their servants happens to be confirmed by Sir Christopher Hatton's sententious secretary, Samuel Cox. 'I never charged you with any kind of wages, nor other gift or bounty of your own whatsoever', he wrote. Accused of selling his master's justice and favour, he unfolded his defence:

> There liveth not so grave nor so severe a judge in England, but he alloweth his poor clerk under him, even in the expedition of matters of greatest justice, to take any reasonable consideration that should be offered him by any man for his pains and travail. It is the poor man's whole maintenance, and without it he could not live ... If this be to sell justice and favour, sometimes to take a gratuity of 10s. for one letter among one hundred, sometimes more, sometimes less, according as the party was benefited, or as myself had deserved, I then confess ... I ignorantly erred, as all the rest of your servants have done.[2]

How many other servants served their masters, as Cox did his, for board, lodgings, and tips, we do not know.[3]

Gratuities were fundamental in Elizabethan Court life. All important officials and many minor ones depended upon them; and though it seems impossible to estimate the proportion of his income that any eminent statesman derived from this

[1] *Cal. Wynn Papers*, p. 7. Also cf. *Hist. MSS. Com., Various Coll.*, vii, 260.

[2] Nicolas, *Memoirs of Hatton*, pp. 389-93. Cf. *Cal. S.P. Dom. 1595-7*, p. 254.

[3] On the death of Heneage, one of his servants, a duchy official, explained to Cecil that he had received £20 yearly, plus diet, lodgings, etc., from Heneage, and £20 from official sources. Further, he had his master's 'honourable speech and letters for himself and friends very readily' — i.e. a source of gratuities. All this he estimated as equal to £100 yearly, which leaves an ample gap for gratuities (*Hatfield MSS.* v, 525).

source, we can safely say that he could not otherwise have sustained his splendour. The household servants of such men were as dependent on these gifts as the staff of a modern hotel on tips.

The Queen, of course, knew what went on. In fact, from time to time we find her diverting a suit to some courtier or lady of the Court — as, for example, to Lady Edmunds in the instance already cited — obviously as a reward. Perhaps there was deliberate policy in her actions — an attempt to spread the benefits of patronage as widely as possible; though her closest advisers, and certain officials such as the Masters of Requests, were strategically too well placed to be victims of much levelling. The Queen's concern was not to stop gratuities but to prevent abuses; to see that her own discretion was not undermined by corrupt conspiracy between suitors and courtiers, and to ensure that bribery did not get the wrong person into office. Her habit was to seek assurance of a man's fitness from those not monetarily or otherwise interested in his appointment. Burghley she seems to have consulted almost invariably. The rivalries at Court also served her well. She took advantage of these to check the plausible arguments of patrons, so promoting efficiency while safeguarding her own independence. From this point of view Court factions were essential to the well-being of the governmental system: there could be no greater disaster than single-faction rule. If she suspected deceit, or perceived that the factions were in unholy alliance to secure some appointment of which she disapproved — as the Essexites and Cecilians united to procure the Solicitorship for Francis Bacon — a common device of hers was to fall back on delays. No one could be sure of obtaining her signature. In 1593, in a suit evidently sponsored by Robert Cecil and presumably carrying a gratuity with it, she refused to grant an office to father and son, saying that 'she would make no continuance of inheritance in any her offices'.[1] Though kept ignorant of many things, she was watchful

[1] Ibid. iv, 364.

and ready to express her wrath at abuses that came to her notice. In 1591 Judge Manwood incurred her displeasure for selling an office in his gift, perhaps at too high a price. He defended himself — very much as Sir John Carey defended his wife in similar circumstances — by citing the more heinous acts of other judges.[1] Corruption and inefficiency would have become rampant without such an alert will and discipline at the centre, reinforced by at least one leading statesman of integrity.

The effect of the system on the structure of politics was profound. In Elizabethan England there were no political parties as we know them. True, from time to time there were political differences among statesmen; but, since privy councillors played a merely advisory role in matters of policy, owed a personal and not corporate obligation to the Queen, and, being resident at Court, were constantly consulted in personal conversation, there was neither the mechanism nor the mentality to foster party politics. 'All these Lords', wrote Sir William Cecil to his friend Sir Thomas Smith in 1565, 'are bent towards Her Majesty's service, and do not so much vary amongst themselves as lewd men do report ... I have no affection to be of a party, but for the Queen's Majesty.'[2] The place of party was taken by faction, and the rivalry of the factions was centred on what mattered supremely to everyone: influence over the Queen, and, through that influence, control of patronage with its accompanying benefits.

The competition at Court was ceaseless. Success not only meant money: it meant power. On it depended the quality and size of a statesman's faction — his entourage of household servants, followers, and clients, thronging his chamber and constituting a minor court within the Court proper. The world saw his greatness reflected therein. Every magnate had his circle of friends and followers, some of whom might don his livery as occasion demanded or pay their respects when

[1] Harleian MS. 6995, fol. 49.   [2] Wright, op. cit. i, 209.

they were in London or he in their locality. It was an association of self-interest, a mutual-benefit society. Members expected their patron to sponsor their interests at Court and cast his mantle over them whenever the prestige of his name or the cogency of his recommendatory letters might help. 'My desire is to be protected ... under the shadow of your wings, as I was by his Lordship', wrote a member of the noble Manners family to Robert Cecil, offering himself as his follower on Burghley's death.[1] If the association did not pay dividends, members might transfer their investment elsewhere, thus weakening the faction they deserted and strengthening a rival one. 'Who will be desirous to come under a roof that threateneth ruin?' asked the Earl of Essex when his prospects seemed gloomy; while on another occasion, when two of his friends were placed in high office and the Council, a follower wrote, 'Those which are lukewarm will trust more in him; and such as be assured unto him will be glad to see he hath power to do his friends good.'[2]

Within this circle, or among those he counted as his friends, a patron did not necessarily take monetary rewards for his services. 'Sir John Stanhope told me it was your practice not to take anything of charge from those you liked best of', wrote one of Robert Cecil's followers, whose gratuity had been declined.[3] But even here there is a qualification to make, for New Year's gifts were no negligible part of a patron's perquisites — nor, for that matter, of the Queen's.[4] Thomas Bilson, the divine, wrote of Burghley's manifold favours, which, as he put it, 'make me careful at this time, when all men acknowledge their patrons', to show some remembrance.[5] And that dauntless beggar, Julius Caesar, who in the opinion of the Dowager

---

[1] *Hatfield MSS.* viii, 310.   [2] Birch, op. cit. ii, 176, 423.

[3] *Hatfield MSS.* ix, 8. Perhaps for the same reason Burghley refused 'a small piece of plate' from Lord Audley, who thereupon sent a horse (ibid. iii, 362-3).

[4] Cf. Collins, *Sydney Papers*, i, 382. In December 1595 there was a rumour that the Queen 'will make both councillors and officers of Household'. A courtier was sceptical; 'but,' said he, 'it will increase the Queen's New Year gifts.'

[5] Lansdowne MS. 77, fol. 44.

Lady Russell had by 1596 'enough already, if these days could acknowledge what is enough',[1] placed his New Year's gifts with nice calculation. In 1591, in addition to Burghley, he sent gifts to the Lord Chancellor, the Lord Admiral, the Earl of Essex, a master of requests, and my Lady Howard. 'It may be that I shall by the next year be enabled to yield a greater gift', he wrote to Burghley.[2] The innuendo was obvious. On the other hand, Burghley refused a cup of gold as a New Year's gift from Sir Thomas Shirley, a month or so before he was appointed Treasurer at War.[3] It overshot the mark, and the recipient had scruples. At his death, Burghley's plate was worth fourteen or fifteen thousand pounds — a fortune in itself, and yet, as a servant-biographer thought, modest in comparison with his opportunities.[4]

With the chief competitors for power it was a vital point of strategy to place their friends and followers in Court offices and the Privy Council, thus surrounding the Queen with persons who would echo the same advice, promote the same suits, and generally enhance the credit, and through that the wealth, of their faction: as one of Essex's followers put it, to 'bring in any of his friends to strengthen him (of which all the world thinks he hath need) or keep out his greatest enemies, who will seek by all possible means to overthrow him'.[5] *Leicester's Commonwealth* contains an acute analysis of the strategy of power, though otherwise one blushes to quote the passage.

In the Privy Chamber, next to her Majesty's person, the most part are his [Leicester's] own creatures (as he calleth them) — that is, such as acknowledge their being in that place from him; and the rest he so over-ruleth,

[1] *Hatfield MSS.* vi, 215.
[2] Lansdowne MS. 47, fols. 8 seqq.
[3] *Hatfield MSS.* iii, 206.
[4] Peck, op. cit. i, 27.
[5] Birch, op. cit. ii, 185.

either by flattery or fear, as none may dare but to serve his turn. His reign ... is so absolute in this place, and likewise in all other parts of the Court, as nothing can pass but by his admission, nothing can be said, done, or signified, whereof he is not particularly advertised; no bill, no supplication, no complaint, no suit, no speech can pass from any man to the Prince (except it be from one of the Council) but by his good liking ... Whereby he holdeth as it were a lock upon the ears of his Prince.[1]

Interesting, but fantastic! The writer maligned the Queen as well as Leicester. She allowed no monopoly, but played the factions one against the other; and there can be little doubt that she paid more heed to Burghley, whose advice was most disinterested and least corrupt. This supreme statesman was wont to tell his intimates 'that he had gotten more by his patience than ever he did by his wit'.[2]

Absence from Court was perilous to faction-leaders. It gave opponents the opportunity of poisoning the Queen's mind with malicious stories; it was their chance to fill vacant offices with their friends. 'I pray you to stand fast for your poor absent friends against calumniators', wrote Leicester to Walsingham, when he was away in the Netherlands,[3] and his absence was seized upon — by Burghley, said the French ambassador — to have Whitgift, Cobham, and Buckhurst, all opponents of his, made privy councillors.[4] The illustration *par excellence* of this strategy is the career of Essex. He failed hopelessly to place his nominees in Court office. 'Not that the Earl meant to stand alone like a substantive (for he was not so ill a grammarian in Court)', wrote Sir Henry Wotton, who once was a secretary

---

[1] *Secret Memoirs*, ed. Drake, p. 52. Cf. *Spanish Cal. Eliz.* iii, 267, and the reference to 'the wonderful power of this man' at Court, in *Cal. S.P. Dom. Add. 1580-1625*, p. 203.
[2] Add. MS. 22925, fol. 29b.
[3] *Foreign Cal. Eliz.* xxi, iii, 233.
[4] *Scottish Cal.* viii, 248.

of his; but the Cecilians frustrated him, 'as very well knowing that upon every little absence or disassiduity, he should be subject to take cold at his back'.[1] And on his last, fateful absence from Court, Essex himself wrote bitterly to the Council from Ireland: 'I provided for this service a breastplate and not a cuirass; that is, I am armed on the breast, but not on the back.'[2]

In its broad lines this analysis of the Elizabethan political scene might have proceeded, not inductively from the printed and manuscript sources of the period, but deductively — as an essay in the logic of human behaviour — from a system of personal monarchy, with immense patronage at the disposal of the Crown, and inadequate salaries in both royal and private households; though whether, in view of man's insatiable cupidity, inadequate salaries constitute an essential element in the argument, is perhaps open to doubt.

There are two weaknesses or dangers inherent in such a system of government. Corruption may get out of hand, or, to employ the Elizabethan distinction, gratuities degenerate into plain bribery; and rivalry at Court may become so intense as to threaten the stability of the state. Our Elizabethan story has light to throw on both.

If our evidence can be trusted, the standard of public morality was declining sharply during the last decade or so of the reign. True, this gloomy view owes much to a unique collection of letters[3] — the correspondence of Michael Hicks, secretary to Burghley and subsequently tied to Robert Cecil; and one cannot but wonder how the picture would look if the correspondence of earlier secretaries had survived. Nor can we close our minds to doubts, knowing that after Burghley's death Hicks went through his papers, and coming across many letters from Sir Robert Sidney offered them to him 'to burn'.[4] Was this a purge? Perhaps not; but if it was, how far did it go?

---

[1] *Reliquiae Wottonianae* (1654), p. 25.
[2] Birch, op. cit. ii, 420.
[3] In the Lansdowne MSS.
[4] *Hist. MSS. Com., Penshurst MSS.* ii, 403.

All the same, if we compare Burghley and his son, Robert Cecil, it is difficult to imagine the father — at any rate in his prime — figuring as Cecil does in many documents. 'You may boldly write for his favour in this matter', John Wynn of Gwydir was told by his London lawyer in 1592. 'You paid well for it.'[1] Two years later we find Cecil writing an obscure letter to Hicks — with instructions to burn it — the gist of which was to keep secret his part in the choice of someone for a post, since he did not wish the Queen to suspect that he thought of anything but her service, nor his enemies to realize what had occurred.[2] Hicks, as this letter indicates, was more than a servant; he was an intimate friend of Robert Cecil. When in 1596 he ended a letter with a 'prayer to give you your heart's desire either in promotion or profit', how much the servant revealed both of himself and his young master![3] In 1603 Cecil was offering him advice on a suit he was making to the Queen. Warning him of the need to secure the Lord Treasurer's support, he told him to go to Lady Glemham, the Lord Treasurer's daughter, and promise her £100 if she 'will win her father to you'. There were two postscripts to the letter, one a caution against being cozened by Lady Glemham, the other a promise to find him a ward to pay for the bribe, whether it cost £100 or £200.[4] Or consider the letter that he wrote Hicks about a wardship which the latter was seeking, and which was reckoned so exceptional a prize that the Court was 'absolutely full of importunity for it'. After putting him gently but firmly in his place for his effrontery in asking for so valuable a gift, in competition with his betters, Cecil — who was now Master of the Court of Wards — explained that he intended to 'draw some benefit' from this wardship for himself, but through a nominee

---

[1] N.L.W., Wynn of Gwydir Papers, 9051 E, no. 135.
[2] Lansdowne MS. 77, fol. 192. Cf. Cecil's letter to the Earl of Northumberland (*Hatfield MSS.* x, 347) where he adopts a high moral tone in contrast with his intimate letters to Hicks.
[3] *Hatfield MSS.* vi, 395.
[4] Lansdowne MS. 88, fol. 105, printed in Ellis, *Original Letters*, 3rd ser. iv, 150-1.

whom no one would suspect of being merely his 'figure'.[1] There is a lack of scruple about these incidents which one can hardly associate with Burghley. Nor can one imagine him advising a suitor, as Cecil did on another occasion, to pay Sir John Stanhope, Treasurer of the Chamber and a follower of his, £100 to speak to the Queen on his behalf.[2]

As for Cecil's merry friend Hicks, he became a wealthy man and played money-lender to courtiers, including Francis Bacon, Fulke Greville, and the Earl of Pembroke.[3] It would not be rash to guess that in the last decade of the reign he received more gratuities than any other servant in England. Many of his surviving letters are from correspondents sending or promising him tokens of their goodwill. One sends £20 and hopes for his favour.[4] Another, desirous to be a clerk of the signet, 'will deliver unto whom he [Burghley] will please to appoint £100, and to yourself 100 angels'.[5] Still another vows that if, through Hicks, Burghley is pleased to move the Queen for his suit, 'I shall ever after be bound to do him and his family honour and service, show myself thankful unto him' — euphemism for a gratuity — 'in sort as I acquainted you, and for your own travail therein assuredly perform what I have promised.'[6] 'A Welsh nag worth five pounds' is another bait.[7] Being so close to two successive masters of the Court of Wards, he was approached by persons seeking wardships;[8] and no doubt Robert Cecil saw that he had occasional bonuses from this source.

To judge the tone of the period, let us glance at a few of the gratuities offered to statesmen — though not necessarily accepted — in the years 1590 to 1603. A receiver-general of

[1] Lansdowne MS. 88, fol. 91.
[2] *Hatfield MSS.* x, 31.
[3] Cf. *D.N.B.*; Lansdowne MS. 88, fol. 23.
[4] Ibid. 72, no. 72.
[5] Ibid. 107, no. 71.   [6] Ibid. 78, fol. 62.
[7] Ibid. 83, no. 39. Cf. also ibid. 77, fols. 36, 164, 168; 87, fol. 214; 88, fol. 79; 107, fol. 46; 108, fol. 19; 109, fol. 119.
[8] Cf. ibid. 77, fols. 112, 180; 87, fol. 37; 108, fol. 41.

the Court of Wards, who had followed the all-too-prevalent practice of holding on to Crown revenue as long as possible, meanwhile employing the money to his own gain, died £25,824 in debt to the Queen — a scandalous episode. His son not only had the effrontery to ask for his father's office, but offered Robert Cecil £1000 to secure the Queen's consent to a certain device for handling the debt.[1] Nothing came of his proposals, but he retained Cecil's friendship. A man offered Cecil £100 a year to join with three other councillors in securing a patent, which was obviously contrary to public interest. Again, it is unlikely that anything came of the offer, though Cecil's relations with this promoter of suits look rather suspicious.[2] Then, in 1597 Sir Anthony Ashley wrote that he had the disposition of a lunatic, and if Robert Cecil would take the wardship for himself, it would bring him 'some thousand pounds per annum', or, alternatively, the lunatic's younger brother would pay him £2000 for it.[3] The same year a man offered him 2000 marks to procure a legal office in Judge Anderson's gift.[4] On this occasion Cecil probably did not even try, for Anderson was the judge who, as John Chamberlain tells us, on the death of a high official in the Court of Common Pleas 'had given the place and sworne an officer before eight a clock the next morning; and within an hour after, came the Queen's letters for another, which by that means were frustrate'.[5] The pursuit of office or wardship in these years grew so feverish that the mere prospect of a death set suitors busy.

[1] P.R.O., Wards Misc. 88, fols. 419b-21; *Hatfield MSS.* iv, 515. There are references to this affair in several volumes of the *Hatfield MSS.*

[2] Ibid. iv, 608, and index to vols. iv and v *sub* Margitts, George. Cf. Margitts' letter to Cecil, October 8th, 1593 (ibid. 384-5): 'I will not leave, with God's help, before your Honour be someways furnished with one good suit or other.' Pressing one particular project, he writes: 'You shall have good assurance for the payment of £5000 in five years, and 500 marks yearly afterwards', and only Burghley and the writer will know 'that you have any dealing in the same'.

[3] Ibid. vii, 4-5. For other references to wardships, cf. ibid. iv, 353, 522-3, 554-5, 597; v, 128; vi, 363, 425 (£1,000 offered to Burghley's secretary, Maynard); vii, 115; ix, 378; x, 107.

[4] Ibid. vii, 210.

[5] N. E. McClure, *Letters of John Chamberlain,* i, 75.

In 1593 no less a person than Sir John Fortescue, Chancellor of the Exchequer and privy councillor, wrote to Lord Keeper Puckering — apparently a corrupt person, whose death few deplored[1] — offering 100 angels for the office of *custos rotulorum* in his county. He explained that he wanted it more 'for credit than commodity', though as he stipulated for nomination of the Clerk of the Peace, he could presumably have made commodity out of it: at any rate, in Devon the clerkship was bought for £300.[2] In 1591 John Wynn of Gwydir, actuated by a feud, tried to rig the choice of sheriff for his county. His agent employed the Countess of Warwick, who 'promised sure to stop' Wynn's enemy, William Williams, and get in his nominee; but she happened to be unwell when the Queen pricked the sheriffs, and as the agent wrote, 'William Williams is sheriff by the means of my Lord of Buckhurst. It is reported he paid dear for it.' However, in the neighbouring shire of Merioneth, Wynn's intervention succeeded. His brother acted as agent in this instance, was more fortunate in his choice of patron, and 'laid out money' as instructed.[3]

This downward trend in public morality was noted by one of Burghley's panegyrists. 'I will forbear', he wrote, 'to mention the great and unusual fees exacted lately by reason of buying and selling offices, both judicial and ministerial, as also the privileges granted unto private persons to the great prejudice and grievance of the common people.'[4] Of course, the bribers were to blame as well as the bribed; and no doubt economic causes were also at work along with social. The growing wealth of the nation, in contrast with that of the state; monetary

---

[1] Birch, op. cit. i, 481, and cf. p. 354.

[2] Harleian MS. 286, fol. 219; *Hatfield MSS.* iv, 517. For other payments offered for local office, cf. *Hist. MSS. Com., Gawdy MSS.* p. 75; N.L.W., Wynn of Gwydir Papers, Add. MS. 464 E, no. 111 (£10 offered to the Earl of Leicester's servant to make Owen Wynn and Thomas Vaughan J.P.s).

[3] N.L.W., Wynn of Gwydir Papers, Panton group, 9051 E, no. 129. For other gratuities, cf. *Hatfield MSS.* iv, 253, 362, 499; vi, 139, 146, 259, 545; vii, 106, 258, 288-9, 332, 349; *Cal. S.P. Dom. 1591-4*, p. 424; *Cal. S.P. Dom. 1601-3*, p. 41; *Cal. Border Papers*, ii, 439.

[4] Additional MS. 22925, fol. 23.

164

inflation; industrial expansion, coupled with the scandal of monopolies; perhaps, also, an undue concentration of money on the domestic market owing to war conditions: all these probably help to explain soaring bribes and the feverish competition for place and favour. It has the appearance of an inflationary movement: too many suitors pursuing too few privileges. Nor must we forget that the Queen was ageing, and her discipline — dependent in any case upon the loyalty and probity of those about her — losing its old resilience. The balance of factions was also weakening, and there was the threatening spectre of single-faction rule. Even Burghley, in the last eight years of his life, when his son so frequently acted as his deputy, seems to have been affected by the new moral climate.

In leaving this tale of growing corruption, we may reflect that pressure tends to concentrate on the weak features of any social system, thus undermining it; and that a new generation does not respond so readily to the restraints of a moral code which it inherits and does not create. The generation coming into power in the 1590s was out of tune with the old Queen and her ways. It fawned, but it deceived. Elizabeth herself voiced this feeling to her faithful antiquary, William Lambarde, in 1601: 'Now the wit of the fox is everywhere on foot, so as hardly a faithful or virtuous man may be found.'[1]

In the first decade of Elizabeth's reign there were occasions when faction seemed to be getting out of hand. But there was then a fundamental harmony in age and outlook between sovereign and statesmen. Leicester was not an Essex, and the loyalty, authority, and uprightness of such men as William Cecil, Nicholas Bacon, and the Earl of Bedford, to mention no others, were sufficient steadying force. Sir Robert Naunton, in his *Fragmenta Regalia*,[2] has an astute comment on the Queen's method of government. 'The principal note of her reign will

---

[1] Nichols, *Progresses of Queen Elizabeth* (1788), vol. ii.
[2] In the essay, 'The Queen'.

be, that she ruled much by faction and parties, which herself both made, upheld, and weakened, as her own great judgment advised.' As Sir Henry Wotton wrote, it 'was not the least ground of much of her quiet and success'.[1]

The 1590s, however, were a political climacteric. The great statesmen and faction-leaders of the reign were passing in rapid succession to the grave; and power had to be transferred to the new generation at a pace dangerous to the digestive capacity of the system. The 'quiet and success' which Elizabeth had derived from the rivalry of the factions were shattered, principally by the nature of the young Earl of Essex, but also by the survival of Burghley, whose unrivalled experience, authority, and subtlety were all concentrated on securing the succession to his very able son, Robert Cecil.

> O grief of griefs, O gall of all good hearts
> To see that virtue should despised be
> Of him, that first was raised for virtuous parts,
> And now broad spreading like an aged tree,
> Lets none shoot up, that nigh him planted be.

So wrote Spenser,[2] and though he was not an impartial spectator, there was perhaps an element of truth in his words. For the followers of Essex, there was certainly a semblance of truth. 'Old *Saturnus* is a melancholy and wayward planet, but yet predominant here', wrote Sir Robert Sidney's man in 1591, warning his master that the way to favour was through Burghley, not Essex.[3] And in 1596, Anthony Bacon, the Earl's right-hand man, described the Cecils as 'the omnipotent couple'.[4] '*Regnum Cecilianum*' or 'Cecil's Commonwealth' was a phrase which had been frequently used.[5]

---

[1] *Reliquiae Wottonianae* (1654), p. 44.
[2] *The Ruins of Time*, ll. 449 seqq.
[3] Collins, *Sydney Papers*, i, 331.
[4] Birch, op. cit. i, 481.
[5] Strype, *Annals*, iii, ii, 380; Add. MS. 22925, fols. 29-30.

But if there was a *regnum Cecilianum* in these later years, it was the creation of the Earl of Essex. This impetuous young man was the architect of his own ruin. He could not live and let live, but wanted everything. He would tolerate no divided loyalties. He virtually reduced the factions to two; and would have reduced them to one — his own. There was no subtlety in his tactics. He recklessly engaged his reputation in the suits he supported, so that failure brought humiliation. Even over an Irish office worth £300, for which in 1593 there was great competition and round sums offered 'in the Chamber and elsewhere', while Burghley planned to suppress it in the interests of economy, we are told that he backed his man with such assurance and publicity that all the Court knew of it.[1] Inevitably he embarrassed the Queen; and as his megalomania developed, feeding on the idolatry of the people for a romantic war-leader, he left her in no doubt that she must resist or be enslaved. He believed that he could carry her mind by storm — his policy of 'hot waters', against which Francis Bacon shrewdly advised him. He would get his way by constant iteration: '*saepe cadendo*', as he termed it.[2] On one occasion Elizabeth bade him go to bed, if he could talk of nothing else. It was impossible for her to follow her old policy of balancing the factions. Instead, she was driven to backing one faction — the Cecilians. At the time of Essex's fall Robert Cecil was Secretary, Chancellor of the Duchy of Lancaster, and Master of the Court of Wards — a unique combination of offices; and if we reflect on the power and patronage they conferred — particularly the rich patronage of the Court of Wards and the Duchy — we can appreciate how near to creating a rival monopoly Elizabeth was forced to go. After the Earl's death she took the Chancellorship of the Duchy away from Cecil.

Never was the danger for a faction-leader of absence from Court more clearly demonstrated. While present, Essex could

[1] Birch, op. cit. i, 130.
[2] Cf. *Unton Correspondence*, ed. J. Stevenson, p. 317.

often by his tantrums prevent the Queen from making unwelcome appointments; but when away, he was too weak to resist his enemies. All Robert Cecil's offices were conferred while his rival was absent on one expedition or another; and news of Cecil's appointment to the Mastership of the Court of Wards, which Essex had strenuously solicited for himself, was one of the gravest blows he suffered during his Irish campaign.

How passionately Essex fought for his friends, Sir Robert Sidney and Francis Bacon! In 1596, when Lord Hunsdon was dying, he promised to put forward Sidney for the great office of Lord Chamberlain — an insensate proposal.[1] Instead, Lord Cobham, his enemy and Burghley's friend, was appointed. Next year, on Cobham's death, he waged implacable battle over the Lord Wardenship of the Cinque Ports, to keep out Cobham's son and put in Sidney. For some months his outrageous behaviour kept the post vacant; but then Cobham got it.[2] He next pressed for the Vice-Chamberlain's office, vacant since the death of Heneage in 1595. Raleigh had ambitions that way; but Essex told him that he would be an enemy to all who sought the office.[3] He so terrified other candidates that the Queen left the office vacant until his death opened the way for a Cecilian. He also promised Sidney a peerage.[4] He got him nothing. The violence with which he pressed his suits for Francis Bacon, first for the office of Attorney-General and then of Solicitor-General, is well known. He tried to make him Master of the Rolls.[5] He failed in all. He could get anything for himself, said a supporter, but nothing for his friends; and Essex's own view in 1599, in the darkening weeks before his departure for Ireland, was that he could 'procure nothing for himself nor any of his friends'.[6]

[1] *Cal. S.P. Dom. 1595-7*, p. 181.
[2] Collins, *Sydney Papers*, ii, *passim*.
[3] Ibid. p. 80.
[4] Ibid. *passim*; *Hatfield MSS.* viii, 29.
[5] Birch, op. cit. i, 488.
[6] *Hatfield MSS.* ix, 10.

As our analysis of the Elizabethan political scene will have suggested, there was another side to this story. Court rivalry was not merely concerned with power and prestige. A leader's own solvency and the livelihood of his servants were at stake. Like a financier in our modern world, he was poised upon a great credit structure. Blow upon it: the result might be ruin. This was Essex's position.[1] Early in his career, in 1589, he confessed to Sir Thomas Heneage that his debts were at least twenty-two or twenty-three thousand pounds, and his revenue no greater than when he came of age. Life seemed to him then, and was, a game with fortune.[2] He obtained the lease of the sweet wines which Leicester had held, and with it the means of raising substantial loans from the wine merchants. In 1597, when it lapsed, statements of his debts were compiled to show that he would be bankrupt if it were not renewed, and his credit with these merchants prolonged.[3] Meanwhile, with the inordinate growth of his household and his splendour, the stakes in the game mounted. He began with two secretaries. In 1595-6 the number was increased to four and then to five — much to the chagrin of the oldest, who, though he gave other reasons for discontent, feared a drastic diminution in gratuities.[4]

Apart from his natural incapacity to accept reverses with equanimity, Essex must have been concerned about the financial effects of continual rebuffs in his major suits to the Queen; and so too must the members of his household, many of whom were ambitious, able men, and some reckless. How long would the indispensable gratuities continue to flow? From this point of view his Irish campaign was a gambler's last throw; and with our knowledge of the great monetary gains which the Master and his friends and servants made out of the Court of Wards, we can appreciate how bitter was the news, which came in the midst of his Irish misfortunes, that

[1] For Leicester's position at his death, cf. Ellis, *Original Letters*, 3rd ser. iv, 75-9.
[2] *Hatfield MSS*. iii, 459.
[3] Ibid. vii, 283, 375-6.
[4] Birch, op. cit. ii, 105 seqq.

Cecil had been appointed to this office. The Earl's mad, unauthorized return to Court was followed by a prolonged disgrace. It brought him face to face with ruin. His licence for sweet wines, as valuable 'in credit as in profit', lapsed: it was not renewed. An incomplete catalogue of his debts at this time showed over £16,000 owing; and his creditors, distrustful as they had cause to be, were pressing for payment and lying in wait to arrest those servants of his who had stood pledge for him.[1] The credit structure was collapsing. His household must have been in worse case. For sixteen months — the duration of his disgrace — there can have been no gratuities. No wonder that the prime villain of the piece, his secretary Cuffe, and others were reckless. The rebellion was an act of financial desperation.

In these last years of Elizabeth's reign, with the inherent flaws of a political system apparent, we are moving into a new age. The accession of James I, a weak sovereign who had neither the character nor the political skill to maintain the discipline of the past, gave rein to the forces of corruption. The episode of Essex was also repeated, though in a different way and with a different ending. This time it was the sovereign himself who encouraged single-faction rule. If Queen Elizabeth had really been infatuated with Essex as tradition pictured her, or as James I with the Duke of Buckingham, then Sir Henry Wotton's *Parallel* between the two favourites would indeed have deserved its name. But Elizabeth strove to maintain the old, balanced order. Under James I it broke down, and the scandal and discontent caused by a putrefying political system helped to provoke the Civil War.

[1] *Hatfield MSS.* x, 110, 128, 312, 348.

THE SAYINGS OF QUEEN ELIZABETH[1]

THE occasion of this article is the publication under the same title of a book by Mr Frederick Chamberlin.[2] Four years ago he achieved considerable popular success by a work on *The Private Character of Queen Elizabeth*, which ran into four printings. Neither book has been reviewed in any serious historical journal, and since Mr Chamberlin's literary programme is by no means complete, it may be useful, before making any excursion of my own into the entertaining field chosen by him, to say something of his more recent work and to assess the scholarship of one whose pretensions are, to put it mildly, a little extravagant.

Mr Chamberlin prefaces his collection of the sayings of Queen Elizabeth with an exuberant introduction, in which he presents himself as the champion of Elizabeth and Leicester against the misrepresentations of former historians. The Queen, he tells us, once said, 'The truth will at last be made manifest', and 'If I had not come along now,' he adds later, 'how many years would have passed before the truth would "at last be made manifest"?' Such passages it is needless to comment upon, as it is needless to rebut his charges against John Bruce, the editor of the *Leycester Correspondence* published by the Camden Society, and against professional historians in general. They are best left to the sober judgment of his readers. But his criticism of Froude is more than mere *obiter dicta*. It pretends to be an elaborate examination of his historical method; and in consequence I must devote a little space to it.

Mr Chamberlin quarrels with Froude because he was

---

[1] Published in *History* (October 1925), x, 212-33.
[2] John Lane, 1923.

critical of Elizabeth, seeing behind her the figure of Burghley, digesting and docketing documents with an amazing capacity for work, drawing up the arguments for and against some policy in that characteristic Italian hand of his, and displaying a solid common sense, which, if seemingly timid and unimaginative, yet gave the turn to the rudder that saved the ship of state from wreck. Mr Chamberlin does not see the Elizabethan age as Froude saw it. Burghley is to shrink under the blast of his criticism, Leicester to take his place as the master-mind of the reign, and the Queen, her name cleansed from scandal, is to stand out peerless. Consequently he attempts to dethrone Froude by submitting his technique to a detailed study.

Faulty as the study is, it shows conclusively that Froude was no respecter of inverted commas; and this is a legitimate and a useful line of criticism. In these days we hold by an exacting historical method, but it would be lamentable if that robbed us of a sense of values. Froude was a great literary artist. He felt the rhythmic possibilities of sixteenth-century prose and made occasional alterations in his quotations that lent an incomparable melody to them. He abridged documents, often without warning. He translated in a free, because an artistic, manner. He felt that history could not be literature were it to consist of documents strung upon a commentary; that both must pass into the crucible of an artistic mind and be fused into one. And yet his sin was not that he amended his documents, which was sound literary instinct, but that he sanctified his own handiwork by inverted commas. It was, however, the fault of another age of historians than our own, and cannot be judged fairly by recent standards. Nor is it serious, once we recognize that Froude is not to be trusted to quote his documents *verbatim*. In fact, it is a venial sin. But if in using his documents the historian inverts or deflects their sense, that cannot be excused. Unfortunately Froude did, and if only Mr Chamberlin had been less concerned with trivial inaccuracies and had enabled us to judge how extensive was

Froude's serious offence, he would have performed a valuable service.

The critic must pay the penalty of submitting his own work to be judged by the standards which he himself sets up. Mr Chamberlin attempts to demonstrate the worthlessness of Froude's quotations by printing alongside of them what he says is the true text. One of his columns he heads, 'What Froude says Elizabeth wrote'; another, 'What Elizabeth actually wrote'.[1] It is perhaps a quibble to remark that Elizabeth neither wrote nor composed the document in question; but be that as it may, when Mr Chamberlin quotes his second column from the *Calendar of State Papers, Scottish Series*, and describes it as 'a correct reproduction of the entire document', he betrays, first that he has not looked at the original document, and secondly that he has not yet realized that generally a Calendar does not reproduce a document *verbatim*.

His idea of what constitutes historical proof is also a measure of his scholarship. 'I am giving to the public', he says on p. vi, 'one of the most epochal facts in all the life of Elizabeth.' It purports to be Elizabeth's own statement of her reason for favouring Leicester, and comes from a letter of Hubert Languet, in which he is retailing the gossip at Antwerp, at a city where, as Guicciardini puts it, one always knew everything that was going on in every other country in the universe.[2] In other words, Mr Chamberlin's evidence is as unreliable as a news-letter. Nor does he improve matters by citing Gregorio Leti in confirmation of it. I can hardly enter here into proof of my estimate of Leti as a historian; but his *Historia ... di Elizabetta* is utterly worthless, and is adorned with letters of his own fabrication.[3] Written between 1680 and 1693, it is obviously not an original authority for Elizabeth's reign.

---

[1] *Sayings of Queen Elizabeth*, p. xxiv.

[2] *Description de Touts les Pays-Bas ...* (1598), quoted by Tawney and Power, *Tudor Economic Documents*, iii, 157.

[3] Mary Wood in her *Letters of Royal Ladies*, and F. A. Mumby in his *Girlhood of Queen Elizabeth*, have both reprinted apocryphal letters from Leti.

The body of Mr Chamberlin's book consists of 'sayings' of Elizabeth. Many are quoted without any reference to their source, and there are few people who would not be tempted to invoke the shade of Macaulay's schoolboy when told that the authority is 'obvious or readily found from its context'. Nor is Mr Chamberlin quite fair to Miss Strickland. Something like half of his 'sayings' are taken from her *Life of Elizabeth*. In most instances he makes no acknowledgment to her, and often he borrows her reference, also without acknowledgment. Here is an example. Miss Strickland's reference is, 'Autograph letter in the imperial collection at St Petersburgh ... '; Mr Chamberlin's, 'Translation from the French original, preserved in the Imperial Autograph Collection at Petrograd. I cannot now vouch for the existence of this MS., but it was at Petrograd before the Great War.'[1] Whatever may be Mr Chamberlin's explanation of his own gloss upon the original reference, the fact remains that the translation which he uses is Miss Strickland's; and since she quotes her documents with much the same freedom as Froude, we have the curious result that she imposes upon Mr Chamberlin throughout his book just those very faults which he criticizes so drastically in his introduction.

Much might be said about the sayings which flow through other channels into Mr Chamberlin's book. He resurrects Sir Nicholas Bacon (d. 1579) to deliver one of the opening speeches in parliament in 1601, and attributes the speech, with what authority I do not know, to the Queen's composition.[2] Some sayings appear more than once in different guises, an example being the famous 'Aye or No' speech of 1593, which again he wrongly attributes to Elizabeth, and the best version of which[3] he does not know. Two sayings are from Carlyle — a 'very reliable' authority, says Mr Chamberlin,[4] who clearly cannot have heard of the Squire papers.

[1] Strickland, *Lives of the Queens of England* (1851), iv, 641 n.; Chamberlin, op. cit. p. 193 n. For another example see ibid. p. 47 n. (Strickland, iv, 644 n.).
[2] Chamberlain, pp. 148-9.
[3] See *Eng. Hist. Rev.* xxxi (1916), 128.　　　　[4] Op. cit. p. 28 n.

And so I might go on; but it is enough to add that as grapes are not gathered of thorns, so sound history does not come from an unsound critical equipment.

One merit Mr Chamberlin's book possesses: it sets us wondering whether the sayings attributed to Elizabeth were really hers. Needless to say, he offers no help to the answer. Whether true or false they went into his collection; and so far as I know there has hitherto been no attempt to set up a canon and apocrypha of stories. The reason is simple. It would involve elaborate criticism of a hundred and one books, and even then we could say no more than 'probable' or 'improbable' about most of the stories. Such criticism I do not pretend for a moment to have undertaken; but in the remaining pages of this article I hope to make a preliminary essay towards a differentiation between the true and the false in regard to a few of the reputed sayings and stories.

It goes almost without saying that some are apocryphal. Wit was in fashion at the Court of Elizabeth, as it is in a community like Oxford, and we hardly need reminding that the men of established reputation in such circles are often strangers to their own fosterlings. At the peace conference of 1919, where there was a company of experts adept at word-play and a few statesmen at the centre of things distinguished politically and not incapable of a *bon mot*, we are told that the epigrams which were invented were fathered with astonishing regularity upon the same few, and especially upon M. Clémenceau. It would be difficult to say what mordant epigrams Clémenceau was responsible for, and what not; and equally difficult is it, and for the same reasons, to tell what sayings were really Elizabeth's. Her wit was equal to them all. She was a woman of ready and vigorous mind and considerable culture, and the figurative style of her writing and speaking gave her excellent practice in turning phrases. She loved metaphor and simile, antithesis and epigram, and sometimes got herself so involved in her conceits that her listeners and correspondents must have been as perplexed about her meaning as her statesmen were. 'No man can knowe the inward entencyon of her harte … but God and her selfe', said her councillors when consulted about the Anjou marriage negotiations;[1] and Walsingham, when advising the Queen on the same project, wisely wrote, 'If you mean it … If you mean it not … '[2]

But even when most involved, her style rarely lacked vigour and distinction, and when passion kept her love of finery in check, she could rise to magnificent heights. Here is a passage ırom a letter to James VI where vigour and affectation struggle for mastery:

> And since it so lykes you to demande my counsaile, I finde so many ways your state so unjoynted, that it needs a skilfuller bonesetter than I to joyne each part in his right place. But to fulfill your will, take, in shorte, theise few words: … Who to peril a king were inventores or actors, they should crake a halter if I were king. Such is my charitie. Who under pretence of bettering your estate, endangers the king, or needs wil be his schoolemasters, if I might appoint their universitie they should be assigned to learne first to obay; so should they better teach you next …[3]

Whilst here, in a brief passage taken from a speech to the Commons, which, though a report only, is a full, and, I believe, a faithful one, and well worth reading in its entirety, her language is simple and forceful:

> As for myne owne part I care not for death, for all men are mortall, and though I be a woman I have as good a courage, aunswerable to my place, as ever my father had. I am your anoynted Queene. I will never be by violence constrained to do any thing. I thanke God I am endued with such qualities that if I weare turned out of the

[1] *Hatfield MSS.* ii, 239.
[2] Ibid. p. 427.
[3] *Letters of Elizabeth and James VI* (Camden Soc. 1849), pp. 76-7.

THE SAYINGS OF QUEEN ELIZABETH

Realme in my peticote I wear able to live in any place in christome [Christendom].[1]

Elizabeth was merely the centre of a Court in which the wit and culture of her age were mirrored, and there were men about her like that imp of a godson, Sir John Harington, who shocked her — so she pretended — by his broad humour, yet amused her and won her love as much by his ready tongue and pen as by his claims as a godson. Inevitably good stories must have been fathered upon her, whether she knew it or not. If she knew, she smiled, no doubt, and let them float down to posterity on the strong support of her fame. Being a very human being, she loved praise, and being a sovereign — and a Tudor sovereign at that — got more of it than was good for her; for if adulation be the common lot of an attractive woman and a prince, only a Diogenes could have resisted a combination of both. 'My heart was never broken till this day', wrote Raleigh to Sir Robert Cecil in an outburst which in its extravagance parodies the eulogies of the Court:

My heart was never broken till this day that I hear the Queen goes away so far off, whom I have followed so many years with so great love and desire in so many journeys, and am now left behind her in a dark prison all alone. While she was yet near at hand, that I might hear of her once in two or three days, my sorrows were the less, but yeven now my heart is cast into the depth of all misery. I that was wont to behold her riding like Alexander, hunting like Diana, walking like Venus, the gentle winde blowing her fair hair about her pure cheeks like a nymph, sometime sitting in the shade like a goddess, sometime singing like an angel, sometime playing like Orpheus — behold, the sorrow of this world once amiss hath bereaved me of all. Oh! love that only shineth in misfortune, what is become of thy assurance? All wounds

[1] *Eng. Hist. Rev.* xxxvi (1921), 516.

have scars but that of phantasy: all affections their relent-
ing but that of woman kind.[1]

The Court cried her praises, and the City, when it was in
the humour, was Echo's voice which Elizabeth kept well
tuned by bewitching it. 'Now, if ever any persone had eyther
the gift or the stile to winne the hearts of people, it was this
Queene', wrote Sir John Hayward, who had little to thank
Elizabeth for save imprisonment and a lucky escape from
worse:

> and if ever shee did expresse the same, it was at that
> present, in coupling mildnesse with majesty as shee
> did, and in stately stouping to the meanest sort. All her
> facultyes were in motione, and every motione seemed a
> well guided actione; her eye was set upon one, her eare
> listened to another, her judgement ranne uppon a third,
> to a fourth shee addressed her speech; her spirit seemed
> to be every-where, and yet so intyre in her selfe, as it
> seemed to bee noe where else. Some shee pityed, some shee
> commended, some shee thanked, at others shee pleasantly
> and wittily jeasted, contemning noe person, neglecting noe
> office; and distributing her smiles, lookes, and graces soe
> artificially, that thereupon the people again redoubled the
> testimonyes of their joyes; and afterwards, raising every
> thing to the highest straine, filled the eares of all men
> with immoderate extolling their Prince.[2]

That Elizabeth had an irresistible way with her the documents of the time prove amply enough. Let me illustrate it by
a letter from Sir William Brown to Sir Robert Sidney, who had
sent him over from the Netherlands with letters to the Queen
in 1601. Like so many of her servants abroad, Brown had
become a disgruntled creature. This Elizabeth knew, and she
set herself to charm him.

---

[1] *Hatfield MSS.* iv, 220. The date is July 1592.
[2] *Annals of Elizabeth* (Camden Soc. 1840), pp. 6-7.

THE SAYINGS OF QUEEN ELIZABETH

I had no sooner kyssed her sacred hands, butt that she presently made me stand upp, and spoke somwhat lowd, and sayd, Com hether Browne; and pronounced, that she held me for an old faithful servant of hers, and said, I must give content to Browne, or som such speeches: And then the Trayne following her, she sayd, Stand, stand back, will you not let us speake but you wilbe hearers? And then walked a turne or twoo, protesting her most gracious opinion of my self: And before God, Brown, sayd shee, they do me wrong that will make so honest a servant be jealous that I should mistrust him ... Having walked a turne or twoo, she called for a stoole, which was sett under a tree, and I begann to kneele, butt she wold not suffer mee; in so much as that after twoo or three denyalls which I made to kneele, still she was pleased to say, that shee wold not speake with me unles I stood upp.

Brown began to explain the position of affairs in the Netherlands: 'Tush, Brown,' said she, 'I know more than thow doest', and thereupon she poured forth her own comment and prophecy. She turned to talk of the French king, and, Brown venturing a remark, 'Tush, Browne,' said she, 'do not I know?' — and so the conversation went on. With a final pat on the back poor Brown was sent away, so deliriously happy that it was only in a postscript to his letter that he remembered he had been sent to England by Sidney on business.[1]

Many other examples could be given of the Queen's genius in winning affection. There was little Byzantine aloofness about her sovereignty. Majesty spoke with the captivating modulations of a woman's voice, employed a woman's every art, and felt with her sensitiveness. She breathed her spirit even into the formal documents of the time, and expressions of loving affection are often found in strange harness with the conventional diplomatic formulae of proclamations and official

[1] Collins, *Letters and Memorials of State* (Sydney Papers), ii, 229-30.

letters. In 1589 Lord Willoughby received a letter under the signet, beginning in the usual form, thanking his troops in France for their services:

> Wee have ... thought good to take knowledge thereof to your comforte, and to let you knowe ... how much we hould ourself bownd to thanck allmighty God for blessing us with subjects of that worthines and valure as you have shewed to be ... And further we will you to make knowen to all the colonels, captaines and souldiars our subjectes ... our princely and grateful acceptance of this their worthy service ... and to assure all and every of them that they shall fynde us myndefull of yt to their comfortes.[1]

And as though she found the formulae of such letters too cold, instead of the simple superscription of her name, she wrote, 'Your most lovinge soveraine, Elizabeth.' To another, extremely formal, signet letter sent to Willoughby she added in her own hand, 'Good peregrin suppose not that your travail and labours ar not gratiusly accepted and shalbe ever kept in good memorye.'[2] And when Cecil drafted a letter of thanks to Lord Hunsdon after his victory over Leonard Dacre in 1570, she set the more restrained language of her secretary to shame by a glowing postscript of her own:

> I doubt much, my Harry, whether that the victory were given me more joyed me, or that you were by God appointed the instrument of my glory; and I assure you that for my country's good, the first might suffice, but for my heart's contentation, the second more pleased me ... ; and that you may not think that you have done nothing for your profit, though you have done much for honour, I intend to make this journey somewhat to increase your livelihood, that you may not say to yourself, *perditur quod factum est ingrato*. Your loving kinswoman. Elizabeth, R.[3]

---

[1] *Hist. MSS. Com., Ancaster MSS.* p. 295.   [2] Ibid., p. 198.
[3] *Cal. S.P. Dom. Add. 1566-79*, p. 246.

Nor did she hesitate to flatter by seeming to deceive her ministers. There is a letter, fortunately preserved by Sir Henry Sidney, which was written to him in 1565. 'Harry,' it begins — and goes on in Elizabeth's most euphuistic style, ending, 'Let this memoriall be only committed to Vulcanes base keping, without any longer abode than the leasure of the reding therof, yea, and with no mention made therof to any other wight. I charge you, as I may comande you. Seme not to have had but Secretaries letters from me. Your lovinge maistris, Elizabeth R.'[1]

Now how can historical science, or, to use Lord Bryce's less pretentious phrase, refined common sense, hope to separate the false from the true in the traditional stories about such a woman as this? *Omnis fabula fundatur in historia*, it has been said. Perhaps; but we must examine the foundations, none the less; and it is only by a critical review of our sources that our problem will be solved, if at all. Let me illustrate the point by examining one of the best known of Elizabethan stories. In 1566 Sir James Melville was sent to England by Mary Queen of Scots to announce the birth of her child. Melville tells us in his *Memoirs* that Cecil first whispered the news to Elizabeth in the course of a dance. Thereupon 'all her mirth was laid aside for that night', and sitting down she put her hand under her cheek and burst out with the moan 'that the Queen of Scots was Mother of a fair son, while she was but a barren stock'.[2]

'When men's memories do arise', said Fuller, who was himself a delightfully garrulous offender, 'it is time for History to haste to bed.'[3] Melville's *Memoirs* were the child of his old age, and though he had some of his papers by him on which to rely, fickle memory played its tricks, and his narrative is by no means reliable. If not conclusive proof that this particular story is false, it is at least sufficient to make us pause in believing it, that the Spanish ambassador, Silva, who was not

[1] Collins, op. cit. i, 7-8.
[2] *Memoirs* (1683), p. 70. The best edition is the Bannatyne Club's (1827).
[3] Fuller's *Worthies* (1811), i, 349.

at all one to miss the chance of retailing such a story, and who saw Melville the day after his audience, merely tells Philip that 'the Queen seemed very glad of the birth of the infant': nor had he a different tale to tell, though he was an assiduous collector of Court gossip, when he wrote again four days later.[1] Other stories go back to Melville for their parentage, the best known of which is probably the amusing debate which he says took place between Elizabeth and himself in 1564 on the relative accomplishments and qualities of his mistress and herself.[2] We cannot say that its pedigree is above suspicion and we cannot test it, although I confess a sneaking desire to keep the tale.

Few of the Queen's sayings are so choice, though their charm depends upon their setting rather than any intrinsic brilliance, as are those connected with her progresses. The supreme moments of her genius were these, and if with their masques and verses her progresses belong to the history of the drama, they are no less part of the unwritten story of government propaganda. Old age failed to cloy her appetite for them, and we find her in her sixty-seventh year resolutely determined to go on her long progress to Tottenham, and with fine spirit replying to the lords who were grumbling at the prospect of the fatigue, by bidding 'the old stay behind, and the young and able to goe with her'.[3] The accounts we have of these progresses are strictly contemporary, written generally immediately after the events, by eye-witnesses.[4] Some are printed tracts, and their sale surely fostered that popular interest in Elizabeth which made her the symbol of a quickening national consciousness. Their evidence is not beyond cavil. Narrators could not have heard all they report. Some of the Queen's sayings must have come from the story of the visit which immediately gained currency in the neighbourhood; and perhaps the writers, no

[1] *Spanish Cal. Eliz.* i, 562, 563.
[2] Op. cit. pp. 49-51.
[3] Collins, op. cit. ii, 210.
[4] They are printed in Nichols, *Progresses of Queen Elizabeth* (1823).

less than the simple folk who constructed the epic in their taverns, did not leave the tale unadorned.

There is a delightful tract describing Elizabeth's passage through London the day before her Coronation,[1] which was in print nine days afterwards. Never was princely play so perfect as on that occasion. It was this which called forth the eulogy from Sir John Hayward that I have already quoted. 'I warrant you it is for gladness,' said the Queen when a gentleman called attention to an alderman who was weeping; and when she was seen to smile and was asked the reason — it was, she said, 'for that she had heard one say, Remember old king Henry theyght'. At Warwick in 1572 she made a perfect speech to the Recorder after his public welcome of her. 'Come hither, little Recorder,' she said: 'it was told me that youe wold be afraid to look upon me, or to speak boldly; but you were not so afraid of me as I was of youe, and I nowe thank you for putting me in mynd of my duty, and that shuld be in me.' And at the same place she sent for a poor man and his wife, whose house had been burnt down by a firework display, comforted them and saw them compensated.[2] At Sandwich she flattered her citizen hostesses at a banquet by taking their food without the usual preliminary tasting, and then had some of the dishes reserved for her and sent to her lodging, a compliment as supreme as it was womanly.[3] There was a similarly incomparable touch at Norwich in 1578. The schoolmaster was very ill at ease at having to make a speech. 'Be not afrayde,' said Elizabeth, and afterwards she purchased a loyal heart at the cost of a small lie, for she told him that it was the best speech ever she had heard. Nor did she stop there. After the Court party had moved on she sent deliberately back to know the schoolmaster's name, capping her conventional courtesies in a way of which she alone was mistress.[4]

[1] Ibid. i, 38 seqq.
[2] Ibid. i, 315, 320.
[3] Ibid. i, 338-9.
[4] Ibid. ii, 155, 159.

I give free rein to scepticism when we come to our next two sources. They are Bacon's *Apophthegms*, and Fuller's *Worthies*. In both, wit or love of a good story prompted most of the tales, and Clio must needs cover her face and hide her blushes, for the inveterate raconteur is without scruple. Everything was fish that came into Fuller's net. His 'bare skeleton of time, place, and person, must', he confessed, 'be fleshed with some pleasant passages'; and consequently he 'purposely inter-laced ... many delightful stories, that so the Reader, if he do not arise ... *religiosior* or *doctior* ..., at least he may depart *jucundior*'.[1] He is not a contemporary authority (he was born in 1608), and even supposing we could believe that his tradi-tional stories had contemporary origins, their parentage would still be doubtful. The *onus probandi* is on the narrator when merry tales are in doubt.

From Fuller come two stories about Sir Walter Raleigh at which one cannot but strain. The first is the famous story of the new plush cloak which he spread in the mud to keep the Queen's feet from being soiled, by his gallantry winning her attention and favour, and gaining, as it has been punningly said, many good suits by the spoiling of a cloak. Where Fuller got the story from I do not know. Naunton, a younger con-temporary of Raleigh's, does not tell the tale, apt though it would have been in his *Fragmenta Regalia*, and I am inclined to think that it was the invention of a later generation wishing to explain so rapid a rise to favour. As an explanation it has the misfortune to be needless. Raleigh may have been intro-duced at Court by Katherine Ashley, a relative of his, or by the Earl of Leicester, and being a man of good parts, mentally and physically, a ready talker and a wit, an introduction was sufficient to make him free of a company loving pride of life, 'the cowrtes vanitie, ambition's puff ball',[2] for, as Fuller puts it, the Queen well knew *Gratior est pulchro veniens e corpore*

---

[1] *Worthies* (1811), i, 2.
[2] Harington, *Nugae Antiquae* (1804), i, 170.

virtus.[1] The other story belongs to his early days at Court and tells that he wrote on a glass window, 'Fain would I climb, yet fear to fall.' Upon seeing it, the Queen completed the distich by subscribing, 'If thy heart fails thee, climb not at all.'[2] It is impossible, and naturally so, to show that a tale of this sort is apocryphal; but if we set out to credit all that we cannot disprove, we shall write strange history, and I am content to state my argument as frank scepticism. Other sayings of the Queen rest upon the uncertain authority of Fuller, amongst which is her reply to Burghley's servant when he bade her stoop as she entered the door at Burghley House to visit the sick minister: 'For your Master's sake I will stoop,' she is made to say; 'but not for the King of Spain's.'[3] This also I would put in our apocrypha.

Bacon's *Apophthegms* contain quite a number of Elizabethan stories, amongst which are some of the Queen's sayings. Most of the apophthegms were dictated from memory by Bacon in 1624. Others appeared only after his death, and though it is probable that they were copied from his papers, one cannot be quite certain of it.[4] Supposing, however, that we accept Bacon's authority for these stories, we must still remember that in collecting them he was not concerned with their historical accuracy, but with their wit or moral, and accordingly neither his scholarly sense nor his position in Elizabethan society can be held to establish the stories as genuine. Only when he was himself an ear-witness need we receive them into our established canon. For example, Bacon tells how Seckford, a master of requests, who had been many times disappointed in his attempts to secure an audience, came at last into the Queen's presence, wearing a pair of new boots. 'Fie, sloven,' said Elizabeth, who disliked the smell of new leather, 'thy new boots stink.' 'Madam,'

---

[1] *Worthies*, i, 496.
[2] Ibid. p. 287.
[3] Ibid. ii, 14.
[4] Cf. editor's preface to the Apophthegms in *Works*, ed. Spedding and Ellis, vii, 113 seqq.

answered Seckford, 'it is not my new boots that stink, but it is the stale bills that I have kept so long.'[1] Now Sir Nicholas L'Estrange, who flourished in the first half of the seventeenth century and collected a large number of stories, tells the same tale in a slightly different form, but tells it of Sir Roger Williams, not Seckford;[2] and it is perhaps one of many stories current even in Elizabeth's lifetime — whether genuine or not, who can say? On the other hand, when Bacon tells of an interview of his with the Queen concerning Hayward's *Life of Henry IV*, the jest in which is not Elizabeth's but his own, we may probably accept the tale as true.[3]

Between Bacon and Sir John Harington there may seem to be little to choose in the way of reliability, and that little in Bacon's favour: I draw a distinction, resting not upon the qualities of the men but upon the character of those writings of theirs in which sayings of the Queen are found. Unsatisfying as the editing of Harington's papers is in *Nugae Antiquae*, they still are his private papers, consisting of letters and diary entries as well as of more definitely literary pieces; and Harington was well placed both to hear himself and to learn of others when the Queen shone in repartee. His parents had earned the gratitude of Elizabeth by their service to her in the perilous days of Mary, a service which brought them into prison; and when their son John was born in 1561 the Queen repaid their loyalty by standing as godmother to him. As the boy grew he became welcome at Court, not alone as the Queen's godson, but as a wit of no small repute. Consequently his tales, when no appreciable time intervenes before their telling, carry a certain weight; but he was too much the established wit to look closely at a good story, and the value of his evidence diminishes considerably when he is engaged upon a literary composition like his *Briefe View of the State of the Church*.

---

[1] Cf. *Works*, vii, 137-8.
[2] Thom's *Anecdotes and Traditions* (Camden Soc. 1839), p. 47.
[3] *Works*, vii, 133.

It is in this work of his, which was written in the latter part
of 1607, that the well-known story is told of Elizabeth's insulting remark to Archbishop Parker's wife. The Queen often
visited Parker. Once, after she had 'greatlie feasted' at his house,
she took her leave, thanking her hostess in the following brutal
words: 'And you, *Madam* I may not call you, and *Mistris* I
am ashamed to call you, so I know not what to call you, but
yet I do thanke you.'[1] The saying, it is true, may not have been
quite so pungent in the sixteenth century, when 'mistress' had
a wider content and moved more frequently in respectable
than in other circles; but if that blunts the point it does not
remove it, and Harington's meaning was obviously ours.
What, then, can be said for and against the genuineness of the
story? There can be no doubt that Elizabeth was strongly,
nay bitterly, opposed to marriage of the clergy: she had a
curious obsession on the subject of marriage, and she horrified
Parker by a tirade against it in 1561, driving the distracted
man to murmur to Cecil, 'oportet Deo obedire magis quam
hominbus'.[2] Also she could show a coarse and venomous
tongue on occasions. Yet even so I find it difficult to believe
in this deliberate insult following upon the enjoyment of
Parker's hospitality; though I confess that if there is one thing
too wonderful for us, it is the way of a woman's mind, and that
the mind of Elizabeth, who, as Sir Robert Cecil said, 'was
more than a man, and (in troth) sometymes less than a woman'.[3]
The late date and studied art of the *Briefe View* make me
sceptical of the stories which are deliberately introduced into it;
and there is this also to be urged against the truth of the story,
that Harington is not a first-hand witness, for he could not
have been above nine years old, and may not have been born,
at the time of the Queen's visit to Parker. I let the reader
decide which way the balance leans. Unfortunately we must

[1] Harington, op. cit. ii, 16.
[2] *Correspondence of Archbishop Parker* (Parker Soc.), pp. 156 seqq.
[3] Harington, op. cit. i, 345.

take our leave of Harington, with but a single story examined. His papers give many glimpses of a Court where men experienced the elations and depressions of a passionate love. When the Queen smiled, he tells us, 'it was a pure sun-shine, that every one did chuse to baske in, if they could, but anon came a storm from a sudden gathering of clouds, and the thunder fell in wondrous manner on all alike'.[1]

I turn from a criticism of various sources which are rich either in the quality or the quantity of their Elizabethan sayings, to discuss a well-known verse with which the Queen's name is always associated. It is the following, and is deservedly famous:

> Christ was the Word that spake it;
> He took the Bread and brake it:
> And what the Word did make it,
> That I believe, and take it.[2]

The problem of its authorship started a discussion in the second series of *Notes and Queries* which dragged its inordinate length over four series of that journal, only to end with no verdict. So far as I know, the verse was first attributed to Elizabeth in Baker's *Chronicle*, where it is said that she gave this answer in Mary's reign when someone tried to catch her in a net by asking what she thought of the words, 'This is My Body.' The chronicle was published in 1643. It contains a list of its authorities, but in none of these does the quatrain appear, and it is highly significant that Speed, who published a chronicle in 1611, does not quote it. Baker, however, was not the first to print it, for it was included in the second edition (1635) of Donne's poems, although modern editors, believing it to be Elizabeth's, have discarded it as spurious. Some light was thrown on the subject by the discussion in *Notes and Queries*. The quatrain apparently was found painted in black letters

[1] Harington, op. cit. i, 362.
[2] Baker's *Chronicle* (1679), p. 320.

on a pillar of the village church at Walton.[1] Also it is to be found, with slight differences of reading, written at the end of a New Testament belonging to Bishop Cosin's library at Durham;[2] and a substantially different version, 'in an Elizabethan hand', occurs on the fly-leaf of a book of Hours at Lambeth.[3] None of these examples is described precisely enough to date it; but the Lambeth version is less pithy and probably more primitive than the version with which we are familiar, and I would therefore suggest that in one form or another the quatrain was current as an anonymous verse for a considerable time before it was given its permanent form. Perhaps it was Donne who rounded it off, and Baker, a friend of his, knowing this version, quoted it from memory. Its connection with Elizabeth is easily explained. Her fame was a magnetic centre for any unattached story that could possibly be fitted into her history, and it was absorbed into her legend probably in the second or third decade of the seventeenth century. Certainly Baker is too late an authority to guarantee his story, and Elizabeth was too hard put to avoid the dangers of Mary's reign to have uttered so equivocal a reply when her loyalty was being tested through her faith: equivocation heightens and does not allay suspicion, and suspicion she wisely was anxious to avoid.

After so much destructive criticism of the Elizabethan legend, it is refreshing to try and rehabilitate one of the Queen's sayings, and that among the most notable. It is the prose version of her speech at Tilbury camp at the time of the Armada in 1588.

---

[1] 6th ser. x, 248. [2] 2nd ser. v, 438.
[3] 5th ser. vii, 111-12. The version reads:
> As christe willed it and spacke it
> And thankeffullie blessid it and brake it
> And as the Sacreid woord dothe make it
> So I beleve and take it
>   My Lyffe to geve
>   Therefor in Earthe to leve
>   No More.

My loving People, we have been perswaded by some that are careful of our safety, to take heed how we commit our self to armed multitudes, for fear of treachery; but I assure you, I do not desire to live to distrust my faithful and loving people. Let tyrants fear. I have always so behaved my self, that under God, I have placed my chiefest strength and safeguard in the loyal hearts and good will of my subjects, and therefore I am come amongst you, as you see, at this time, not for my recreation and disport, but being resolved, in the midst and heat of the battle, to live or die amongst you all, to lay down for my God, and for my Kingdom, and for my People, my honor, and my blood, even in the dust. I know I have the body but of a week and feeble woman, but I have the heart and stomach of a King, and of a King of England too, and think foul scorn that Parma or Spain, or any Prince of Europe should dare to invade the borders of my Realm; to which, rather than any dishonor shall grow by me, I my self will take up arms, I my self will be your general, judge, and rewarder of every one of your vertues in the field. I know, already for your forwardness, you have deserved rewards and crowns; and we do assure you, in the word of a Prince, they shall be duly paid you.[1]

In a recent number of the *English Historical Review*,[2] Mr Miller Christy, when examining the various accounts of the Queen's visit to Tilbury, cast a doubt upon this version of the speech. He was unable to trace its source, and its language seemed to him more like that of a report drawn up afterwards by some skilled literary hand. In fact, the speech first appeared in print in the *Cabala*, an anonymous collection of the letters of illustrious persons, the first edition of which was in 1651; and it is part of a letter from Dr Leonel Sharp to the Duke of Buckingham. Sharp was a divine whom we know to have been

---

[1] *Cabala* (1691), p. 343.   [2] xxxiv (1919), 55.

chaplain to the Earl of Essex, to Queen Elizabeth, and to Prince Henry.[1] In 1614-15 he was in disgrace and was imprisoned in the Tower; and this letter, written probably after Buckingham's marriage expedition to Spain in 1623, like others, was meant to ingratiate the writer with the Duke. In it Sharp discusses England's policy towards Spain, and draws upon his memory of events in Elizabeth's reign, giving in that connection an account of the Queen's visit to Tilbury. 'The Queen', he writes, ' ... made an excellent oration to her army, which, the next day after her departure, I was commanded to redeliver to all the army together, to keep a publick Fast ... This I thought would delight your Grace, and no man hath it but my self, and such as I have given it to ... '[2]

I see no serious reason for rejecting the speech. The letter itself is probably genuine, despite the fact that we know only too little about the collection in which it appears; Sharp's statement that he was at Tilbury, waiting upon the Earl of Leicester — presumably as chaplain — may be accepted; and his story of the way in which he came by the speech is circumstantial and natural enough. That James Aske's account of the delivery of the speech, in his *Elizabetha Triumphans*,[3] seems not to square with Sharp's, is no strong argument against the latter's story, which, at any rate, will fit in with Deloney's verse narrative.[4] Then, so far from agreeing with Mr Christy's stylistic argument, I think that some of the phrases have every appearance of being the Queen's, and the whole tone of the speech is surely very much in keeping even with the few Elizabethan quotations that I have had room for in this article. Since the Queen, like Mr Micawber, revelled in her own words, it is very probable, if Sharp's tale be true, that it was she herself who ordered the speech to be re-delivered to the troops, in which event she would certainly not have entrusted

[1] Cf. *Dict. Nat. Biog.*
[2] *Cabala*, pp. 343-4.
[3] Printed in Nichols, *Progresses*, ii, 545 seqq.
[4] *Works*, ed. F. O. Mann, pp. 474 seqq.

her phrases to another's memory; and so I have little doubt that Sharp's version is a copy, at two or three removes, of a speech actually written by Elizabeth herself.

Legend clouds over us as we turn from the incidents of the Queen's life to those of her death, for there is a dramatic sense in popular story which demands of its famous people that they shall die fittingly, so acquitting themselves on their death-beds as to point a moral or adorn a tale. The biographer of Elizabeth may, like Mr Chamberlin, choose as the Queen's last words a highly moral reflection — 'My lord, the crown which I have borne so long has given enough of vanity in my time'; or he may finish his portrait of a frivolous woman with the cry, 'A million of money for a moment of time': only, if he does, he will be the dupe, in the latter instance of someone, I know not whom, and in the former of the egregious Leti. Mr Chamberlin devotes four pages of his book to the sayings of what he calls 'the inevitable hour'. I might dispose of most of them by an individual examination of their sources, but such a method of attack would be involved and wasteful, and it will be more useful and equally effective if I review the various accounts of Elizabeth's death, separating the reliable from the unreliable.

One counsel of safety there is in such a review, and one only — to start from strictly contemporary narratives, that is, from letters written actually during the illness. Much the most informative are the dispatches of the French ambassador, Beaumont,[1] who evidently drew his bulletins from the Court, despite the fact that Cecil and the Council, nourished on an inherited fear of what might befall at the Queen's death, were at first doing their best to prevent news leaking out and alarming the country. It is an ordinary death-bed tale that the dispatches tell, unadorned by terrible visions and with few random flashes of Elizabethan temper. Unable to sleep, parched in throat and body, and plunged in a deep melancholy;

---

[1] Included in Baschet's transcripts at the Public Record Office.

refusing for days to enter what she instinctively felt would be her death-bed, spurning medicine, and having little taste for food, the Queen gradually sank, plagued by the solicitations of doctors and councillors, until she passed into a stupor and the end came. Chamberlain, writing to Carleton on March 30th — the Queen died in the early hours of March 24th — says nothing more; and the moment we venture beyond some such general outline to fill in any details, especially of words which Elizabeth may have spoken, we are in a whirl of uncertainty, for gossip got to work immediately. 'Even here', says Chamberlain, writing six days after her death, 'the papists do tell strange stories as utterly voyde of truth, as of all civill honestie or humanitie.'[1]

One problem with which I must deal, before examining the set narratives of Elizabeth's death, is whether she did or did not name a successor. There is no hint that she did in any letter written during her illness. Beaumont appears to have been in touch with the Earl of Northumberland, and was told by him in all secrecy that the councillors had determined to proclaim James the moment Elizabeth was dead;[2] but as late as the day following her death he states definitely that she had named no successor.[3] Eleven days later his news was different. Nottingham and Cecil had seen him and had told him that a few days before her death Elizabeth had said to them in confidence that she recognized no other successor but James, and did not want her kingdom to fall into the hands of rascals. When they later asked her to confirm this before other councillors, being speechless she made a sign by putting her hand to her head.[4] The story may be true. Cecil certainly did announce that Elizabeth had named James as her successor;[5] and perhaps we should believe him. But one contemporary at least looked a

---

[1] S.P. Dom. Jas. I, i, no. 6.
[2] Beaumont to Villeroy, March 18th/28th.
[3] *Venetian Cal.* vol. x, 1603-7, pp. 15-16.
[4] To Villeroy, April 4th/14th.
[5] Baildon, *Les Reportes del Cases in Camera Stellata*, pp. 164, 227.

little askance at the tale,[1] and it may be that it was an invention given currency after Elizabeth's death to justify the action of the Council. It has found its way into the narratives of her death, sometimes with elaborations.

Of these narratives the most sober and the best known is Sir Robert Carey's.[2] Carey was about the Court during Elizabeth's illness, waiting for the moment when he was to set forth on his famous ride to Edinburgh, harbinger of a flock of time-servers hastening north to worship the newly-risen sun. He saw the Queen twice during her last days, and, apart from his own knowledge, had a sister in waiting on Elizabeth and a brother at Court, from whom to draw further information. His narrative, I have said, is sober. It contains one remark of the Queen's only. Its sobriety makes it an admirable check on other accounts; for considering what his sources of information were, and considering also that he did not write his *Memoirs* until about 1627, by which time the legend of Elizabeth's death was practically complete, his deliberate rejection of the details which we find in other narratives — 'false lies', he termed them — is strong argument against their authenticity.

There are four of these narratives which I must notice. All but one may be dismissed without much discussion, for they were not written by eye-witnesses. The first is an account found in the State Papers[3] — a fact which goes for nothing in the way of reliability — in the Cotton manuscripts,[4] and elsewhere. Written during the year 1603, its distinguishing feature is that it elaborates the story about the naming of a successor. We may certainly reject the additional remarks of the Queen

[1] Ellis, *Original Letters*, 2nd ser. iii, 195.

[2] In his *Memoirs*, best edition, 1808. The narrative is reprinted in Firth, *Stuart Tracts*.

[3] S.P. Dom. Jas. I, lxxxvi, no. 150.

[4] Titus, C. VII, fol. 57, printed in Nichols, *Progresses*, iii, 607-9. There is also a copy in the Petyt MSS. at the Inner Temple, which Isaac Disraeli printed in his *Curiosities of Literature*. As Camden used the Cotton copy, Disraeli's argument is invalid.

which it gives. The second account[1] apparently was written in November 1603 by one formerly in the service of Lord Burghley. It contains a sober enough description of Elizabeth's illness, adding one or two ordinary remarks of hers in which I neither believe nor disbelieve, since persons having 'good means to understand the truth of things', from whom the remarks profess to come, are often licensed deceivers, striving to live up to their reputation, and disarming one's critical faculties. But even this writer quotes from the apocrypha. 'It is credibly reported', he says, 'that not long before her death she had a great apprehension of her own age and declination by seeing her face (then lean and full of wrinkles) truly represented to her in a glass, which she a good while very earnestly beheld: perceiving thereby how often she had been abused by flatterers.' For its point the tale needs the explanation which is found in another narrative,[2] to the effect that for twenty years she had only seen herself in a false mirror, made to deceive her sight. This legend furnished a piquant story to Ben Jonson, who told Drummond that the Queen's ladies 'painted her, and some-tymes would vermilion her nose'.[3] Our third narrator is Camden. It is easy to recognize that in his account of Elizabeth's death, in addition to the tradition of the time, he used the first narrative referred to above and the fourth narrative, which we must next examine; and it is enough to add that the less this writer is regarded as an original authority, and the more as a historian whose sources can and ought to be discovered, the safer a student will be.[4]

With the fourth narrative I come to the real problem of our sources. It is an account, existing in manuscript at Stonyhurst College and endorsed in the hand of Robert Persons — or Parsons — the Jesuit, 'The relation of the lady Southwell ...

[1] B.M. Sloane MS. 718, part only printed in Ellis, op. cit. pp. 189 seqq.
[2] The Southwell narrative, dealt with later.
[3] *Conversations*, ed. R. F. Patterson (1923), p. 30.
[4] Cf. in this connection Camden's account of the trial of Mary Queen of Scots, and my remarks thereon in *Eng. Hist. Rev.* xxxviii, 446.

primo Aprilis, 1607.'[1] Lingard, who was the first of modern historians to use it, did not know that part of it had actually been printed, but in fact Persons first referred to it in a tract of his, *The Judgment of a Catholic English-man*, published in 1608,[2] and when challenged by Bishop Barlow to leave his innuendoes and produce his evidence,[3] printed more than half of the narrative, omitting all names, in his *Discussion of An Answer*, a pamphlet that appeared in 1612.[4] It is the most vivid of all the accounts of Elizabeth's death, revelling in witchcraft and nightmare, decking itself out in sayings of the Queen, and working to a climax of horror, so that the sceptic might be inclined to dismiss it as worthless without more ado. But 'improbable' and 'impossible' are not synonyms, and however sceptical he may be, the historian must attempt to justify his scorn by a process of reasoning.

We may accept Persons' statement that the narrative is the relations of a lady named Southwell. She was Elizabeth, daughter of Sir Robert Southwell, goddaughter to Elizabeth, and granddaughter of Lady Nottingham, a young woman of surpassing beauty, romantic in temperament and career, and, at the time of the Queen's death, one of her maids of honour. In 1605 she set the Court of James in a flutter by eloping to the continent, disguised as a page, with Sir Robert Dudley, who left his wife behind. Abroad the two lived together irregularly until the Pope granted Dudley a dispensation, and they were married. Elizabeth Southwell is said to have eloped on the pretext of religion: at any rate, both she and Dudley became Catholics.[5] Consequently our narrative is that of an eye-witness, written, however, four years after Elizabeth's death by a romantic young woman who had turned Catholic. The first question

---

[1] Printed, apparently in full, by Tierney in his edition of Dod's *Church History*, iii, 70 seqq. Lingard, Miss Strickland, and Beesly print it in part.

[2] pp. 31-2.

[3] *An Answer to A Catholike English-man* (1609), p. 86.

[4] pp. 217-20.

[5] *D.N.B.*, under Dudley, Sir Robert; J. T. Leader, *Life of Sir Robert Dudley* (Florence, 1895).

one naturally asks is whether it was tendentious. The reply
may be found in the words of Persons: 'It will remayne to
posterity', he said, 'as a dreadfull patterne of a miserable end,
after a lyfe of so much joylitie.'[1] Obviously, to him it was a
sermon. But I would not make too much of the point, for if
this was her aim Mistress Southwell did not make the best
of her opportunity. None the less, neither its author nor the
circumstances under which it was written encourage trust in
the narrative.

But we may use stronger arguments in criticizing it. In the
first place, Sir Robert Carey probably had read the account
in Persons' *Discussion*. What Elizabeth Southwell knew — and
more — Carey's sister, Lady Scrope, must have known; and
yet Carey repeats none of the stories. Implicitly they are part of
the 'false lies' which he denounces. Especially is this true of
one story, for it was to Lady Scrope, according to the narrative,
that Elizabeth said, 'she saw one night her own body, exceedingly lean and fearful, in a light of fire'. The argument from
Carey may be strengthened by an argument from other sources.
The Southwell narrative closes with a gruesome tale. Elizabeth,
it relates, gave instructions that her body should not be em-
balmed, but despite her wishes it was opened by her surgeons
at Cecil's secret command. The account continues:

> Now, the queen's body being cered up, was brought
> by water to Whitehall, where, being watched every night
> by six several ladies, myself that night watching as one of
> them, and being all in our places about the corpse, which
> was fast nailed in a board coffin, with leaves of lead covered
> with velvet, her body burst with such a crack, that it
> splitted the wood, lead, and cere-cloth; whereupon, the
> next day she was fain to be newtrimmed up.

The French ambassador,[2] the Venetian ambassador,[3] and

[1] *The Judgment of a Catholic English-man*, p. 32.
[2] Beaumont to the King, March 29th/April 8th.
[3] *Venetian Cal.* x, 2-3.

Chamberlain,[1] all refer in their letters to the body lying at Whitehall, all three state definitely that it was not opened, as was customary, and, needless to add, they do not mention the gruesome story of it bursting. If in consequence it be reasonably certain that part of the Southwell narrative is false, then my point is made, for it becomes impossible to distinguish between the false and the true in the greater part of the account except by the test of probability, and it is just that test which it will not stand. And so I would reject all the set narratives of Elizabeth's death except Carey's, either as adding nothing new of which we can be certain or as most likely false, and with them reject most of the sayings in Mr Chamberlin's four pages.

Here my essay must end. It has touched only the fringe of the subject. There is the whole range of ambassadors' dispatches, there are Foxe and Naunton and a traveller's tale in Hentzner, none of which I have criticized. And beyond contemporary authorities lies a less reputable but extensive collection of sayings which has grown continuously, aided by the prolific Leti and by wits of all centuries and many localities.[2] To take the formidable weapon of historical criticism to some of these might seem like taking a sledge-hammer to a pea-nut; whilst so far as the more securely-based stories that I have overlooked are concerned, they may be criticized along the lines that I have already indicated. Neither space nor the purpose of this essay allows of it being exhaustive.

[1] S.P. Dom. Jas. I, i, no. 6.
[2] Cf. *Notes and Queries*, 5th ser. iv, 139.

ENGLAND'S ELIZABETH[1]

T|HIS is November 17th, 1958. Four hundred years ago today, Queen Elizabeth 'of glorious memory' — Good Queen Bess, as she was affectionately known to generations of Englishmen — ascended the throne of England. And here are we — you of the New World, where the name of Virginia establishes your interest in the occasion, and I from the Old World, unable to resist the call to the ghost to go west — here are we met to commemorate the day. In the words of the simple ballad writer, composed in 1600:

> Now let us pray
> and keep holy-daye
> The seaventeenth day of November;
> For joy of her Grace
> in every place,
> Let us great prayses render.

But why should we? you may ask. It is my business to supply the answer.

First of all, we are associating ourselves with an old English tradition that lasted for two centuries. It was about ten years after Elizabeth's accession that villagers and townsmen in England took to ringing their church bells and rejoicing on November 17th. The custom began spontaneously. So far as I know, there were no precedents, though in Catholic England there had been saints' days galore. After a few years, the Anglican Church adopted this popular innovation, making a Protestant holyday of November 17th; and as the cult of the

[1] A lecture delivered at the Folger Shakespeare Library, Washington, on November 17th, 1958, the fourth centenary of the accession of Queen Elizabeth I; published by the Folger Library 1958.

199

Queen intensified, the day was celebrated throughout the land in a pleasing variety of ways, ranging from elaborate tilts at Westminster, where the royal Court assembled, to the simple service, bell-ringing, and bonfires of the rural village.

Like its origins, the history of the day is unique. The death of the Queen naturally brought the November holiday to an end and her successor, James I, cashed in on the idea by transferring the celebration to his Accession Day in March. But soon the people of England, growing disgusted with the Scots, losing confidence in the government, and renewing their old fear of Catholicism, began to feel that England's golden age was in the past, and consequently revived their celebration of November 17th with the ringing of bells and public joy and sermons in commemoration of Queen Elizabeth's Day. The dynamic of a people — which is to exult in the present — turned to the nostalgia of memory and regret; witness the title of a tract published in 1642 and devoted to praise of Elizabeth's virtue and her government — *The humble petition of the wretched, and most contemptible, the poor Commons of England, to the blessed Elizabeth of famous memory.*

In the second half of the seventeenth century, when the later Stuart sovereigns in their folly flouted the prejudices of the nation and brought the Protestant establishment into apparent danger, a new intensity was imparted to the celebration of Queen Elizabeth's Accession Day — the Birthday of the Gospel, as it was often called. With the aid of Opposition politicians, the annual festival in London was turned into an occasion for fantastic anti-Papist processions, ending in the burning of effigies on a huge bonfire. Guy Fawkes Day — that other Protestant festival, held on November 5th, the anniversary of the Gunpowder Plot, and still celebrated by English children with fireworks and 'guys' — was completely outclassed by the rejoicings and ceremonial of Queen Elizabeth's Day. 'The feast the factious rabble keep', Dryden termed it. London maintained its day of bigotry into the eighteenth century, while in the countryside the more restrained and appropriate practice of bell-ringing continued on this day, certainly to the end of the third decade of that century. Gradually, however, the atmosphere changed and the fame of Queen Bess dwindled, leaving Guy Fawkes in command of November. By the early nineteenth century, the vestigial remains were a day's holiday at two of London's ancient schools and also — oddly enough — at the national Exchequer.

We are no longer stirred by the crude passions that roused the London mob in the seventeenth and eighteenth centuries. But the instinct of a people which made a Thanksgiving Day of November 17th: that surely interests us. Posterity has never wavered in regarding the Elizabethan period as one of the golden times of history. How indeed could it, when the age gave birth to such immortal names and achievements as those of Sidney, Spenser, Bacon, and Shakespeare; Hawkins, Drake, and Raleigh? What a people's instinct did was to associate this astounding flowering of an age with a single event — the accession of Elizabeth Tudor to the throne of England.

The people were right. Consider the alternative: imagine that Queen Mary Tudor, Elizabeth's sister, had lived the normal span of life and produced an heir to the throne. Tied to Spain and Catholicism, England's story — Europe's and America's as well — would have been very different. The enterprising minds and personalities of high Elizabethan days were associated with the fresh ideology of that age — Protestantism. In the circumstances we have envisaged, it seems certain that the energies of such men would have found an outlet and been absorbed in civil dissension. As it was, Mary's brief reign hovered on the brink of civil war, and the gloom cast on the nation by subordination to a foreign king, along with the priestly cruelty of burning heretics at the stake — it would have been less offensive to call heresy treason and use the gallows — all this was tolerable only because Mary was childless and ailing, and a bright future seemed at hand in the person of Elizabeth. Otherwise England, not France, would probably have inaugurated the Religious Wars of the second half of the century, and under a Catholic government they would have been as prolonged as the French Religious Wars. How could the literary achievements of the period have come out of such a setting? How could its maritime saga have been enacted with the King of Spain still King of England? How could Virginia and New England have been what they were and are without the Elizabethan background? What would have been the story of Francis Drake or Walter Raleigh? Would Shakespeare have written his plays?

Let us broaden our speculation to include the continent of Europe. Had premature death and childlessness not brought the rule of Philip and Mary to so abrupt an end, the Council of Trent would still have met, the Catholic Church would still have shed its uncertainties, and the Counter-Reformation would still have been launched on the strong basis of renewed confidence. But official England — Scotland, too, for the Reformation could not have prevailed there without Elizabeth's assistance — would have been on the Catholic side, instead of opposed to it. What difference that would have made, it is perhaps hard to say; but the difference would certainly have been considerable. As this profound struggle between the rival ideologies of those days developed, the leaders of the Counter-Reformation came to think of Queen Elizabeth as their prime enemy, while to Protestants throughout Europe she was their principal protector. She intervened diplomatically, financially, and militarily in support of the Protestant cause in France and the Netherlands, as well as in Scotland. One may doubt whether the revolt of the Netherlands could have prospered without her, or the Huguenots in France have continued their struggle to win in the end the Edict of Nantes. And if she had not so engaged the attention and resources of the Counter-Reformation, could Geneva have cocked a snook with such effrontery and undermined the French State with its genius for subversive practices? There is a moral as well as a material side to Elizabeth's influence. Her fame and fortune were in themselves of incalculable survival value for the cause of Protestantism in Europe.

We should not be misled by the peaceful and uneventful accession of Queen Elizabeth into thinking of November 17th, 1558 as an ordinary transfer of the throne from one dead monarch to her natural successor. The exiles returning to England after their flight abroad from the Catholic regime of Mary Tudor, the citizens of London in their welcome to the new Queen, and the majority in the House of Commons when the first Parliament of the reign assembled — all these, and many more, saw the occasion as the overthrow of one ideology and the victory of its rival: we might almost say, a revolutionary *coup d'état*. And, in fact, there is evidence to suggest that Elizabeth was organized to fight for her throne, if the need had arisen.

To ardent Protestants, the miraculous preservation of their Queen from all the perils of her sister's reign was the admirable work of God's own hand. In an oration, written for the accession, John Hales imagined God saying to Englishmen: 'Ye see, my people, what I have done for you ... I have not only discovered mine, yours, and my land of England's enemies ... but I have also taken away their head and captain, and destroyed a great number of them, that ye should not be troubled with them; and some of them I have left, that ye may make them spectacles and examples, to the terror and fear of their posterity.' Addressing Elizabeth, Hales told her that if she fulfilled her destiny, carrying out the revolution fully and quickly, then all men would confess that she was 'of God specially sent and ordained. And as the Queen of Sheba came from afar off to see the glory of King Solomon — a woman to a man — even so shall the princes of our time come — men to a woman — and kings marvel at the virtue of Queen Elizabeth.'

Here, in this elation of spirit after a depressing reign, lay the potential dynamic of the new age. I have said 'potential'. If it were to be a case of replacing one persecuting ideology by the fanatical impulses of another — if, in the words of John Hales, the Elizabethan government were to make of Catholics 'spectacles and examples to the terror and fear of their posterity' — what chance would there be of national unity? The rule of the saints is not conducive to common happiness. And yet from these godly men — supremely from them — could come a new inspiration. To harness this to the broader emotion of patriotism; to nurse the ardour of men like Hales and yet restrain their harmful fanaticism; to cultivate the Puritan sense of a divine purpose guarding and promoting the welfare of England, as God in the Old Testament had watched over Israel — to do this and at the same time qualify that exclusive spirit by tolerance, here was the problem of statecraft.

It called for exceptional ability and a genius for leadership; and since that leadership, in a period of personal monarchy, had to come from the sovereign, and the sovereign was a woman, ruling men who believed the regiment of women to be monstrous, it also called for extraordinary will-power. Happy fortune too was needed: a combination and succession of accidents, not least of which was the long life of the Queen. Elizabeth's reign might be interpreted as a gamble, a gamble of hers with time. She preferred to run the gravest risks rather than act against her deeper promptings. 'Safety first' was not her motto. Her ministers — all of them, including the ablest and most trusted — wrung their hands in despair over her. 'To behold miseries coming and to be denied remedies!' moaned Lord Burghley. 'Our remedy', wrote Sir Francis Walsingham, 'must be prayer, for other help I see none'. 'If we prosper', echoed another Councillor, 'it must be, as our custom is, by miracle.' In such a situation, what wonder, when peril after peril was successfully avoided and the reign progressed with resounding fortune, if that biblically minded generation, which in 1558 regarded Elizabeth as the ward of Providence, perceived God's eternal vigilance in the preservation of his servant Elizabeth and his chosen Englishmen? Her enemies were just as impressed; but they thought her the daughter of the Devil. The sober fact is that if she had died twenty years sooner she would probably have left a name of infamy in history; and she knew it. Our generation, which watched Sir Winston Churchill's leadership of England during the late war and has read Lord Alanbrooke's diary, can appreciate all this.

The harnessing of the revolutionary spirit began almost at once with the religious settlement made at Elizabeth's first Parliament. It was a Protestant settlement, but with comeliness and tradition preserved and fanaticism excluded. We know too little about its story, but all that little shows that it was the personal policy of the young Queen, stubbornly forced through a reluctant, radical House of Commons. The Anglican Church, now four hundred years old and venerable, was uniquely the creation of this woman. Though not so conservative as she wished, it has certainly proved, what she wanted it to be, amazingly comprehensive. At all times it has harboured high, low, and also moderate churchmen. It might be regarded as the symbol of her rule. The Deborah of the revolutionaries certainly failed them. Rather than be a party leader, she chose to lead the nation. In so doing she created a left wing of discontent.

The paradox of the Elizabethan age is that its flavour and dynamic came from this left or Puritan wing, and came through a romantic attachment between them and their Queen. It was an attachment for which I think the closest parallel in our history is that between Englishmen and Winston Churchill in our own time.

What is the explanation? As in the case of Winston Churchill, undoubtedly the supreme art and deliberate policy of the Queen. But there were more specific reasons — reasons of an accidental character. The first was the Queen's failure to marry, the consequent lack of an heir, and the uncertainty about the succession to the throne. If no religious problem had existed, Mary Queen of Scots would have been the obvious heir apparent; but she was a Catholic, the spearhead of the opposing ideology, and English Protestants would on no account tolerate the prospect of her succession. The future of Protestantism therefore continued as it had during Mary Tudor's reign, linked indissolubly with the life of Elizabeth. Whatever her shortcomings, she remained the Deborah of the saints: they had no other choice. If she had married and borne a child, the radicals would almost certainly have transferred their hopes to the heir, and the romance would have turned sour. Everyone knows that Elizabeth was the Virgin Queen; it is not often realized how vital to her success that role was.

The second reason for the romantic attachment of Queen and people was the mounting concentration of the Catholic Counter-Reformation against Elizabeth and her England — the cold war of the two rival ideologies of that age, with its hot spots. The crucial event was the flight of Mary Queen of Scots to England in 1568, after her lurid tale of misadventure in her own country. Thenceforward, until her execution in 1587 put an end to this frightful danger, the alternative, Catholic Deborah was in England, a focus — though captive — for every plot and scheme of the counter-revolution. Granted a similar revolutionary climate and a similar life-or-death struggle, who could be confident that, even in our modern civilized days, a bloody end would not be put to such an intolerable situation in less than twenty hazardous years? Elizabeth's statesmen, Parliament, and people exerted their utmost pressure to exact that solution, and exact it rapidly, from their Queen. Her obstinate refusal was an even more personal policy than her religious settlement. She pursued the *via media* in politics as well as religion, gambling with her own life and the country's apparent welfare for the sake of rooted principles and instincts. We may doubt whether any masculine ruler would have shown such compunction.

Even before the arrival of Mary Queen of Scots in England, an attack of smallpox, from which it was feared that Elizabeth would not recover, had reminded English Protestants of the slender thread upon which their world depended. As the cold war developed and Catholic missionaries penetrated into England, undermining the ideology of the nation and recruiting what their militant leaders abroad regarded as a potential fifth column to be called into action on the day the cold war became a hot one, and as plot succeeded plot, with the purpose of killing the Queen and replacing her by Mary Queen of Scots, the reaction of Protestant England, quite understandably, was passionate in the extreme.

Increasing danger imparted a new and peculiar intensity to the bond of affection between Elizabeth and her people. She herself cultivated the relationship with consummate art, playing her part, on set occasions, with the skill of a born actress. She was as sensitive to public relations as any modern publicity agent. She wrote her own speeches for Parliament, fining and refining her phrases like the most finicky stylist. When, for example, at the final crisis over Mary Queen of Scots, two of these speeches were needed for propaganda purposes at home and abroad, she secretly worked over the printer's text herself rather than permit a mere report to be printed. Her courtly progresses through the countryside — her summer holidays — were episodes in publicity, marked by most elaborate and artificial entertainments and relieved by innumerable touches of the unconventional. 'Stay thy cart, good fellow! stay thy cart, that I may speak to the Queen', cried a worthy lawyer to the royal coachman, holding up the long, courtly train on progress in Huntingdonshire. 'Whereat', we are told, 'her Majesty laughed as she had been tickled', and gave the good man 'great thanks and her hand to kiss'. She wooed her Londoners unceasingly, on set occasions and as numberless minor opportunities presented themselves.

> The people flocked there amain,
> The multitude was great to see;
> Their joyful harts were glad, and fain
> To view her princely majesty,

> Who at the length came riding by,
> Within her chariot openly;
> Even with a noble princely train
> Of lords and ladies of great fame.
> Her Majesty was glad to see
> Her subjects in so good a case,
> Which then fell humbly on their knee,
> Desiring God to save her grace.
> And like a noble prince that day
> For them in like sorte did she pray;
> And curteously she answered still,
> I thank you all for your good will.

Her court was a community in itself, thronged with visitors, especially on Sundays, come to see the Queen, perhaps to catch her eye and be spoken to.

For their part, the people admired her qualities of mind and heart — her 'magnanimity', as they often termed it, using that word in its etymological sense, which, alas, it has now lost.

> The peerles pearle of princes all,
> So ful of pitty, peace, and love,
> Whose mercy is not proved small,
> When foule offendors doo her moove,
> A phenix of moste noble minde,
> Unto her subjects good and kinde;
> A moste renowned virgin queen,
> Whose like on earth was never seen.

Patriots felt profound content in the thought that their country was personified in her, much as Englishmen, in our time, felt about Winston Churchill. As their mutual perils were overcome and their enemies confounded, the conviction deepened that God had indeed chosen her as His handmaiden and her people as His people. In the Parliament of 1587, Job Throckmorton —

who may have been that pamphleteering genius, Martin Marprelate — told the story of a Frenchman, who, hearing of a vital English success, rapped out an oath and said, 'I think God be sworn English: there is nothing will prosper against the Queen of England.' 'With what affection that wretched man spake it', commented Throckmorton, 'I know not. But sure, we that have lived in the eyes of all men, so choked, as it were, with blessings of God beyond desert, we that have lived to see her Majesty's life, so dear unto us, pulled out ... even out of the lion's jaws in despite of Hell and Satan, may truly — not in any pride of heart, but in humbleness of soul to our comforts — confess that indeed the Lord hath vowed himself to be English.' All such emotions led Englishmen to worship Elizabeth this side of idolatry and to make of her a cult, which, with its feminine ingredient, was converted into a patriotic romance.

The cult of the Queen was expressed in the literature of the age, in courtly pageantry, and by artists in her portraits. Much, of course, was highly artificial, though that does not mean that it was necessarily false, and the ballads were usually simple enough. The parliamentary debates of the high Elizabethan period — from the arrival of Mary Queen of Scots to the post-Armada years — throb with the pride of Englishmen in their sovereign. Even the most obstreperous Puritans — indeed, they above all — rejoiced in her. 'It makes my heart leap for joy to think we have such a jewel,' declared one of them in the House of Commons. 'It makes all my joints to tremble for fear when I consider the loss of such a jewel.' Job Throckmorton pictured, in apocalyptic mood, England's supreme bliss: that, if it so pleased God, the last day of Queen Elizabeth's life might be the last day of this earth, and 'that when she fleeteth hence ... we may then behold ... Jesus sitting in his throne of judgment, to our endless and everlasting comfort'.

In 1585, when England was horror-stricken by the assassination of William the Silent and its own Catholic plots, a Sussex Puritan lawyer, who had sat in Parliament, recorded similar sentiments in a draft will, written on the flyleaf of the family's Wycliffe Bible:

> I heartily pray the Almighty God to send a long, prosperous and happy life and reign to our good Queen Elizabeth, and to send us all grace that we may all live in his fear as good and dutiful subjects to our said gracious Sovereign Lady and Queen, and all die before the sorrowful days of England shall come, if God should take her from us before the end of the world. And that if for our sins he shorten her days, as he did the days of good King Edward [VI], that yet he will grant me the grace to die at her feet before her, and that at the end of all things, which is at hand, we may joyfully rise again to life everlasting, with perpetual joy and felicity. Amen. Amen.

Thus, there was this cult of the Queen as the symbol of patriotism and the Protestant ideology. The other aspect of England's reaction to its perils was the desire to promote political security by penal laws, increasingly drastic as the danger became more acute. The State in those days was inevitably ideological. How far it went along the totalitarian road depended on policy. Quite early, Elizabeth's Councillors and Parliament wanted to enforce attendance at Communion in church by statute, in order, as one Puritan Member said, that 'the very secrets of the heart in God's cause ... must come to a reckoning, and the good seed [be] so sifted from the cockle that the one may be known from the other'. The Queen vetoed that Bill, and when in a later Parliament an attempt was made to revive the measure, she interfered to stay its course. Though requiring outward conformity to the law, she abhorred all inquisitional practices and would open no windows into men's souls.

By 1580 the cold war was hotting up, and the infiltration of Catholic missionaries was reinforced by the beginning of Jesuit missions. The menace had to be dealt with, and when Parliament met, statesmen and both Houses drafted what they regarded as the necessary legislation. They wanted to stop the missionaries by making their work treasonable and their converts traitors, to prohibit saying or attending Mass under the severest penalties, and to bar Catholics from entry into the professions. With these and other proposals they would have imposed (or tried to impose) orthodoxy in their ideological State as ruthlessly as the totalitarian regimes of our contemporary world. The Queen intervened to prohibit many of their proposals, scale down the penalties of others radically, and insert a secular instead of a doctrinaire principle into the Act.

As the drama unfolded, the pattern remained the same. In 1584, for example, after the assassination of William the Silent, the people of England, knowing that papal approval had been given for the murder of Elizabeth, joined in a Bond of Association, devised by Privy Councillors, the avowed intention of which was to use lynch law against the Catholics' prospective Queen, Mary of Scots, in retaliation for plots to kill their own Queen. In the following Parliament, when it was planned to give statutory sanction to this lawless agreement, Elizabeth interfered to amend both statute and Bond of Association in the interests of decency.

Liberal-minded historians of the past — not so imaginative as we necessarily are about the passions aroused by a prolonged ideological struggle — have deplored the anti-Catholic penal legislation of the Elizabethan period. By enlightened nineteenth-century standards it was indeed shocking, though the critics seldom realized that the crucial question for those days was how the law was administered. All the same, this legislation was mild — astonishingly mild — compared with the penalties that Privy Councillors, Lords and Commons did their utmost to secure. Their obstacle was always the Queen.

It was the same at the other extreme. In the passionate

atmosphere of the time, doctrinaires of the left — the Puritans — acquired an authority and following out of proportion to their number or their gospel. In the name of truth and patriotism they wanted to reform the Anglican Church root and branch to obtain what had been denied them in the Settlement of 1559, and even to go the whole hog in Protestant ideology. It is the perennial story of revolutions, except in the sequel. In the name of patriotism, if not of truth, they generally found a majority of fellow travellers in the House of Commons ready to back them, and substantial sympathy for many items of their programme in the House of Lords and among Privy Councillors. After all, what surer defence was there against the enemy than a nation legislated into Protestant godliness? The saints seemed to have the right answer to the country's grave political problem.

Elizabeth would not budge an inch. Always at hand, always vigilant, she argued, threatened, sent prohibitory messages, imprisoned offenders in the Tower, and wielded her legislative veto. Then, when the doctrinaires, having secretly built up a subversive Presbyterian movement within the Church itself, tried to legislate the revolution into existence, she disciplined them with rigour and put up her best orators in the House of Commons to expose their conspiracy. It was deliberate, consistent and personal action, and undoubtedly saved the Church of England.

What does all this amount to? Surely that in a period of passion Elizabeth prevented the ardour of fanatics, the vengeful indignation of patriots, and the panic fear of many from running away with policy. She resisted even the ruthless logic of her statesmen. Lord Burghley was probably the most moderate of her Councillors, as he was the most responsible and the one she trusted most. Drawing up the pros and cons of problems, as was his habit, he found himself supporting many of those parliamentary measures that the Queen vetoed or amended. 'The Queen's Majesty', he told Walsingham in 1571, 'hath been always a merciful lady, and by mercy she hath taken more harm than by justice, and yet she thinks that she is more beloved in doing herself harm. God save her to his honour long among us.' Doubtless there were those near Elizabeth who whispered advice against the majority opinion of Council and Parliament; but we know enough about some of the most striking instances to be sure that the overwhelming weight of authority was against her. In this sense she may often be said to have gambled with the fate of the kingdom. It is worth asking how this could be.

In the first place, the constitution of the country was personal monarchy. The sovereign received counsel or advice, but all decisions were hers. One of the remarkable features of Elizabeth's rule is the extent to which she kept both major and minor decisions in her own hands. Again, she chose her own Councillors. Their superlative quality is equally remarkable. Even her 'favourites' were men of parts and were made to work hard. Legend and history have been wrong about one of these favourites, Sir Christopher Hatton, and I think we are due for a reassessment of another, the famous Earl of Leicester. She was an almost infallible judge of men, and if with her temperament and perversity she gave her servants many headaches, she was loyal to them and won their genuine devotion. 'She is our God in earth', wrote Lord North in 1575. 'If there be perfection in flesh and blood, undoubtedly it is in her Majesty. For she is slow to revenge and ready to forgive. And yet ... she is right King Henry, her father. For if any strive with her, all the princes of Europe cannot make her yield. Again, whoso humbly and lovingly submitteth himself to her desire, she doth and will so graciously receive and recompense him, as every [person] that knoweth her doth honour and entirely love her.' Elizabeth did not discard her statesmen, much less ruin or execute them, as her father did. In this she set a new, a civilized example to princes.

It is an interesting reflection that masters who have the faculty of choosing servants of outstanding ability usually remain none the less masters. To diagnose why this was the case with Elizabeth is easy. A person of exceptional intelligence and studious, inquisitive temperament, she was educated in the rigorous manner of the Renaissance by the finest scholars of the time. She was a cultured woman, the intellectual peer or superior of her advisers, and had the requisite linguistic and historical knowledge to keep even foreign policy in her hands. Moreover, in her youth she had passed through a school of experience where everything — even her life — depended on her wit and intelligence. Her political instinct was already mature when she came to the throne at the age of twenty-five, and over the years, judging solely by results, she made so few blunders that time could only confirm and justify her trust in it. Her greatest statesman, Lord Burghley, who was inclined at first to share contemporary prejudice against a woman ruler, was brought at length to acknowledge her surpassing wisdom. The divergences of policy between him and his mistress seem often to have been divergences between logic and instinct. Perhaps her greater trust in instinct was a feminine trait, though experience, as so often can be said of instinct, was a predominant ingredient. She worked hard and conscientiously at her job and lived for it, with mind and emotion. She had every reason for self-confidence except that of sex, and her masterful nature and birth compensated here. Tradition has portrayed her as unprincipled. It is a superficial judgment, bred of ignorance. In fact, no sovereign or statesman has clung more obstinately and daringly to certain fundamental principles, though in small things few women have tantalized men more frequently by their mutability.

It was principle, deep-rooted in instinct, that led Elizabeth to restrain the passion of an angry nation against Catholics and stand adamant against the dreams of doctrinaires. For this, surely all who in any degree owe something to English civilization still remain indebted to her. Our tradition is one of tolerance. In England the fanatic has never got his way. We have had a Civil War: it did not go to the extremes normally experienced in such strife. We have had our revolutions: that in 1688 is always known as 'Glorious', it was so bloodless and respectable; and the one we are going through now is so good-tempered that only when we stop to think do we know that we are in it. For explanation, we need not, like our Elizabethans, invoke God's Englishman. I suppose we might agree that the Bible and the English Common Law largely deserve the credit. But with the Bible, it is the New and not the Old Testament. Elizabethan Parliaments, in their bloody moods against Catholics and Mary Queen of Scots, quoted the Old, not the New, Testament and got the bishops and ecclesiastical lawyers to fortify their petitions to the Queen with precedents and vengeful injunctions from it. As for the Common Law — which, like the Bible, is an American as well as a British heritage — two of its great principles are the rule of law and the rights of individuals. 'The King is under the law', said the medieval Bracton; and his successors have echoed him. The Bond of Association of 1584 against Mary Queen of Scots was the negation of law, and if the legal system, by this and other devices, had been prostituted to the use of passion, what a precedent would have been set! In its nature, passion does not endure; but laws and the way political institutions are used tend to have a prolonged existence and far-reaching effects. It is alarmingly easy to inject poison into the body politic. Recovery may be slow, and no one can foretell when it will be complete.

'Nothing in the world', complained the Earl of Leicester to Sir Francis Walsingham in 1582, 'grieveth me more than to see that her Majesty believes this increase of Papists in her realm can be no danger to her. The Lord of his mercy open her eyes.' That the Queen, at this critical time in our history, remained sensitive to civilized feelings and resisted her advisers is surely cause for us to salute her memory on this, her day. Politically it was folly. She was much too intelligent not to grasp the force of the advice she was given and success alone could justify the responsibility she assumed. By the mercy of God and the devotion of her people success was granted her.

The devotion of her people! Inevitably I return to that theme. It was as Gloriana, Belphoebe, and other conceits of the Elizabethan imagination; it was as an orator who in her great Armada speech spoke these words, 'I know I have the body of a weak and feeble woman, but I have the heart and stomach of a King, and of a King of England too'; who, later, in her Golden Speech told her Commons, 'Though God hath raised me high, yet this I count the glory of my crown, that I have reigned with your loves'; it was also as one whose impromptu dressing-down of an insolent Polish ambassador, spoken in Latin, thrilled that generation and remained a memory in early Stuart Parliaments; and finally it was as one who, in her last State address to the Realm, rendering a final account of her stewardship, could phrase her peroration in words magical and moving in their simplicity, 'This testimony I would have you carry hence for the world to know: that your Sovereign is more careful of your conservation than of herself, and will daily crave of God that they that wish you best may never wish in vain' — it was as such a person, a great woman in a great office, with an unsurpassed gift for romantic, intrepid leadership, that she won the adoration of her subjects and conjured from individuals and the nation as a whole their utmost genius. She was, wrote Francis Osborne some fifty years later, 'the choicest artist in kingcraft that ever handled the sceptre in this northern climate'.

Let two of the supreme minds of all time, both Elizabethan, both in reflection after the Queen's death, when sycophancy cannot be thought to have smirched their praise; let these two — William Shakespeare and Francis Bacon — speak her panegyric.

Shakespeare's appreciation comes in the form of a prophecy by Archbishop Cranmer at Elizabeth's christening:

Let me speak, sir,
For heaven now bids me; and the words I utter

Let none think flattery, for they'll find em truth.
                    ... She shall be —
But few now living can behold that goodness —
A pattern to all princes living with her,
And all that shall succeed her: Saba was never
More covetous of wisdom and fair virtue
Than this pure soul shall be: all princely graces,
That mould up such a mighty piece as this is,
With all the virtues that attend the good,
Shall still be doubled on her; truth shall nurse her;
Holy and heavenly thoughts still counsel her;
She shall be lov'd and fear'd; her own shall bless her;
Her foes shake like a field of beaten corn,
And hang their heads with sorrow; good grows with her.
In her days every man shall eat in safety
Under his own vine what he plants; and sing
The merry songs of peace to all his neighbours.
God shall be truly known; and those about her
From her shall read the perfect ways of honour,
And by those claim their greatness, not by blood.

Here is Francis Bacon's encomium:

Elizabeth, both in her nature and her fortune, was a wonderful person among women, a memorable person among princes ... The government of a woman has been a rare thing at all times; felicity in such government a rarer thing still; felicity and long continuance together the rarest thing of all ... A womanish people might well enough be governed by a woman; but that in England, a nation particularly fierce and warlike, all things could be swayed and controlled at the beck of a woman, is a matter for the highest admiration ... There are some times so barbarous and ignorant that it is as easy a matter to govern men as to drive a flock of sheep. But the lot of this Queen fell upon times highly instructed and cultivated, in which it is not possible to be eminent and excellent without the greatest gifts of mind and a singular composition of virtue ... To crown all, as she was most fortunate in all that belonged to herself, so was she in the virtue of her ministers. For she had such men about her as perhaps till that day this island did not produce. But God, when he favours kings, raises also and accomplishes the spirits of their servants ... As for her memory, it is so strong and fresh, both in the mouths and minds of men, that now death has extinguished envy and lighted up fame, the felicity of her memory contends in a manner with the felicity of her life ... The only true commender of this lady is Time, which, so long a course as it has run, has produced nothing in this sex like her, for the administration of civil affairs.

'The only true commender of this lady is Time'. And Time — to adapt to this occasion of ours a remark made by Elizabeth during her Coronation procession — 'Time hath brought us hither.'

THE DIPLOMATIC ENVOY[1]

AMBASSADORS became a necessity among men when Pandora's box was opened and the evils escaped into the world. So say sixteenth-century authors of manuals for ambassadors, claiming an antiquity for the art of diplomacy as remote as society itself and the distinction of *meum* and *tuum*. They might have added that it was the reopening of Pandora's box, when princes were consolidating the nation-state, that made resident ambassadors a necessity in Europe and gave the art its modern significance.

The nursery of European diplomacy was Italy. Not only did the Papacy develop a ceremonial attaching to the dispatch and reception of envoys so elaborate as to become an intolerable nuisance to officials in Rome, but among secular states Venice won a prestige for its service by careful regulation and sustained tradition that was unique. By common consent it had no need of the manuals that the development of diplomacy inspired: it was itself the mirror for ambassadors. The orders governing the conduct of Venetian envoys date back to the thirteenth century and were revised and expanded from time to time. But until the middle of the fifteenth century the embassies to which they referred, as the embassies of other secular states, were what later would have been called missions or special embassies. It was in 1479 that Venice sent an ambassador to reside at the court of France. At the Duke of Burgundy's court she had a resident ambassador rather earlier, but extended the practice to England only in 1496. Princes followed the example — slowly, however, and with suspicion. For long an ambassador's

[1] A lecture, one of a course on historical sources to students in the Honours School of History, delivered in the University of London (at King's College), on May 14th, 1928; published in *History* (Oct. 1928), vol. xiii, no. 51, pp. 204-18.

principal business was to supply his government with information, and the contemporaries of Philippe de Commynes were prone to think that ambassador might be more simply spelt spy. This coming and going of embassies, Commynes remarked,[1] is by no means safe:

> It is unavoidable, but, if my advice be sought, here are the precautions that I would take. If they come from true friends of whom there can be no suspicion, treat them with good cheer and grant them frequent audience, but dismiss them soon, for friendship among princes does not endure for ever. If from hostile courts, send honourably to meet them, lodge them well, set safe and wise men about them to watch who visits them and keep malcontents away, give them audience at once and be rid of them. Even in time of war one must receive envoys, but see that a keen eye is kept on them, and for every one sent to you, do you in return send two, and take every opportunity of sending, for you can have no better spies, and it will be hard to keep a strict watch over two or three.

This represents an attitude of mind that hindered the development of permanent diplomatic relations; but if Ferdinand of Aragon and Henry VII of England shared Commynes' distrust, the intricate diplomacy of the new century and the interminable disputes of commerce drove their successors to follow where Venice had led.

The establishment of resident ambassadors at the various European courts brought into existence a class of documents of bulk, interest and importance such as to vie with that other great class of documents created by the new monarchy, the domestic state paper. My purpose here is to give you some idea of the content and worth of these documents, and perhaps you will forgive me if I do not pretend to knowledge of them in more than a very limited period of history — the Elizabethan.

[1] *Mémoires*, III, viii.

Their bulk may be indicated by the fact that though Elizabeth had fewer resident ambassadors abroad than France, Spain and several less important states — this because of her religion — yet the foreign state papers of the reign fill some 300 volumes at the Public Record Office, and much besides exists in the way of semi-official correspondence between ambassadors and leading statesmen. We must recollect that similar great collections once existed in the more important states of Europe, and smaller ones in the archives of minor states; and though acts of God and of man have made sad havoc of documents, the volume of material still in existence is enough to startle the most intrepid of researchers. Glance at the footnotes to Lucien Romier's two large volumes on *Les origines politiques des guerres de religion* and you will obtain some notion of the wealth of diplomatic correspondence in Italian archives bearing on a very short period of French history.

Bulk we may accept; but what of the information these documents contain? It is still the business of an ambassador to keep his government informed of events and opinion in the country where he serves, and a Walter Page, in his admirable comments on English society, may emulate the great Venetian ambassadors of the sixteenth century. This duty has, however, lost its ancient importance, for nowadays the various movements of national thought find their expression in print and can generally be interpreted by foreign governments without an ambassador's help. The raison d'être of an ambassador today is the preservation of peace, not the supplying of news; and it is in the reversal of the order of these duties that he is chiefly distinguished from his sixteenth-century predecessors. The dispatches of ambassadors in those days were virtually the sole regular source of foreign news that had much value, and since the diplomacy of Elizabeth and her fellow-sovereigns had to be framed upon this news, the success or failure of their representatives depended upon the constancy and accuracy of their reports. What little leisure a zealous ambassador had may be judged from the fact that one, a Venetian, who was resident at Rome, wrote 394 dispatches in 365 days! All were not as model as he. But in addition to writing his official dispatches, it was often essential for an ambassador to keep up a regular correspondence with one or more of the influential councillors at home. For example, our ambassadors addressed an occasional letter to the Queen herself, and frequent ones to the secretary charged with foreign affairs — for a long time, Walsingham. This was his official correspondence. Burghley, however, was a power at Court and needed information, not merely to frame his policy but to maintain his dominance in the Council, which was founded on his knowledge of affairs. An ambassador dare not ignore his wishes, and when that ambassador was Sir Edward Stafford, who belonged to Burghley's party at Court and was disliked by Walsingham, the correspondence with Burghley became almost as voluminous as the official dispatches to Walsingham, and certainly more intimate.

In his role of foreign correspondent to his sovereign an ambassador had to see to the organizing of his news service. Hotman, in his sixteenth-century manual *The Ambassador*,[1] advises him to set about this at once on his arrival at the foreign court. He ought to see that he is kept posted with the news from other countries; but this was of negligible importance beside the necessity of penetrating by every means in his power into the secrets of the country where he was serving. He must intrude his agents wherever information was to be had. He must entertain at table, which, says Hotman, obligeth many people, and especially those who to have a free recourse thereunto, or to draw from the ambassador some dozen of crowns, smell out all the news and report them unto him. He must suborn both high and low: money maketh the closest cabinets of princes to fly open. In fine, he must establish a secret service of his own.

Let me give one or two illustrations. De Spes, the Spanish ambassador in England, writes in 1570 of a friend, whom he

[1] English translation, London, 1603.

has always found to be true, who has undertaken to make for him a note of all that passes in the Council, keeping himself as free as possible from other things in order the better to remember. Perhaps it was that secretary of the Council to whom he had alluded before.[1] Mendoza, the successor of De Spes, had an agent employed in Walsingham's office whose death was a great loss to him, for in addition to his knowledge of Walsingham's affairs (which, says Mendoza, was absolutely trustworthy), he heard many things that went on in the Queen's chamber through a lady with whom it was almost impossible for Mendoza to communicate after his death. In consequence, the ambassador continues, 'I have to lose much time in finding out what goes on, and have, so to speak, to go about begging for intelligence.'[2] Perhaps the most remarkable example of spying that I have noted — if it is to be taken at its face value — is an instance of one Spanish agent spying on another in 1572. The one agent wrote to Alva on December 22nd detailing a conversation which he had had with Burghley. 'This conversation', he writes, 'took place in his [Burghley's] room on the 19th instant, only he and I being present.' On the same day the other — and rival — agent also wrote to Alva telling him that this conversation had taken place on the 19th. 'What passed between them,' he adds, 'and the answer given to him I leave for Guaras to tell, as no doubt he will write to your Excellency about it; although I have heard the whole of the conversation from a person who overheard it.'[3]

It was also the custom for sixteenth-century sovereigns to dispense pensions through their ambassadors to certain councillors and others at foreign courts. As one might guess, it was not a practice that Elizabeth liked to follow, her scruples, however, being financial, not moral. And even with Philip II there was many a slip and much delay between promise and performance. But by this means both Spanish and French

---

[1] *Spanish Cal. Eliz.* ii, 248; cf. ibid. 93, 96, 227.
[2] Ibid. 663, 653.   [3] Ibid. 452, 454.

ambassadors obtained claims on a number of courtiers. That they secured Court gossip and news in consequence is no doubt true, but that their pensioners betrayed state secrets I think it well not to believe except when there is conclusive proof. Dr Conyers Read, following Martin Hume, has argued that our ambassador in France, Sir Edward Stafford, sold important state secrets to the Spanish ambassador there for a bribe. If true it is peculiarly infamous, but for my own part I have not been able to bring my credulity to this leap and do not believe that the facts are quite as Dr Read thinks. It was, however, not pensioners amongst the nobility who told ambassadors most, but malcontents. The religious and political dissensions of the time gave Elizabeth, Philip II and Catherine de Medici their chance of weakening one another by encouraging the discontented in each other's realms, the result being that an ambassador's residence was apt to become a resort or a centre of intrigue for rebellious nobility. De Spes and Mendoza, Spanish ambassadors in England, flagrantly abused their positions by their intrigues, and so did the English ambassador, Sir Nicholas Throckmorton, in France.

If it was the business of an ambassador to penetrate the secrets of a rival Court, it was the concern of that Court to bamboozle the ambassador and in its turn to discover any intrigues in which he might be engaged. An ambassador might even have his correspondence waylaid. Spy was set against spy, and bluff against bluff. The age of Machiavelli knew that there is nothing on occasions so sure to deceive as the plain truth. Or, alternatively, that to misinform one's ambassador lent to his report of a lie all the semblance of truth. If princes wish to deceive their adversaries, said Guicciardini, let them begin by deceiving their own ambassadors: their words will seem more free and be more calculated to inspire confidence.[1] The authors of those early manuals for ambassadors loved to enumerate the qualities demanded of an ambassa-

[1] Quoted by Janet, *Histoire de la science politique* (5th edition), i, 544.

dor by his office. They would have him to be a divine, astrologer, logician, an excellent orator, as learned as Aristotle, and as wise as Solomon; and to these requirements the practice of the age added the subtlety of the serpent. No wonder that Hotman remarks, 'The perfect image of an Ambassador ... was never amongst men.'

However, I must not leave a jaundiced impression of an ambassador's activities in your minds. Spies and intrigue were more or less important according as the relations between two courts were strained or friendly. My remarks may or may not amount to a caricature of any particular embassy. Let me add that they really do not misrepresent such embassies as those of De Spes and Mendoza in England or Throckmorton in France. Their point, however, lies not in their sufficiency or insufficiency as a portrait of a sixteenth-century ambassador, but in the caution they must engender when we are assessing the value of his dispatches as historical evidence.

I turn to make that assessment. And it is not with the obvious — the value of diplomatic correspondence for diplomatic history — that I shall deal, but with the less obvious, for it has become increasingly less important in later times — its value for domestic history. I have already said that an ambassador had to report — generally at intervals of a few days — whatever news he could ferret out: Court gossip, meetings of the Council, the trend of policy, events and rumours of importance in the country; and if he was a wise man, and was writing to Elizabeth or Catherine de Medici, he would flavour his letters with lengthy descriptions of Court ceremonies, personalia and lighter gossip. His dispatches constituted a fairly elaborate Court diary and a less elaborate diary of national events.

It is this fact which gives diplomatic correspondence its peculiar value for sixteenth-century history. We should suffer gravely without it in England, for in those days we were very much behind the continent — at any rate behind Italy and France — with our historical literature. It is astonishing, if explicable, that we have no memoirs at all to set beside the great wealth of France. Brantôme, Marguerite de Valois, Monluc, are three amongst scores of French memoir-writers of the sixteenth century. Memoirs are, of course, notoriously untrustworthy. These were written late in life, and generally to the greater glory of the writer or to set his career in a more agreeable light. The Italian wars produced quite a number of would-be Caesars dictating their Commentaries in the enforced idleness of old age, imprisonment or unemployment. And in all the memoirs facts have been distorted by the tricks of memory and the passing of time. With all their faults, however, they give us a picture of Court life in France and a survey of events for which in England we are dependent on the dispatches of foreign ambassadors. Not indeed that French historians can ignore similar dispatches. Anything in the nature of a diary has very obvious advantages over a memoir, and however strong may be one's cautions against too easy a faith in an ambassador's facts, they were recorded at the time and avoid the snares that beset facts in memoirs.

England boasts no memoirs for the sixteenth century, but she can boast great wealth in domestic state papers and private correspondence. This is due to Providence. We have had no social revolution and have preserved our county families singularly well. Only moth and rust — unless we add the death duties of the last few years — have entered in and destroyed. But neither from domestic state papers nor private correspondence could one reconstruct a connected story of events at Court, and over discussions of important state affairs hangs an almost impenetrable cloud. No records were kept of them. We have a very occasional memorandum of Council discussions made by Burghley, but matters of state were *arcana imperii*, and those sharing the secrets divulged them and forswore themselves at their peril. On the other hand, it was the business of an ambassador to discover what had been said and done in Council, and however uncertain his reports may be, they present, I think, a more connected story than we could piece together from other sources. Similarly with the intrigues of conspirators. It was the height of folly for them to commit their thoughts or plans to paper, but the confidences which they whispered into the ears of ambassadors were immediately transmitted by the latter to their sovereigns. To take a single instance: the Duke of Norfolk, at the time of the Ridolfi Plot, would have cut a still sorrier figure if only Elizabeth had had before her the dispatches of the Spanish ambassador. Norfolk ultimately bolted out a good deal of the truth after repeated examinations before his trial, but his confessions can be checked and supplemented from the Spanish and French ambassadors' dispatches.

I have said enough to suggest the peculiar position which diplomatic correspondence holds among the historical sources for the sixteenth century. This, however, implies no estimate of its reliability; and let me say at once that, indispensable as such correspondence is, I nourish the deepest distrust of it. In the first place, ambassadors in England were almost always in a country whose language they could not understand. The manuals of the time give lists of languages which the perfect ambassador ought to know. Latin, Italian, French, Spanish, German are included, and one Italian writer even includes Turkish. None thought to include English, and even as late as 1716 a manual could omit our language from the tongues of diplomacy.

Now an ambassador, unable to understand the language of the country, was half blind and dependent on others to lead him — a fruitful source of half-truths and misconceptions. How difficult communication was may be illustrated by the following examples. The first is from the *Spanish Calendar* and refers to an interview between De Spes on the one hand and the Admiral and Cecil, the Secretary, on the other. 'The Admiral', says De Spes, 'spoke first, and briefly said in French that he and the Secretary had been sent by the Queen, but that as he did not speak much Latin the Secretary would communicate her Majesty's message in that tongue, which he [the Admiral] understood, although he had little practice in speaking it.'[1] It is easy to imagine what flounderings there would have been had Cecil not borne the brunt of the conversation, and easy to imagine, not only how useful Cecil's linguistic knowledge was to him in the competition to control affairs, but how useful the Queen's was to her. Elizabeth spoke Latin, French and Italian and understood Spanish. Her accomplishments have more than the interest of cultural frills, though her love of showing them off and her courtiers' love of indulging her whim might prevent one from realizing it. They are indeed as much the explanation of her control of policy as her masterly temper. As a woman in the age of John Knox she would have been hard put to it to direct policy had she not been as able as the best of her councillors, and more able than most of them, to conduct the interviews with foreign ambassadors. My impression is that she kept a closer monopoly of these interviews than other sovereigns of her age, who were apt to refer ambassadors to their councillors — closer even than Catherine de Medici. But I must return to my examples of an ambassador's linguistic difficulties. I take my second from the same year, from the French ambassador, La Mothe-Fénelon's correspondence. Fénelon had the Duke of Norfolk, the Earls of Arundel and Leicester, Lord Howard of Effingham, Cecil, and other lords of the Council to dine with him. He notes that Cecil translated his speech into English for the benefit of the Councillors and that after they had conferred together, Norfolk said a few words in English and then told Lord Howard of Effingham to explain them to Fénelon in French.[2]

The information that an ambassador collected was a rather indiscriminate mass of rumour and gossip, truth and falsehood, sometimes with a good leavening of official bluff. For example, while the Ridolfi Plot was brewing Sir John Hawkins, with the

---

[1] *Spanish Cal. Eliz.* ii, 117.
[2] La Mothe-Fénelon, *Correspondance diplomatique*, ii, 132.

full cognizance of Burghley, was offering to go over with his ships to the Spanish side and betray his country; this in order to penetrate the plot. He easily tricked the credulous Spanish ambassador and even convinced the more cautious Philip. 'I have written to your Majesty', says De Spes, 'of the great desire which Hawkins expresses to serve you ... and I can discover nothing suspicious about it. He has gone to Plymouth, taking artillery and munitions from London, leaving a person here in case I should wish to call him back ... He may render great service by manning his ships with a very few men and filling them up with others chosen by your Majesty.'[1]

Similarly, in the negotiations which Burghley had with a Spanish agent in October and November 1572, when events in the Netherlands made our strained relations with Spain seem dangerous, I am sure that he was often mildly pulling the agent's leg; and I have frequently suspected, in reading the diplomatic correspondence of the time, that the seemingly disloyal overtures of a councillor like Leicester to some ambassador were moves in a game of bluff. Doubly a foreigner by his ignorance of the language, it was difficult for an ambassador to sift the true from the false, and if his relations with the Court were unfriendly his sympathies tended to go out to malcontents, and the eddies of faction ever threatened to destroy his discretion. The effect of keeping such company upon a particularly intemperate mind may be illustrated by the following quotation from a dispatch written by De Spes:

The principal person in the Council at present is William Cecil, now Lord Burghley. He is a man of mean sort, but very astute, false, lying, and full of artifice. He is a great heretic, and such a clownish Englishman as to believe that all the Christian princes joined together are not able to injure the sovereign of his country, and he therefore treats their ministers with great arrogance.

[1] *Spanish Cal. Eliz.* ii, 329; cf. 346, 351.

This man manages the bulk of the business, and by means of his vigilance and craftiness, together with his utter unscrupulousness of word and deed, thinks to outwit the ministers of other princes. This to a certain extent he has hitherto succeeded in doing. Next after him, the man who has most to do with affairs is Robert Dudley, Earl of Leicester, not that he is fit for such work, but because of the great favour with which the Queen regards him. He is a light and greedy man who maintains the robbers and lives by their plunder. He is ungrateful for the favours your Majesty has granted to him, and is greatly inclined to the French party, from whom he receives an allowance. The other man who has his hand in the government is the Lord Keeper of the Great Seal. He is an obstinate and most malignant heretic, and, being Cecil's brother-in-law, always agrees with him. The Admiral does not interfere very much in arranging matters, but he is a very shameless thief without any religion at all, which latter also may be said of the Earl of Sussex ... The Earl of Bedford also belongs to the Council. In person and manners he is a monstrosity and a great heretic. There are others of less authority than these men, lawyers, creatures of Cecil who only repeat what he says.[1]

Once more, perhaps, I have overdrawn my picture, or rather, put in the shadows and omitted the rest. All is not gloom, but he who would sail in uncharted seas must keep a sharp look-out for rocks, and I have known quite eminent historians founder.

It remains for me to give you a rather fuller conception of the information contained in diplomatic sources. I turn first, as every sixteenth-century diplomat would have done, to the *Relazioni* or Relations of the Venetian ambassadors. In origin they are the reports on their missions which ambassadors had to make on their return home, and there is a decree of the

[1] *Spanish Cal. Eliz.* ii, 364.

Venetian Grand Council as early as 1268 concerning them. Had they continued to be mere reports on the details of a diplomatic mission, they would not have become the famous and unique documents that they are. In fact, they might have been confined, as was more or less so in other states, to ambassadors returning from special missions, since resident ambassadors gave full reports of their negotiations in their dispatches and it was generally needless — and indeed impracticable when the residence had been of long duration — to review their work on their return. Consequently, it was a happy accident that led the Venetians to add to their reports a geographical, social and political description of the country from which they had returned. The pattern became established custom, and I imagine that it was with the introduction of resident ambassadors that what had been a mere frill became the very substance of a 'Relation'. The document was read before a solemn gathering of the Doge and Senate within a fortnight of the ambassador's return, and was listened to with critical interest. Tradition and the fame which these reports won throughout Europe in the sixteenth century established very high standards, and one can see the effects of emulation in the formidable length to which some of them grew in the second half of the century. Though formally they were confidential documents, manuscript copies got abroad. They were sold in Rome at 15 pauls per hundred sheets, and contemporary transcripts are to be found in the great libraries of England and other countries. A group of *Relazioni* was actually published at Cologne in 1589.[1]

No doubt it was largely the commercial character of the Venetian state and the high level of its culture, but it was also the traditions of a great service which made its ambassadors the ablest and most detached of observers. Their Relations have these advantages over travellers' descriptions: first, that there are very many more of them — for a country like France they recur at intervals of a few years; and secondly, that their

[1] Cf. Introduction to *Venetian Cal.* vol. i.

231

authors were generally shrewder observers, lived longer in the country they are describing, and had peculiar advantages in noting and collecting their information. It is true that a foreigner is almost sure to go wrong in some measure in commenting on institutions, which are too elusive to understand readily. But against native writers must be set a freshness of view that notes points which are so familiar to an inhabitant that they cannot become objective.

Let me sample one or two of these Relations for you. The earliest known, written about 1500, concerns England and opens in the following matter-of-fact way:

> Magnificent and most illustrious Lord!
> The Kingdom of England is situated in the island named Britain, which ... is in the Ocean, between the north and the west. Her form is triangular, like that of Sicily, and she lies, though at a considerable distance, over against Germany, France and Spain ...

On Englishmen its comment is as follows:

> The English are, for the most part, both men and women of all ages, handsome and well-proportioned; though not quite so much so, in my opinion, as it had been asserted to me ... ; and I have understood from persons acquainted with these countries, that the Scotch are much handsomer; and that the English are great lovers of themselves, and of everything belonging to them; they think that there are no other men than themselves, and no other world but England; and whenever they see a handsome foreigner, they say that 'he looks like an Englishman', and that 'it is a great pity that he should not be an Englishman'; and when they partake of any delicacy with a foreigner they ask him, 'whether such a thing is made in *their* country?' ... [1]

[1] *Italian Relation of England*, edited by C. A. Sneyd (Camden Soc. 1847), pp. 7, 20.

From a Relation of the year 1551, which is admirable in its description of our institutions, I take the following account of the mode of holding parliament:

When they are assembled in the place appointed for this purpose, which is very vast and extremely handsome, after celebration of the mass the King makes the Lord Chancellor state the causes which have rendered it necessary to assemble the Parliament. In the next place, the King desires the inferior order, that of the burgesses, to elect as usual an able and eloquent member to announce their suits and grievances. This mover is styled Speaker of the Parliament, because as president of that order he prescribes the mode and place for speaking. These orders being separated one from the other, they commence regulating matters, as aforesaid; and first of all they inscribe in a bill[1] whatever has to be treated, after which they read the bill three times in three days, one day always intervening between each reading, for the purpose of giving time to the House in question to consult. The bill having been read, any member who pleases is at liberty to speak, but in turn, one after the other, nor is it allowable to interrupt anyone speaking. The arguments on both sides having been heard they proceed to vote, and all those who assent to a motion exclaim 'Aye, aye,' those who reject it exlaiming 'No, no.' If the number of one side is doubtful the Speaker counts it one by one, and thus the majority conquers the minority, and the deliberation being noted in a bill, is sent by three or four members selected from that House to the Upper House, wherein the whole affair is discussed in like manner. If the bill is disapproved they immediately tear it; if approved, it is kept until the last day of Parliament, when in presence of the King all bills of the sort are read; and if the King assents to them they all

[1] I have substituted 'bill' for the translator's 'book'.

become so many lasting and immutable laws; but if any of the bills do not please the King, they then say that the King will consider, and the matter is referred to another time.[1]

I might go on indefinitely quoting from these descriptions of England. Certainly I must not omit the fine portraits of Mary and her sister Elizabeth, drawn by the Venetian ambassador in 1557.

Queen Mary ... is of short stature, well made, thin and delicate, and moderately pretty; her eyes are so lively that she inspires reverence and respect, and even fear, wherever she turns them; nevertheless she is very short-sighted. Her voice is deep, almost like that of a man. She understands five languages, English, Latin, French, Spanish and Italian, in which last, however, she does not venture to converse. She is also much skilled in ladies' work, such as producing all sorts of embroidery with the needle. She has a knowledge of music, chiefly on the lute, on which she plays exceedingly well. As to the qualities of her mind, it may be said of her that she is rash, disdainful and parsimonious rather than liberal. She is endowed with great humility and patience, but withal high-spirited, courageous and resolute, having during the whole course of her adversity been guiltless of any the least approach to meanness of comportment; she is, moreover, devout and staunch in the defence of her religion ... The cabal she has been exposed to, the evil disposition of the people towards her, the present poverty and the debt of the Crown, and her passion for King Philip, from whom she is doomed to live separate, are so many other causes of the grief by which she is overwhelmed. She is, moreover, a prey to the hatred she bears my Lady Elizabeth, and which has its source in the recollection of the wrongs she experienced on account of

[1] *Venetian Cal.* v, 342-3.

her mother, and in the fact that all eyes and hearts are turned towards my Lady Elizabeth as successor to the Throne.

My Lady Elizabeth ... is a lady of great elegance both of body and mind, although her face may rather be called pleasing than beautiful; she is tall and well made; her complexion fine, though rather sallow; her eyes, but above all her hands, which she takes care not to conceal, are of superior beauty. In her knowledge of the Greek and Italian languages she surpasses the Queen. Her spirits and understanding are admirable, as she has proved by her conduct in the midst of suspicion and danger, when she concealed her religion and comported herself like a good catholic. She is proud and dignified in her manners; for though her mother's condition is well known to her, she is also aware that this mother of hers was united to the King in wedlock, with the sanction of the holy church and the concurrence of the primate of the realm.[1]

France — the France of the religious wars — offered a fine field of observation for the Venetians, and had I not been addressing an English audience it would have been from the French Relations that I would have drawn my main illustrations. The comments on persons are often notable. Catherine de Medici, says one ambassador, writing in 1561, in her role of mother keeps the king under her control. She allows no one but herself to sleep in his chamber; she never leaves his side. And her difficulties as regent are well analysed by another ambassador. 'It is sufficient to say', he writes, 'that she is a woman, a foreigner, and a Florentine to boot, born of a simple house altogether beneath the dignity of the kingdom of France.' Good also is this comment on Antony, King of Navarre: He is said to be intelligent and to talk well, but he is vain, imprudent and inconstant in his actions, readily enters upon great schemes,

---

[1] Ellis, *Original Letters*, 2nd ser. ii, 236-7; cf. *Venetian Cal.* vi, ii, 1043 seqq.

yet lacks the capacity to see them through. My final excerpt seems to me to be singularly penetrating. It is one of those simple but fresh comments which are the very essence of imagination. It was written in 1569 in the course of one of the religious wars. 'I believe', says the ambassador,

I believe that in these troubles the Pope has gained more than he has lost; for before the religious dissensions there was so much licence of manners and so little respect for the Roman court that his holiness was regarded rather as a great Italian political power than as the head of the Church and universal pastor. But as soon as the Huguenots appeared, the catholics began to have a new respect for the pontiff and to recognize him as the true vicar of Christ, and the more the Huguenot party scoffed at him the more their faith increased.[1]

The Venetian ambassadors alone wrote these descriptive reports of the countries where they had resided. I know of only one exception, and that is a Relation of the State of France, written by Sir George Carew upon his return from his embassy there in 1609, and addressed to James I. It was avowedly an imitation of the Venetian Relations, but owed its existence to the ambassador's initiative and to that alone. It did not inspire an English series of Relations; nor indeed could there very well have been such a series without that form of audience for a returning ambassador which was peculiar to Venice. We may deplore the solitary character of the Venetian tradition, but it is more just to count our blessings than cry our losses; and, in fact, in their passing comments upon persons and affairs, the ordinary dispatches of an ambassador supply part at least of the picture that a Venetian deliberately drew. In Sir Edward Stafford's dispatches from France there are many touches which put together give us a portrait of Henry III — an

[1] *Relations des ambassadeurs vénitiens*, ed. M. M. Tommasio (Collection de documents inédits), i, 425, 549, 431; ii, 163.

unstable king, at one moment coercing even his mother, at another letting politics go hang while he mortified the flesh in religious processions. 'He is so strange a man of disposition', writes Stafford on one occasion, 'and so unknown in his proceedings, that no man can settle any judgment upon his actions. He is become, since Monsieur's death (whom he stood in fear of) to care for nobody, and so keepeth every one about him in awe that mother, counsellors, mignons and all quail when he speaketh.' He 'beginneth to reform marvellously the orders of his house', is the report a few weeks later; 'maketh three chambers afore they come to his inner bedchamber; in the first, to be gentlemen, modestly apparelled; in the next, men of greater quality; in the last, the princes and knights of the order of the Saint Esprit ... Into his private bed-chamber nobody to be allowed but who is called in, but only Epernon and Joyeuse, the Marshal Retz and Villequier ... ; all others being quite cut off, not to come in but when they are called for.'[1]

As we might expect, the most entertaining of all passages in the dispatches of ambassadors resident in England are those which describe their audiences with the Queen. Upon her progresses among her own people every faculty Elizabeth possessed was set in motion, and so it was at these audiences. At her accession to the throne she knew how to check the arrogance of the Spanish ambassador and remind him that her power depended upon the affection of her people and not upon the goodwill of his master; she could parry offers of marriage with maidenly yearnings for a cloistered life, and then pout because Philip II could not wait a month for her answer: 'Your Lordship', writes the ambassador, 'will see what a pretty business it is to have to treat with this woman, who I think must have a hundred thousand devils in her body, notwithstanding that she is for ever telling me that she yearns to be a

---

[1] *Foreign Cal. Eliz.* xix, 126, 184, 302.
[2] *Spanish Cal. Eliz.* i, 119.

nun and to pass her time in a cell praying.'[2] She knew how to receive the French ambassador after the Massacre of St Bartholomew, surrounded by her Court in profound silence, with a solemn and severe air, and yet without hostility, for she did not dare to break openly with France. She knew too how to trounce an insolent Polish ambassador, summoning her wrath and her Latin and rising lion-like from her chair. Infinite were her wiles. 'She caressed me more than I can describe', writes Mendoza, on one occasion; and on another he tells how at his last audience with her she gave the Portuguese ambassador a ring from her own finger, 'no doubt as a keepsake, for she is very clever at such little witcheries as these, when she thinks she can gain a point by them and disarm those with whom she is dealing. I fancy', he adds, 'she has fully succeeded in this with the ambassador.'[1]

These and many other such passages are to be found in the diplomatic correspondence of the time. I would counsel you, when next you read any well-documented history of the period, to note how many of the facts of domestic history are dependent on this type of source. It is not that the facts are best expressed in any ambassador's words. Too often it is that he provides our only evidence, and though I advise you to look the gift horse in the mouth, I would have you retain your gratitude.

And so I would end, but for a duty that I owe to our sixteenth-century ambassador. His was not a happy lot. His profit and loss account was a statement in two terms of which one was never operative. His equipment had to be costly, else he lost respect; his table had to be free and bountiful and his news service efficient, else he failed in his principal duty. He had to follow the Court in its perambulations and incur loss, fatigue and danger. One Venetian tells a vivid story of the alarms through which he passed when the Huguenots attempted to seize the king at Meaux. In Paris he kept his servants armed, water ready in the street lest his house was fired over his head,

[1] *Spanish Cal. Eliz.* ii, 691, 663.

sentinels posted and himself ready at every sound to spring from his bed and escape. Another tells of the inordinate price of victuals, of unhealthy lodgings, of dangers from soldiers and brigands.[1] Their pay was often irregular and never adequate, and they were lucky if their private estates were not hopelessly mortgaged at the end of an embassy. In 1511 an ambassador from the Low Countries in Spain had to slip out of the country and desert his post for lack of money. The consolation for the ambassador was that his reward came in some future appointment or grant from the state. The consolation for us is that what is generally assumed, so far as our ambassadors are concerned, to have had a peculiar source in Elizabeth's parsimony, was really the common practice of the time. We are an insular folk in our historical judgments.

[1] Tommasio, op. cit. ii, 199; i, 359.

THE BIOGRAPHICAL APPROACH
TO HISTORY[1]

Fᴵʀsᴛ, a word about the title of this paper. I am not going to discuss the merits or demerits of biography as a form of historical writing. In other words, I am not speaking as the author of *Queen Elizabeth*. I was told that at a Thursday-evening conference at the Institute of Historical Research, devoted to the question of a new edition of the *Dictionary of National Biography*, some speakers were inclined to regard biography as outmoded: to be classed with the Dodo or Queen Anne. If that view was taken, I should have liked to join issue on it: I am a staunch friend of the *D.N.B.*, though whether the time has arrived to rewrite the *Dictionary* is an arguable question, and I think I should argue 'No.'

My old master, A. F. Pollard, who did his best work as a biographer, was opposed to biographies as research theses — I mean biographies in the conventional sense. So, if I remember aright, were Tout and others of that generation. It is a prejudice that I have inherited and retained. If I examine my prejudice, I find that it is not against biography itself, which in any case we must have, and which can be as exacting and searching a discipline as most types of history. It is against young people writing of life before they have gathered sufficient experience to interpret it.

This leads me to a reflection — a provocative one, maybe — with which to end an irrelevant prologue. Between the two world wars, biography had a remarkable vogue. *Littérateurs* and their publishers scanned history for interesting persons, hitherto unsung or uncursed, or insufficiently cursed. I doubt

[1] A paper read at the Anglo-American Historical Conference held at the Institute of Historical Research on July 14th, 1950, and published in *History* (Oct. 1951), n.s. xxxvi, 193-203.

if there has been anything quite like the craze. Even Jane Shore, to cite one of the most conspicuous examples which came my way as a reviewer, found her biographer. And when an author's sources failed him, we had monologue and dialogue, and much else into the bargain, invented to liven up the story. I remember how in one book Wolsey communed at night with his soul in a remarkable monologue, unknown to the *Letters and Papers of Henry VIII* or any other historical source. The vogue began with Lytton Strachey, who caught or created — something of both, I think — the post-war mood for 'debunking'. His imitators were legion. None equalled the master in quality; some — perhaps most — were pitiable flounderers. Nevertheless, I think that history may have gained rather than lost by this prostitution of the subject. Although Lytton Strachey, through inability to judge sound historical scholarship, based his *Elizabeth and Essex* on a naive, if learned-looking book on Queen Elizabeth's health, and though he did not always know how to interpret his sources, I am an admirer as well as a critic of his work. He and the abler of his imitators were expert in interpreting human beings: they took psychology seriously, as the literary critic, indeed, must. Their historical portraits may have been partly or largely fictional, but they lived. For our part, as professional historians, our traditions and scholarship ensure that our portraits are factual. May we not learn something from the literary experts and make them also live?

But this prologue has gone on too long, and I must turn to my subject. I toyed with the idea of calling my paper, 'The demographical approach to history'. Two or three considerations deterred me. I am not sure that I know what 'demographical' means, and in any case it is a loathsome word. 'The biographical approach to history' it therefore is, though I hope you will not mind if I become surreptitiously 'demographical'.

I do not know how old this type of historical approach may be. The first modern book in my range of reading to apply it was Charles Beard's *Economic Interpretation of the American*

Constitution, the basis of which was a series of biographical studies of the framers of the constitution, keyed into the two rival economic interests of creditor and debtor in the United States. How much of Beard's thesis has survived subsequent critical examination, I am unaware; but clearly, within properly controlled limits his method was a great and promising advance upon what we may call the conventional approach to constitutional history, just as the latter was upon the legal-minded approach of still earlier generations. In England, I remember when we used to see reviews in the weeklies signed 'L. B. Namier' and heard of a formidable and mysterious biographical card-index. We pitied the *littérateur* and the weaker brethren who strayed into his field: we also enjoyed the reviews. And at last came the two volumes on *The Structure of Politics at the Accession of George III.* It is a book which in retrospect must be regarded in this country as one of the supremely influential historical works. Pollard's *Evolution of Parliament* stimulated a remarkable amount of research, but Namier's book began a new historical method.

I suppose that indirectly Marx has had something to do with this new approach, just as Darwin influenced the earlier generation of institutional historians — as witness the title of Pollard's *Evolution of Parliament.* Pollard himself in his last years started what I may call the Namier method in dealing with the Reformation Parliament. He got far with the biographical foundations, but the synthesis never came; and I often wonder whether this was owing to physical or to psychological causes. Was he too much a Darwinian to change over to new methods? Of course we must not press the ideological explanation too far. After a period of frontal attacks on institutional history, a new generation of scholars was bound to try a flank attack, if only in the hope of fresh victories. And I do not doubt that Professor Namier would argue, as I should in my own case, that all he was doing was getting at the facts.

Human beings are the stuff of history. Their social activities, whether political or otherwise, are the result of environment and personal qualities, in which I include personal interests. And to these two I would add that third, strange factor, group behaviour, which almost justifies the personification of abstractions like the State. For as Rousseau has taught us — and we have only to look around to see it justified in a way that would have horrified him, as it horrifies us — the general will is not the arithmetical sum of individual wills. I mention this third factor, not because I propose to dwell on it, but because the biographical approach to history, with which I am concerned, is essentially the method of discovering the 'arithmetical sum of individual wills'; and if we allow ourselves to become mere mathematicians, ignoring the elusive forces that enter into group behaviour, we shall err as surely as our predecessors did in confining themselves to a frontal approach to institutional history.

I state the obvious when I say that we cannot fully understand the nature and functioning of any human group without knowing about the individuals who compose it. This knowledge must come from a series of biographies. But that is not all. We must first know what questions we hope to answer from the biographies, and if at all possible the necessary information must be got. This is a very different proposition from writing ordinary biographies. Indeed, we may have very little interest in the usual contents of a biography. Some of the facts we seek may be difficult to come by; they may seem insignificant and in themselves dull. Once more I may be stating the obvious; but not without provocation. The historians on Colonel Wedgwood's committee dealing with a biographical study of parliament could never get this fundamental thesis home, and he went on compiling biographies without the preliminary enunciation of questions. Such procedure prevents the vital, broad questions being answered; and the answering of these is in my view the principal — I would almost say the sole — justification for the prodigal labour of compiling hundreds of biographies. All facts are not born free and equal. They may be to the antiquary, but not to the historian.

When the same questions are asked and — if possible — answered in each biography, the results can and should be summarized and given in tabular form as statistics (if a mere historian, without the pale, may use that word). It is from these tables, plus the biographies and all the direct evidence commanded by previous scholars, that we can hope to fashion a new and illuminating interpretation of our subject.

For my own part, I am gradually having the parliaments of Elizabeth's reign — and before quitting I hope to add the two preceding reigns — studied in this way. Facts which can be expressed in tabular form include: the social class to which members belonged; their occupation—for example central or local officials, lawyers, etc.; their education; their age; their religious affinities, if ascertainable; their previous and subsequent parliamentary experience; their family relationships; the location of their residence or estates in relation to the constituency. I need not linger to point out the supreme importance of such information for parliamentary history. If only we had similar studies over a long range of time we should be able to trace the infiltration of the gentry into borough seats; changes in the educational quality of the House of Commons and the sort of experience found there; the balance of political, economic, class, and religious interests; and so on. And we could relate these to the parliamentary story and to the legislation that was passed. Nor must I forget to add that for the sixteenth century, and doubtless other centuries, it is only through biographies that one can obtain much of the evidence for an electoral history of the House of Commons. There is direct evidence for a number of elections in the Elizabethan period: for a surprising number, one might perhaps say. But this simply sets the pattern. More often than not the story comes by inference from facts in the biographies. When I wrote my recent book, *The Elizabethan House of Commons*, though I had a shrewd idea of the truth about that notorious problem, the Cornish boroughs and their connection, if any, with packed parliaments, I lacked the evidence to deal with it in detail. So far as the sixteenth century is concerned, the secret will yield itself only through deliberately designed biographical studies of all the Cornish members over a long period of time. A student of mine is tackling the problem along these lines; and I am confident that we shall at last crack this doughty nut.

A study of the members of one parliament makes an almost ideal subject for a research student. The biographical work introduces him to an extraordinarily wide range of sources and secondary material; and what is more, links the material for local history with that for national history. There are no immature disquisitions on character. The results are matter-of-fact; but the pursuit of them has plenty of human interest and gives an admirably broad sense of the structure of society. There is also synthesis, which I regard as highly desirable for the research student. In the hands of the second-class student — and let me add in parenthesis that we should not depreciate such people, who can render great help in extending the frontiers of history and who may, as teachers, carry into the schools the inspiration and enthusiasm, as well as the knowledge, that comes from creative, scholarly work: as I was saying, in the hands of the second-class student the synthesis may be jejune and faulty; but the tables and biographies remain, and if compiled with accuracy — and their factual character helps to induce this — they are invaluable. On the other hand, the finest mind can be stretched by the work to the limits of its ingenuity, critical capacity, and imagination.

Biographies — compiled, shall I say? in the mass, and on this plan — when they come to be studied reveal many facts that can be correlated; many social similarities and differences which in themselves are worth pursuing. They suggest fresh studies, though they may not supply the complete answer. For example, I feel the urge, as a result of my parliamentary work, to probe into the social affinities and implications of university and legal education in the sixteenth century. I should like to trace the invasion of the universities by the country gentry and to establish the facts about what I regard as one of the most important developments in English life — the use of the Inns of Court as finishing schools for the gentry, divorced from any intention of legal practice. Such a study might seem formidable, for it involves biographies on a wholesale scale, though in this particular instance there are Wood and Cooper and Venn to help us. But the archaeologist, with his system of sample trenches, shows us how to tackle the over-large job. We can take our samples at intervals of time, though the sample must always be a complete unit — for example, in the instance I have cited, we must include everyone at the universities and Inns of Court in a particular year.

My work has been the application of the biographical method to parliamentary history — the obvious field of inquiry for an Englishman. But, as my previous remarks indicate, there is a great area of history where the method is also applicable. One could, with great profit, study the Church, especially its higher dignitaries, along these lines. One of my American students this year has been applying the biographical method, as well as the more conventional one, to a study of the episcopacy during the great Reformation divide. He thought that he saw a correlation between the reactions of the bishops to the Reformation and training in the Roman civil law. Whether his facts will ultimately justify such a thesis, I do not know. All that I am concerned with is that here is an approach which may contribute to our understanding of a significant historical theme. Then again, how much I should like to see the information in Miss Garrett's valuable biographical census of Marian exiles supplemented by the necessary facts and thrown into tables showing the social class to which each exile belonged, his vocation, his residence — whether it was in town or country and its geographical location — etc. etc. I imagine that the result would cast a great deal of light upon the political and religious history of the time and in particular on the Elizabethan Puritan movement. One could also study in this way the legal profession, from judges down to barristers, the justices of the peace, the royal household — either in the form of the Court or one or more of its administrative organs — and so on. The essence of the game — if I may use its jargon — is to 'biograph' everyone, ask the right questions, and assemble the facts in tables where their significance may be readily grasped.

In a different way, the biographical approach (by which I mean the compilation of a number of biographies) can be amazingly effective in solving many otherwise insoluble problems in ordinary biography. This of course is particularly true in periods when relatively little direct evidence can be found about many important people. The underlying facts are that men have friends and enemies, and that their activities, in one way or another, are so often related to those of a group. Biographical studies of a man's acquaintances may shed invaluable light on the life of the individual; or it may prove·profitable to study someone as a member of a group rather than in isolation. Professor A. W. Reed's *Early Tudor Drama*, which deals with a group round Sir Thomas More, is a conspicuous example of the interaction of several biographical studies. Indeed, it is literary historians, and particularly those interested in Shakespeare, who, for very obvious reasons, make most use of this method. Dr Leslie Hotson's work proceeds along these lines, and in the course of long years of research he has compiled a card-index which deserves, in the best sense of the word, to become fabulous. Historians — or at any rate, modern historians — who usually are concerned with men who have left more ample records of their careers, are not often driven to multiple biographies in order to write one biography; and after all, life is finite and a sense of proportion in research is essential. But it is worth noting that a young American scholar, Mr Zeeveld, has recently thrown interesting and fresh light on Henry VIII and Wolsey, Pole, and Cromwell by a group study of a number of humanists. Others, no doubt, will follow his example.

And now I come to that horrid thing whose name must be whispered — 'demography'. I think there is immense scope for studying people in their social units and classes. I do not mean conventional social history, but something that I might describe as a mixture of institutional history, sociology, and social history. Let me explain. In the Elizabethan period the social and administrative unit *par excellence* was the county, and the politically significant class the country gentry. I should like to see one county taken (with others to follow), each family planted on its land, each family made the subject of a biography, with the same questions asked — all the questions that one could imagine as being interesting when generalized. I should like to elicit information about wealth and movement, social, political, and administrative activities, social, political, and geographical antecedents, size and sex of family, education, marriage, length of life; to ask many of the questions that the peripatetic takers of the census in America seem to be asking just now. I should like, in my own period, to extract through these biographies all that can be obtained about clientage — the political and social relationship of patron and dependant, which prevailed in the sixteenth century — and to investigate the nature and extent of local faction, its influence on local affairs and its connections, if any, with national politics. In that stimulating essay called *A Room of One's Own*, you may remember that Virginia Woolf asked questions about women in the past — and waited for an answer. I should ask them, and ask more of them; and I should obtain the answers, or most of them. I should have this information tabulated and probe into all the conceivable correlations.

What a task! you will say. But each county will make an admirable subject for a research student. The first thesis will face all the difficulties and bear all the blemishes of pioneer work. But improvement will come. And if the teacher is, as we are in London, happily situated in having sufficient students to form a seminar, and if two or more such theses can be constantly under way, then the students will develop a special technique which they will hand on from one to another, encouraging and helping one another. This is co-operative work of the kind achieved when the *D.N.B.* was being written; and I well remember how often A. F. Pollard used to talk of the skill so gained and preserved in the *D.N.B.* office and of the loss to scholarship when that organization was dispersed. Since 1945 I have secured this continuity in the study of Elizabethan members of parliament. There have been two or more students at work each year, overlapping one another. They find confidence and happiness working together; they certainly do better work than they would in isolation; and yet all are stretched to the limits of their varying ability.

Of course, what really interests me is the pattern that emerges when the results of these individual pieces of work are put together; when the synthesis is made of answers to identical questions, asked over a period of time or over a series of separate counties or communities. And I look beyond my Elizabethan period. If we could have similar syntheses arising from similar studies throughout the range of a nation's history, what a remarkable master-study would ultimately be possible! Naturally, some of the questions one would need to ask would change in the course of the centuries, as would their relative importance. Such changes would in themselves throw into relief points of supreme significance. I hasten to add that I am not urging the organization of historical research on a vast scale. I am essentially an individualist and am as hostile to making sociological historians of us all as I am to converting us into bibliographers. Let the spirit blow where it listeth, and example, not committees, guide our interests.

I came to this type of investigation as an institutional historian; and in these latter years the repercussion of the contemporary world has made me more and more want to get behind the formal architecture of constitutions to the men who worked them; to the way politically significant people lived, to the nature of their interests and the conflicts they provoked, to the reflection of all these facts in the social and institutional structure of society; shall I say, to realities? Asking myself, as I constantly do, how far a Hitler or a Stalin is master of his political system or becomes merely another victim of inherent, unplanned, and perhaps unforeseen tendencies in it, I want to look at the past in the same way. And I think that if historians can by this type of inquiry elicit and explain the inherent tendencies in various political or even social and economic systems, they may be adding to the available wisdom of mankind: which, after all, is their supreme function.

For example, I am not satisfied, as my predecessors might have been in rosier days, with describing the personal monarchy of the sixteenth century in terms of what the monarch could and could not do according to the law and custom of the constitution, plus a factual account of what was done. I see the monarch as the principal dispenser of patronage in society, and I want to discover the effect of the competition for this patronage on the structure of Court life, of politics, and of national life in general. My attention, in consequence, is directed to what I have ventured to call clientage, which in the sixteenth century might be regarded as a vestige of feudal days, but can also be viewed as a response to the system of personal monarchy. And let me here interpolate that in my post-war reading about the Hitler regime, I was struck by its resemblance to personal monarchy in the sixteenth century, with many of the stresses and strains familiar to me in Elizabethan history. If it be possible — and I imagine that the biographical approach would alone make it possible — I should like to discover through whose influence every Elizabethan official got his job; to find out in which great courtier's orbit he moved. And I should expect in this way to reach a new understanding of Court politics. Certainly, I should be able to explain much that has seemed very puzzling and unconvincing when tackled along old, conventional lines.

Let me cite another illustration. I am interested in the payment of officials. Pursuing the older approach to constitutional history, Pollard, with his mind always alert for details — and, incidentally, what a privilege it was to be trained by that great scholar, who, though concerned with the large picture, never missed the detail! — noted the wages paid to officials by the Crown. But it is not simply formal wages that interest me. These were supplemented by a system of fees and gratuities which often — perhaps usually — made the total income many times the amount of the formal wage. Now it is the effect of such a system upon society that awakens my curiosity: the tendency towards corruption, the means and effectiveness of controlling this, the result on the efficiency of the service, the danger of corruption getting out of hand. One can see this last danger clearly in the closing years of Elizabeth, and corruption was rampant under James I. Would a series of such studies, analysing the weaknesses of society at various periods, show — as one might expect — a tendency in human affairs for increasing pressure to be exerted on the flaws of any system, distorting its purpose and in the end breaking it down? If so, knowledge of this is valuable. If not — well, there is at any rate virtue in asking the question.

It will be noticed that my questions are always concerned with individuals — with individuals in groups, in the mass. I do not deny that many of the questions could be pursued by direct attack — by seeking directly for the items of evidence, instead of obtaining them through the medium of biography. Nor do I deny that the direct attack must be employed. But the merits of the biographical approach are several. As we construct these group biographies significant points emerge as common elements in the evidence; points which were not likely to reveal their significance in a non-biographical approach. This has certainly been my experience — to a degree that I can hardly exaggerate. My second point is that very many questions in their nature presuppose biographies: the facts are unobtainable without at least skeleton biographies. Then again, the tables showing the prevalence of the phenomena in which one is interested postulate a biographical basis.

Admittedly there is danger in the method. I well remember a convulsive review by the late Professor Hearnshaw of a book which reduced to statistical form a study of aids to the teaching of history in American schools: 'So many per cent used maps, and so many per cent used intelligence!' But folly will out whatever the approach to a subject. Perhaps it shows itself in stark nakedness in this particular approach. But is that a disadvantage?

Let me conclude by assuring you that I am not advancing the proposition that all history is biography. Some history — very fruitful history — is biography.

THE VIA MEDIA IN POLITICS

AN HISTORICAL PARALLEL[1]

WE are living in an age of ideological conflict and are troubled by the strains it imposes on society. The totalitarian state spreads alarm; we fear doctrinaires with their subversive organizations; we suspect fellow-travellers; we endure the Cold War; we think of quislings and the fifth column as instruments of foreign conquest. The fanatic's way of life we know to be dynamic; and though we say 'It shall not happen here,' we are not inclined, after our experience of the last twenty years, to boast that it cannot happen here. We are at odds about the policy we should pursue. Passion breeds passion; and unless we feel deeply about our own ideals, inevitably we are at a disadvantage against the enemies of society. Moderation, which is a liberal virtue, takes on a watery appearance. It seems uninspired and inglorious, prone to defeat.

In such a dilemma it may be useful to turn to history, which is the treasury of recorded experience. History never repeats itself, but it offers analogies. Just as the historian, consciously or unconsciously, uses the present to understand the past, so there is a reverse process. It is the most weighty of the justifications for the writing and study of history; and a nation which is historically minded is more likely to be fortunate in its affairs than one which is not.

For an analogy with our own times we cannot do better than turn to the Elizabethan period in English history. Such terms as fifth column, fellow-traveller, cold war, and the totalitarian state may be of recent origin, but the ideas for which they stand were as familiar to the Elizabethans as they

[1] Published under the title 'Elizabeth I and her Cold War' in the *Saturday Review* (New York), October 1st, 1955.

are to us, and their ordeal was as long drawn out as ours. In their case, moreover, we know the outcome and can judge more or less dispassionately. By common consent it is one of the great success stories of history.

Few historians nowadays would hesitate about ascribing the chief credit for this success to the Queen herself. In her own day her prime enemy, Pope Sixtus V, acclaimed her as great. Her Protestant subjects had no doubt about it. They believed that they were living at the summit of their country's glory; and their temper and achievements proclaimed the dynamic character of the age. Nevertheless, the Queen's policy, which she pursued with impressive tenacity, was that of the *via media*: one we do not normally associate with exuberance and glory. To examine the situation which confronted her, explain her policy, account for its success, and, above all, discover why the spirit of the nation, so far from being deflated, was never more buoyant: this surely cannot be an exercise remote from our present-day interests.

When Elizabeth I came to the throne in November 1558 she found her country, and the western European world in which it was set, divided by the great conflict of the Reformation. In due course and after much suffering, men learnt to separate religion from the State, at least to the extent of tolerating divergent creeds. But for the sixteenth century, inheriting the medieval conception of the Christian Commonwealth, that solution of the problem was beyond comprehension and therefore outside practical politics. Church and State, for the time being, were indissolubly joined, and the Reformation imposed the choice of Catholic or Protestant. In other words, the State was ideological in an age of conflicting ideologies. Its problems were similar to ours; and since the Catholic Church, like Communism today, was universal in its claims and international in its organization, the parallel with our predicament was very close.

Elizabeth may be described as Protestant by destiny and

upbringing. Educated by able Renaissance scholars of liberal outlook, experience during the short reigns of her brother and sister deepened her distrust of fanaticism. She was only twenty-five when she came to the throne, but for five years she had watched Mary Tudor govern the country as a Catholic devotee, and had learnt much from her own personal danger. If ever there was a lesson that passion and politics do not mix well, it was that reign. Instead of making England united and Catholic, as was fondly hoped, Mary had intensified faction, alienated moderate and patriotic men, and cast a gloom over the nation by the clerical character of her government, the excessive use of the stake against dissidents, and the subordination of English to foreign interests.

Several hundred of the most active Protestant divines and laymen fled abroad to escape her persecution. There, developing the single-mindedness of the revolutionary, they lived for the day when they would return, destroy Catholicism, and build their new Jerusalem in its place. Their hopes were centred on Elizabeth, their Deborah; and they looked to her to justify the blood of the martyrs by setting up a more extreme Protestant regime than the country had yet known. A counter-revolution was what they wanted; and the mood of London citizens, as Elizabeth's Coronation procession and other events demonstrated, was similar. When the first parliament of the new reign met in January 1559, the House of Commons proved to be like-minded.

Elizabeth understood what was expected of her and rose to her destiny to the extent of deciding on an immediate break with the Papacy, in this proving more courageous than some of her advisers. But beyond, caution ruled. With her eye on danger from abroad and disunity at home, she proposed to defer doctrinal changes; and, indeed, so far was she from sharing the crusading ideals of her triumphant supporters, that for her ultimate settlement she wanted a Church as conservative, comprehensive, and tolerant as possible. She even hoped to carry the more moderate of Mary's bishops with her: which would have rendered her less dependent on the radicals. In the event, the bishops refused to co-operate and so the Elizabethan Religious Settlement — the famous *via media* of our history books — emerged from a stubborn struggle between the Queen and a pressure-group of Marian exiles, directing the agitation of the House of Commons. Elizabeth was forced to make concessions — they can be seen in the Anglican Prayer Book of today — but she denied the radicals their thorough reform. It was in this opportunist way that the Anglican Church, which time has made so venerable, came into being.

Thus at the outset fanaticism was checked. The advantages of the policy were quickly apparent. During the early, critical years of the reign, while Elizabeth was consolidating her authority, Catholic forces abroad were not provoked into attempting her overthrow, Catholics at home remained quiescent, national instead of factional sentiment was fostered, and domestic peace was preserved. England escaped the religious wars of western Europe. That was one of the signal achievements of the reign: a miracle profoundly appreciated, though few grasped its secret. True, the radicals proved troublesome. They persisted in regarding the Settlement as a temporary measure, dictated by expediency. They practised nonconformity in defiance of the law, and they maintained their agitation. The Queen, however, knew that she could rely on their loyalty; and had time and circumstance permitted, they might have ceased to be a serious political problem.

The opportunity of unfolding its merits in peaceful isolation was unfortunately denied to the religious *via media*. England was drawn into the great storm of the Catholic Counter-Reformation and subjected to strains quite as severe as those we ourselves have endured. The Religious Wars broke out in France, continuing intermittently for a generation. The Netherlands revolted against Catholic Spain; and that struggle lasted even longer. Protestant zealots in England became convinced that at the Council of Trent and subsequently at a Franco-Spanish conference a universal Catholic conspiracy had been planned, its object to root out Protestantism by every means, in every country.

Then, in 1568, occurred the event which was to end all hope of insularity: the flight of Mary Queen of Scots to England. Mary was a Catholic. Through her mother she was a daughter of the House of Guise, leaders of militant Catholicism in France. It could be argued that she was the rightful Queen of England: certainly, on ground of mere descent, she had the best title to be Elizabeth's successor. And Mary as Queen of England foretold a return to Catholicism, the nightmare of all good Protestants. She instantly became a focus for discontents, political as well as religious. Her mere presence revived Catholic hopes and attracted conspirators, both foreign and English. The relative tranquillity of the first decade of the reign was ended. English statesmen foresaw the peril, but the alternative of allowing this dangerous woman to leave the country was even more perilous. 'Our good Queen', wrote one of them, 'has the wolf by the ears.' The Queen of Scots was kept in honourable captivity, and remained a captive till her execution in 1587.

In little more than a year trouble matured with the Northern Rebellion, a coalescence round Mary of political and religious discontent. More serious than that, the Papacy seized the opportunity to issue a Bull deposing Elizabeth, thus openly ranging international Catholicism against Protestant England. It was the beginning of a period of cold war and aggressive devices, similar to those we ourselves have experienced in our time. English Catholics fled to the continent, where they were trained for the English mission field and sent back secretly to convert their countrymen. Throughout the 1580s the Papacy and the Guise party in France were busy planning the invasion of England by an international Catholic army, to be aided by a revolt of English Catholics: the Enterprise of England, as it was called. The ever-increasing band of missionaries, however innocent their intentions, were, from the standpoint of the Enterprise, a stratagem of war. They were recruiting a fifth column, to be called into action at the Pope's command when the invaders landed.

Against this general background there occurred plot after plot, beginning with the Ridolfi Plot of 1572. Plans were made and remade for the assassination of Queen Elizabeth and ultimately — as the English government discovered — received the official blessing of the Holy See, through the Papal Secretary. Add the Massacre of St Bartholomew in France in 1572, and the assassination of William the Silent by a Catholic fanatic in 1584, and we have a picture of the times as seen by Elizabethans: ideological warfare without scruple or limit, the sort of nightmare experienced by many of our contemporaries.

The reaction of the nation and the policy of the Queen are both of interest to us today. They are best seen in Parliament, where, as each phase of the danger developed, new legislation was required for the defence of the Queen's person and the country. One notes the constant extension of the law of treason; and it is worth reflecting that in the ideological State treasons inevitably multiply.

The general scene is of an angry, fanatically-tempered House of Commons, supported in some of their most extreme proposals by the more sober-minded House of Lords and Privy Councillors. It is not surprising. Nothing stood between Protestant England and the threat, bordering on certainty, of Mary Queen of Scots obtaining the throne, with the backing of international Catholicism — nothing, except the life of Queen Elizabeth. And that life was subject to the hazards of epidemic illness and assassination. The religion, the careers, the fortunes, possibly the lives of these men were at stake. They wanted to root out Catholicism in England by any and every means, stop the missionaries by merciless laws, answer terror by terror. Many spoke and acted as if the only good Catholic was a dead one.

Standing against Parliament and her Councillors, often in stark isolation, was the Queen. She proved herself a *politique*: which is not to say that she was indifferent about her faith. Her own experience in her sister's reign, reinforced by temperament, had taught her the principles by which to rule. They might be comprehended in the phrase, civil obedience. The State was Protestant; the law demanded attendance at church; the people must conform. But she would be content with outward obedience. She was opposed to forcing conscience, 'Her Majesty', as Francis Bacon expressed it, 'not liking to make windows into men's hearts and secret thoughts.' She had assured her people of this in 1570, at the time of the Northern Rebellion; and when, in the Parliament of 1571, both Houses, with the cordial support of bishops and Councillors, passed a bill to compel attendance at the Communion service — in order, as one Puritan zealot declared, that 'not only the external and outward show' but 'the very secrets of the heart' should come to a reckoning — the Queen vetoed the bill. The relevance of such an incident to our own days needs no stressing.

The Queen continued to restrain her Parliaments. In 1581, when the first Jesuit mission and other events had invested the Catholic threat with a new intensity, Lords and Commons joined to frame a bill imposing orthodoxy on the country with the ruthlessness of a modern totalitarian regime. Missionaries and their converts, without qualification, were to be guilty of treason; and for other Catholics there were Draconic provisions. Elizabeth intervened to reduce the penalties, and so qualified the treasonable offence that it was made dependent, not on the simple act of conversion but on treasonable intention. Here she applied her second principle of policy, namely — as Bacon defined it — that matters of conscience cease to be such when they exceed their bounds and become matters of faction, involving overt threats to the established government. It was a principle that she extended to the Puritans as well.

Needless to say, these Parliaments of Elizabeth would have

destroyed the focus of all troubles, Mary Queen of Scots, long before 1587 if they had been allowed. The Queen's reaction to their fearful anger makes one of the most astonishing stories of the reign. In 1572, after the Ridolfi Plot, Privy Council, Lords and Commons united in a passionate determination to attaint and execute Mary. When Elizabeth demurred, they repeated their demand with all the vehemence and argument they could devise; and it was only after a second, emphatic denial that they turned, in disgust and tears, to the milder alternative of excluding her from the succession to the throne. At the end of the session, Elizabeth confounded them all by vetoing their second bill. Next, in 1585, following further plots and the assassination of William the Silent, Council and Parliament wanted to fight the cold war, now degenerating into murder, with its own weapon. They proposed to legalize lynch-law against Mary. Elizabeth intervened to amend the bill in the interests of decency. Even after the Babington Plot, when the nation could no longer be denied its vengeance, the Queen did her utmost to avoid the inevitable. No historical legend could be more ironic than the one, still cherished by Scotsmen, which saddles Elizabeth with unalloyed responsibility for the execution of this unfortunate woman.

In such an atmosphere it is not surprising that the Religious Settlement of 1559 was threatened by radicalism. We in our day have witnessed the expansion of Communist sympathy during the struggle with Nazism and Fascism. The Marian exiles had won the support of the House of Commons in the revolutionary mood at the opening of the reign. That mood, renewed by the cold war, restored the alliance of Puritan clergy with Members of Parliament. After all, a distinguishing feature of Puritanism was hatred of every vestige of Popery; and, on the political side, that was the flamboyant symbol of patriotism. The men who pressed most relentlessly for the execution of Mary Queen of Scots and urged ruthless legislation against Catholics were also earnest Puritans. In this curious

world of conflicting ideologies, Queen Elizabeth found herself —
like American statesmen in recent years — fighting a triangular
duel and suffering from the shots of the other two duellists,
Catholics and Puritans. The latter, though the most ardent of
her supporters, gave her almost as much trouble as the common
enemy.

In the 1570s the Puritan party among the clergy developed
a younger left wing of extremists, who became Calvinist and
wanted to change the polity of the Anglican Church, substitut-
ing Presbyterianism for the episcopal and hierarchical system
inherited from Rome: a change so far-reaching in its political
and social consequences that revolution is the only adequate
term for it. Their programme suited the times. Its claim to be
the apostolic form of the Christian Church caught the prevalent mood of truth-seeing, just as the doctrinaire character
of Communism has attracted visionaries in our generation.
Similarly with its sombre and severe discipline: this was the
spiritual complement to the totalitarian regime desired by the
fanatics in Parliament. Moreover, in the city of Geneva these
Puritans had a contemporary working model of the new
Jerusalem, as infectious in its influence as Russia in our time.

The parallel carries further. One of the conspicuous features
of Communism is its party organization and discipline. The
same is true of Elizabethan Presbyterianism. Both might be
described as singularly well adapted to subversive, minority
movements. Both have made remarkable use of propaganda.
Though primarily a clerical concern, the Elizabethan movement won wide support from the gentry, and even included
Privy Councillors among its patrons and sympathizers. Many
laymen were convinced adherents; still more were fellow-
travellers.

To Queen Elizabeth, Puritanism was an abomination. She
hated and scorned its doctrinaire character, disliked its radicalism, and detested its inquisitorial discipline. Long before its
conspiratorial nature and secret organization were revealed,

and while some of her bishops and statesmen, beguiled by its lively virtues, were playing the role of fellow-travellers, she sensed the danger. Puritan divines briefed their supporters in the House of Commons and maintained a constant agitation there; but Elizabeth was adamant in resisting every parliamentary effort to interfere in Church affairs. The struggle reached its climax in the Parliament of 1587 when the Puritan extremists, who had set up their secret presbyteries and were undermining the Church from within, attempted to impose their revolution on the country by legislation. The Queen imprisoned the group of M.P.s responsible, and set her best orators to expose the true character of their bill, thus shocking fellow-travellers into some awareness of the company they had been keeping. A few years later, having uncovered the secrets of the Puritan clergy's organization, she was able to strike at its leaders and destroy a very dangerous conspiracy.

It remains for us to assess the merits of the Queen's policy. The history of the reign — in particular the parliamentary history — leaves no doubt that but for Elizabeth's firm rule the period would have been much more cruel and bloody. Her statesmen — including the moderate Lord Burghley — were always bemoaning her merciful nature, perilous to herself and the country. We have observed in the totalitarian states of our own time that ideological regimes tend to evoke the worst instincts in men and bring brutes to the fore. The administration of the Elizabethan penal laws, in any case, was not free from tyranny: nor, be it added, from astonishing lenity. The career of that notorious hunter of Catholics, Richard Topcliffe — a cultured gentleman, but a fanatic and sadist — shows that the Gestapo and the OGPU, with their abhorrent methods, are not so much the product of particular countries or a particular era as of a political system. But there would have been many more Topcliffes in Elizabethan England if Parliament had had its way and a different sovereign been on the throne. If life had been made intolerable for ordinary Catholics, their patriotism would have been submerged under fear, hopelessness and passion. They knew, however, that their Queen was no fanatic, and though they suffered from recusancy fines and other troubles, they continued to be Englishmen first. Only the exiles and a few extremists of their faith welcomed the Spanish Armada.

Even more important: the damping down of ideological passion enabled the nation, when dangers eased, to recover balance. Fanaticism is not an enduring feature of civilized society. A new generation rarely experiences the same exaltation of spirit as the old: unless, indeed, the same causes persist; and perhaps, even then, only reluctantly, since it is not of their own creation. How foolish the first Stuart kings were, who provoked a new Catholic scare and so revived old passions. As Elizabeth's reign moved into its fourth decade, the execution of Mary Queen of Scots, the successful — nay, glorious — weathering of the international storm at the time of the Armada, and the gradual passing of the generation that had known persecution under Mary Tudor and endured the long nightmare of the cold war under Elizabeth, all made for a relaxation of tension. A new mood is perceptible, strikingly perceptible, where the fanaticism of the high Elizabethan period was most apparent — in Parliament. The Parliament of 1593 saw two government bills introduced against Catholics. They emerged as a bill against Protestant sectaries and only one against Catholics — the last anti-Catholic bill of the reign, with its penalties reduced by a Parliament, now closer in sentiment to the Queen and more tolerant than her Privy Councillors.

If Parliament had had its way in the 1570s and 1580s and fastened on the community a merciless totalitarian system, with the consequent inflammation of passions and the inevitable momentum or inertia, as also the vested interests, that any regime acquires, who can say when the country would have recovered? Certainly, a very different, a spiritually impoverished England would have emerged. To inject poison into the body politic is to take grave risks.

One question remains: How was it that a Queen, so anti-pathetic to Puritanism, managed to preserve and nurture in her people an exuberance of spirit derived largely from the emotions she opposed? Accident enters into the answer. She was all these zealots had. There was no obvious successor to look to. They cherished her as parents do an only child. As an explanation of Elizabethan England, this, however, is utterly inadequate. Positive qualities were there, lots of them: personality, ability, complete absorption in her country and task. Her people were left in no doubt that she was, as she claimed to be, 'mere English'. Moderation can be a gutless policy. We have biblical authority for disliking people who blow neither hot nor cold: and an occasional hot-gospeller did not hesitate to quote the passage to Queen Elizabeth. But her moderation was the reverse of gutless. As she knew and was repeatedly told, it increased the risk to her own life immeasurably: thus, incidentally, inspiring more passionate love. In fact, her policy was a calculated and courageous gamble — trusting, for example, to outlive Mary Queen of Scots, rather than destroy her; trusting that the threatened storm would not come or could be weathered, rather than consent to courses detestable to her. Had her gamble failed, the name of Queen Elizabeth — as Peter Wentworth was bold enough to tell her — would have been infamous.

This woman was as vital as Winston Churchill, and, like him, made romantic leadership an art of government. The name 'Gloriana' and the phrase '*via media*' seem odd companions. But the liberal way of life is richest and fullest, and it was well for England that when men's passions led them from it, Queen Elizabeth preserved the tradition. Her Puritan fanatics had no more obstinate opponent: she, in turn, had no more devoted worshippers. It is the strangest paradox of her reign and the supreme tribute to her greatness.

INDEX

INDEX

INDEX

269

INDEX

Ridolfi Plot, the, 227–8, 258, 260
Rochelle, La, 70–1
Romier, Lucien, 221
Roussillon, 64
Rousseau, Jean Jacques, 243
Rozel, M., 20
Russell, Bertrand, 127
—— Bridget, Lady Russell, 157–8
—— Francis, Earl of Bedford, 165, 230

SACHEVERELL, DR HENRY, 102
Sackville, Thomas, Lord Buckhurst, 159, 161, 164
St Andrew's Parish, Holborn, 97
St Bartholomew, Massacre of, 22, 37, 57, 59, 62, 65, 67–73, 75, 83, 88, 111, 238, 258
St Denis, Abbey of, 13
St Germain, Peace of, 63–4
St Paul's Cross Sermon, 98, 101
St Quentin, 39
Sandwich, 183
Savoy, 56, 82
—— Duke of, 85
Scrope, Lady (Philadelphia Carey), 197
Sea-Beggars, the, 64
Seckford, Thomas, Master of Requests, 185–6
Sens, 55
Seymour, Edward, Duke of Somerset, 35
Shakespeare, William, 121, 201–2, 216–17, 247
Sharp, Dr Leonel, 190–2
Shirley, Sir Thomas, 158
Sidney, Sir Henry, 181
—— Philip, 201
—— Sir Robert, 160, 166, 168, 178–9

Silva, Don Guzman de, Spanish ambassador, 181–2
Sixtus V, Pope, 81, 107, 254
Smith, Sir Thomas, 118, 133, 156
Sorbonne, the, 83
Southwell, Elizabeth, 195–8
—— Sir Robert, 196
Speed, John, 188
Spenser, Edmund, 126, 148, 166, 201
Spes, Guerau de, Spanish ambassador, 222–5, 227, 229–30
Stafford, Sir Edward, 222, 224, 236–7
Stalin, 113, 250
Stanhope, Sir John, 157, 162
Stow, John, chronicler, 113, 126
Strachey, Lytton, 241
Strasbourg, 140
Strickland, Agnes, 174
Swift, Jonathan, 102

Taillé, the, 32, 34
Tawney, Professor R. H., 129
Temple Bar, 102
Thirty Years War, the, 12
Throckmorton, Job, 208–9
—— Sir Nicholas, 130–1, 137
Thynne, Sir John, 135
Tilbury, 189
Times, The, 105
Topcliffe, Richard, 262
Tottenham, 182
Tout, Professor T. F., 240
Tower, the, 105, 138, 191, 212
Trent, Council of, 47–8, 111, 202, 257
Triumvirate, the, 50, 53, 55–6, 77
Tuscany, 68
Tyndale, William, 20

271